Better Homes and Gardens®

Make-Ahead
COOKING

Better Homes and Gardens® Books
Des Moines, Iowa

All of us at Better Homes and Gardens® Books are dedicated to providing you with the information and ideas you need to create delicious foods. We welcome your comments and suggestions. Write to us at: Better Homes and Gardens Books, Cookbook Editorial Department, 1716 Locust St., Des Moines, IA 50309-3023.

If you would like to purchase any of our books, check wherever quality books are sold or visit bhgbooks.com

Our seal assures you that every recipe in *Make-Ahead Cooking* has been tested in the Better Homes and Gardens® Test Kitchen. This means that each recipe is practical and reliable, and meets our high standards of taste appeal. We guarantee your satisfaction with this book for as long as you own it.

Pictured on front cover: Creamy Chicken Enchiladas (see recipe, page 63)
Cover Photo: Pete Krumhardt, Photographer; Dianna Nolin, Food Stylist

Better Homes and Gardens® Books
An imprint of Meredith® Books

Make-Ahead Cooking
Editor: Jan Miller
Associate Art Director: Lynda Haupert
Contributing Editors: Shelli McConnell, Spectrum Communication Services, Inc.
Writer: Wini Moranville
Recipe Development: Bev Bennett, Ellen Boeke, Linda Henry, Better Homes and Gardens® Test Kitchen
Copy Chief: Terri Fredrickson
Managers, Book Production: Pam Kvitne, Marjorie J. Schenkelberg
Contributing Copy Editor: Brenda Witherspoon
Contributing Proofreaders: Emmy Clausing, Jacquelyn Foster, Elizabeth Popplewell
Photographers: Pete Krumhardt, Scott Little
Food Stylists: Jill Lust, Dianna Nolin
Electronic Production Coordinator: Paula Forest
Editorial and Design Assistants: Judy Bailey, Mary Lee Gavin, Karen Schirm
Test Kitchen Director: Lynn Blanchard
Test Kitchen Product Supervisor: Marilyn Cornelius
Test Kitchen Home Economists: Judy Comstock, Marilyn Cornelius, Maryellyn Krantz, Tami Leonard, Jill Moberly, Kay Springer, Colleen Weeden, Lori Wilson, Charles Worthington

Meredith® Books
Editor in Chief: James D. Blume
Design Director: Matt Strelecki
Managing Editor: Gregory H. Kayko
Executive Food Editor: Jennifer Dorland Darling

Director, Retail Sales and Marketing: Terry Unsworth
Director, Sales, Special Markets: Rita McMullen
Director, Sales, Premiums: Michael A. Peterson
Director, Sales, Retail: Tom Wierzbicki
Director, Book Marketing: Brad Elmitt
Director, Operations: George A. Susral
Director, Production: Douglas M. Johnston

Vice President, General Manager: Jamie L. Martin

Better Homes and Gardens® Magazine
Editor in Chief: Jean LemMon
Executive Food Editor: Nancy Byal

Meredith Publishing Group
President, Publishing Group: Stephen M. Lacy
Vice President, Finance and Administration: Max Runciman

Meredith Corporation
Chairman and Chief Executive Officer: William T. Kerr

Chairman of the Executive Committee: E. T. Meredith III

Make It Easier,
Make It Ahead!

Few things in life are more satisfying than enjoying a meal with family and friends. *Better Homes and Gardens® Make-Ahead Cooking* is filled with 165 recipes that will enable you to enjoy this simple pleasure more often with less stress. Each chapter offers a do-ahead strategy for every cooking need. Choose from an assortment of recipes to help you keep pace with a hectic schedule, whether you need a jump-start on a casual dinner party, a satisfying meal for a busy weeknight, or a sweet treat to brighten a child's day. Make your holidays stress-free with a survival kit filled with menus, timetables, and food gifts to share with friends and neighbors.

Every recipe and tip has been tested to perfection by the experts in the Better Homes and Gardens® Test Kitchen. Be confident that if a recipe did not yield delicious, high-quality results—whether it was made ahead or eaten immediately—it didn't make it into this book.

Go ahead, whenever you have a little time, linger over these recipes and choose a few to make. Tomorrow, next week, or perhaps a month from now, you'll be glad you did.

Contents

Make-Ahead Essentials 6

From hints for quick cooking and easy entertaining to tips on food safety and storage, here are the essentials from the experts in the Better Homes and Gardens® Test Kitchen.

For Friends And Family 10

It's easy to welcome everyone around the table—and join in the fun yourself—when so many good foods are ready and waiting ahead of time.

Make a Bonus Batch 52

What's more satisfying than a home-cooked recipe? Knowing that extra helpings are securely stashed away for a future feast.

Leftover Transformations 82

You'll love the way the starring ingredient of one recipe makes two delicious (and decidedly different) return engagements.

Make-Ahead Essentials

In these pages you will find simple pointers for making your time in the kitchen as efficient as possible, planning tips for your next entertaining experience, and up-to-date food storage information.

Cook Smart

Overbooked and overwhelmed? Time is precious. So when you plan to cook in advance, make the most of your time in the kitchen. Follow these simple suggestions:

● **Put cooking first on your to-do list.** You'll be surprised how quickly the recipe will come together. It's easy to burn up half an hour reading the mail or checking phone messages. Save those chores for later and focus on the task at hand.

● **Read the recipe completely.** This should eliminate delays searching for missing ingredients or last-minute trips to the grocery store.

● **Overlap steps to accomplish two things at once.** Chop vegetables, measure ingredients, open cans, or prepares sauces while waiting for water to boil, meat to brown, or appliances to preheat.

● **Clean as you go.** Before you start any preparation, fill the sink with hot, soapy water.

● **Let time-saving appliances and techniques work for you.** Use a food processor to slice and chop vegetables or grate cheese. The microwave is an easy, no mess method for melting butter or chocolate and toasting nuts. Because a toaster oven takes little time to preheat, it toasts buns and rolls quickly. Use kitchen scissors to snip fresh herbs or dried fruit, a garlic press to crush garlic, and a mini ice cream scoop for drop cookies.

● **Purchase shortcut ingredients to cut minutes off your prep time (see Key Ingredients, right).** Or visit your local deli or bakery for instant appetizers such as specialty cheeses or olives, and simple side dishes or breads to embellish your meal.

Key Ingredients

Keep a supply of time-saving ingredients on hand for those occasions when you don't have time to spare. Choose a few from the list below:

● Pre-cut fruits and vegetables
● Pre-washed, packaged salad greens
● Boned and skinned fish
● Boned and trimmed meat
● Rice pilaf mixes
● Pasta mixes
● Packaged hot roll mix
● Canned stock or broth
● Instant bouillon granules or cubes
● Canned beans (cannellini, Great Northern, pinto)
● Refrigerated mashed potatoes
● Refrigerated or frozen cheese-filled pasta
● Refrigerated mango
● Frozen chopped onion, or sweet pepper or loose-pack vegetables
● Frozen bread dough
● Frozen peeled shrimp
● Bottled minced garlic
● Bottled roasted red sweet pepper
● Bottled lemon juice

Entertaining Thoughts

If you're planning to serve dinner for eight at 8 p.m. or to have the neighborhood gang over for the big game, take a few minutes to plan—it will save you time. Consider the following when making preparations for your next social function:

● **Stay in your comfort zone.** You should enjoy yourself too. Prepare items that are within your comfort and skill level. Balance the number of make-ahead recipes with those that require a few last-minute finishing details. Round out your menu with convenience and purchased items when necessary.

● **Limited resources.** Keep it simple. There is no need to rent additional flatware, serving pieces, tables, and chairs—serve the number of people you can accommodate easily. Make sure you have adequate refrigerator or freezer space for the recipes that are prepared in advance.

● **Invest a little time.** Work out a time schedule so you know in what order to prepare the food. All of the recipes in this book include thawing (if necessary) and reheating instructions. Allow enough time to follow storage and serving instructions for the best results. Make sure your oven will hold everything that must be reheated; check to ensure oven temperatures for reheating are similar.

May We Recommend?

If you create a menu, here are a few pointers to guide you:.

● **Consider the occasion.** A party menu that works for a formal dinner may not work for a casual gathering of friends.

● **Combine interesting, contrasting colors and textures.** Think visually how colors and shapes work together. How will you serve each dish?

● **Balance rich, highly flavored foods with simple fresh items.** If you serve a rich, cheesy main dish, dessert should be light and refreshing.

● **Avoid repeating flavors.** Even when two recipes aren't served at the same time, consider how each dish adds character to a meal.

Menu Planning Made Easy

Use one of these suggestions or one of the six menus and preparation timetables in the Stress-Free Holidays chapter that begins on page 144.

Overnight-Guest Fest
Apple Harvest Cinnamon Rolls, page 22
Mexicali Potato Brunch Bake, page 186
Fresh fruit
Coffee or hot tea

Picnic in the Park
Lahvosh Roll, page 51
Assorted fresh veggies and chips
Fresh strawberries
Crackled Sugar Cookies, page 227

Simple Sunday Supper
Mustard Crisp Chicken, page 46
Marinated cucumbers
Three-Cheese Orzo Salad, page 29
Tomato bread with butter
Chocolate and Peanut Butter Bars, page 223

Dinner for Four
Herbed Beef Pinwheels, page 40
Mixed greens with balsamic vinaigrette
Crusty seed or multigrain bread with butter
Ultimate Nut and Chocolate Chip Tart, page 205

Summer Barbecue
Gingery Apricot-Glazed Pork Ribs, page 127
Corn-on-the-cob with herb butter
Coleslaw
Rhubarb Hand Tarts with Vanilla Ice Cream, page 212

Meatless Made Elegant
Three-Cheese and Artichoke Lasagna, page 49
Caesar-style salad
Rustic Italian bread
Chocolate-Raspberry Cheesecake, page 219

Fridge and Freezer Facts

Follow these basic guidelines to ensure the best flavor, texture, aroma, and overall enjoyment from the food you store.

Cold Enough for You?

To make sure your freezer and refrigerator maintain the proper temperatures for safe food storage, use refrigerator and freezer thermometers.

● **To check refrigerator temperature:** Place the thermometer in a glass of water set in the middle of the refrigerator. Check the temperature in 5 to 8 hours. If the temperature is not between 34°F and 40°F, adjust the refrigerator temperature control according to the manufacturer's directions, and check again in 5 to 8 hours.

● **To check freezer temperature:** Place the thermometer between frozen food packages. Check in 5 to 8 hours. If the temperature is not 0°F or colder, adjust the freezer temperature control according to the manufacturer's directions, and check again in 5 to 8 hours.

Exposing a Dangerous Myth

Food safety experts are often asked whether cooked foods should stand at room temperature to cool before they're refrigerated or frozen. The answer? No! Room temperature falls directly within the danger zone of temperatures (between 40°F and 140°F) at which harmful bacteria develop. Foods requiring refrigeration should be properly frozen or refrigerated as soon as possible and should never stand longer than 2 hours at room temperature.

Cool it Quickly

Whether you are preparing hot food for storage in the refrigerator or the freezer, it is essential to cool the food quickly for two reasons. First, it decreases the chance for harmful bacteria to grow, keeping your food safe to eat. Second, if freezing food it allows the food to freeze faster, preventing the formation of large ice crystals that may ruin the flavor and texture of foods. For quick cooling follow these guidelines:

● Divide cooked foods into small portions and shallow containers for rapid cooling. A general rule: For soups and stews, divide into portions that are 2 to 3 inches deep. Stir soups and stews to speed the release of heat. For roasts and whole poultry, divide into portions that are 2 to 3 inches thick. Place the smaller portions of hot food directly into the refrigerator to chill rapidly.

● If the final destination is the freezer, transfer cooled food from the refrigerator to the freezer. Arrange containers in a single layer in the freezer until frozen. This allows the cold air to circulate around the packages, freezing the food faster. Stack them after they are completely frozen.

Wraps and A-OK Containers

Not all wraps and containers are created equal. Follow these guidelines when purchasing storage containers and wraps for the refrigerator or freezer:

● **Airtight food storage containers with tight-fitting lids:** Most containers, even disposables, provide adequate protection in the refrigerator. However, when shopping for freezer-safe containers, check for a phrase or an icon on the label or container bottom indicating they are designed for freezer storage.

● **Baking dishes:** When freezing, use freezer-to-oven or freezer-to-microwave dishes, and cover the surface with plastic freezer wrap or heavy-duty foil (See Foil Foibles, page 9).

● **Glass jars with tight-fitting lids:** All major brands of canning jars are acceptable for use in the refrigerator or freezer. If freezing liquid and semiliquid foods, leave headspace in the jar so the food can expand as it freezes (½ inch for pints and 1 inch for quarts).

● **Self-Sealing Storage Bags or Plastic Wraps:** Storage bags and wraps are available in all colors and sizes. Make sure you include products appropriate for both the refrigerator and the freezer in your cupboard.

● **Regular or Heavy Aluminum Foil:** When freezing food, use only heavy aluminum foil (see Foil Foibles, page 9).

Foil Foibles

A word of caution: Do not use foil to wrap foods that contain acidic ingredients, such as tomatoes. Acid reacts with the aluminum foil, giving the food an off flavor. To refrigerate or freeze a casserole that contains tomatoes or another acidic ingredient, first cover the food with plastic wrap, then with foil. The plastic wrap will prevent the reaction between the foil and the food during storage. The foil can be used as a cover when heating; remove the plastic wrap before heating.

A Perfect Fit

When freezing food prepared in a casserole dish, use the following method to avoid tying up the dish in the freezer for weeks. Line the dish with heavy-duty foil three times the width or diameter of the dish. If the casserole contains acidic foods place a layer of plastic wrap on top of the foil (see Foil Foibles). Center the foil, coat with nonstick cooking spray. Assemble the casserole. Bring the longer sides of the foil together over the food. Seal with a double fold; freeze. Once frozen, lift out the foil-covered food. Wrap tightly with heavy foil and return to the freezer. To thaw the casserole, put it back in the casserole or baking dish and follow recipe directions for thawing and baking.

Be Label Conscious

Ever peer into the freezer and wonder just what's inside that foil-wrapped package? Eliminate those mysterious packages. Using a wax crayon or waterproof marking pen, take a moment to properly label food before freezing. Labeling also helps you remember which packages are the oldest and which should be used first. Include the following:
- The name of the item or recipe
- The quantity, weight, or number of servings
- The date it was frozen
- Any special information about its use

Follow recommended storage times included in each recipe. See the Food Storage Charts on pages 236 to 239 for additional guidelines.

To Freeze or Not to Freeze

These foods lose flavor, texture, or overall quality when frozen:
- Whole eggs in the shell, whether raw or cooked
- Cooked egg whites and yolks, as well as cake icings made with egg whites
- Cottage and ricotta cheeses
- Sour cream
- Mayonnaise
- Custard and cream pies or desserts with cream fillings
- Battered and fried foods
- Soups and stews thickened with cornstarch and flour (which tend to lose their thickening capacity when frozen)
- Soups and stews made with potatoes, which can darken and become mushy when frozen
- Luncheon meats
- Stuffed chops or chicken breasts
- Store-cooked convenience meals

Thoughts on Thawing

Here are few general guidelines on thawing foods.
- The recipes in this book that offer freezing options include information on the best way to thaw and reheat the food. Follow these instructions for optimum quality.
- Generally, thaw all frozen foods in the refrigerator—never at room temperature. A few exceptions include recipes for breads and sweets that specifically call for thawing at room temperature.
- Some foods may be successfully thawed in the microwave; follow your microwave manufacturer's directions.

Rules For Reheating

Make-ahead cooks need to heed special precautions when reheating leftovers or any food that has been refrigerated or frozen. Reheat food to a safe internal temperature before serving. To do so, invest in a good food thermometer (see tip, page 129, for varieties available), and follow these guidelines:
- Bring sauces, soups, and gravy to a full boil.
- Heat other leftovers to 165°F.

Herbed Beef Pinwheels (page 40)

For Friends
and Family

Here's a great range of appetizers, breads, main dishes, and more—from the kid-friendly to the crowd-pleasing to something just right for tonight. Best of all, each recipe boasts its own clever make-ahead strategy to make it easier than ever to gather around the table with the people you enjoy the most.

In This Chapter

To Make Ahead

Prepare Wonton Dippers as directed through step 2. Arrange unfried wontons in a single layer in freezer container. Seal, label, and freeze up to 2 months. Store Hoisin Dressing in an airtight container in refrigerator up to 3 days or label and freeze up to 2 months.

To Serve

Thaw wontons overnight in refrigerator. Fry as directed. Thaw Hoisin Dressing overnight in refrigerator before using.

Wonton Dippers

Prep: 40 minutes **Cook:** 1 minute per batch **Makes:** 32 wontons

1 cup dried shiitake mushrooms	1 beaten egg white
¼ pound fresh or frozen crabmeat, thawed and flaked, or ½ of an 8-ounce package flake-style imitation crabmeat	1 tablespoon soy sauce
	2 teaspoons grated fresh ginger
	1 teaspoon toasted sesame oil
	½ teaspoon Oriental chili paste
2 tablespoons finely chopped carrot	¼ teaspoon salt
2 tablespoons chopped green onion	¼ teaspoon pepper
2 tablespoons finely chopped water chestnuts or celery	32 wonton wrappers
	Cooking oil or shortening for frying
2 tablespoons snipped fresh cilantro	1 recipe Hoisin Dressing (below)

1 In a small bowl soak mushrooms in enough warm water to cover for 30 minutes; drain and finely chop. For filling, in a medium bowl combine mushrooms, crabmeat, carrot, green onion, water chestnuts, cilantro, egg white, soy sauce, ginger, sesame oil, chili paste, salt, and pepper.

2 Place 1 teaspoon of filling slightly off-center on a wonton wrapper. Fold wonton wrapper in half to enclose filling and release any trapped air; moisten edges with water and press to seal. Place finished wonton on a baking sheet lined with waxed paper. Cover lightly with plastic wrap while filling and sealing the remaining wonton wrappers.

3 In a 3-quart saucepan or wok heat 1½ to 2 inches oil over medium-high heat to 365°. Fry wontons, a few at a time, in the hot oil about 1 minute or until crisp and golden, turning once. Drain on paper towels. Serve with Hoisin Dressing.

Hoisin Dressing: Stir together ⅓ cup hoisin sauce, ¼ cup rice vinegar or red wine vinegar, 1 tablespoon soy sauce, 1 tablespoon Chinese-style hot mustard or Dijon-style mustard, 1 tablespoon grated fresh ginger, 1 teaspoon sugar, ½ teaspoon pepper, and 2 cloves garlic, minced.

Nutrition Facts per wonton: 72 cal., 4 g total fat (1 g sat. fat), 3 mg chol., 184 mg sodium, 7 g carbo., 0 g fiber, 2 g pro. Daily Values: 3% vit. A, 1% vit. C, 1% calcium, 2% iron

Mandarin Beef Buns

Prep: 40 minutes **Rise:** 20 minutes **Bake:** 15 minutes **Makes:** 24 buns

1 tablespoon cooking oil	1 teaspoon shredded orange peel
2 cups shredded cooked beef or pork	⅓ cup thinly bias-sliced green onions
¼ teaspoon crushed red pepper	¼ cup hoisin sauce
1 cup chopped bok choy, Chinese cabbage, or green cabbage	1 16-ounce package hot roll mix
2 tablespoons grated fresh ginger	1 beaten egg
	Sesame seed

1 For filling, in a large skillet heat oil over medium heat. Add beef and red pepper; cook and stir for 3 minutes. Add bok choy, ginger, and orange peel. Cook and stir 2 to 3 minutes or until bok choy is wilted. Stir in green onions and hoisin sauce. Remove from heat; cool.

2 Meanwhile, prepare the hot roll mix according to package directions. Divide dough into 24 portions. Shape each portion into a ball. On a lightly floured surface roll or pat each ball into a 3½-inch circle.

3 For each bun, place about 1 tablespoon of the filling in the center of a dough circle. Moisten the edges of the dough with water and bring up around filling, pinching the edges together to seal.

4 Arrange the filled buns, seam sides down, on 2 lightly greased baking sheets. Cover; let rise in a warm place for 20 minutes. Brush buns with beaten egg and sprinkle with sesame seed. Bake in a 375° oven about 15 minutes or until golden. Serve warm.

Nutrition Facts per bun: 126 cal., 4 g total fat (1 g sat. fat), 28 mg chol., 188 mg sodium, 16 g carbo., 0 g fiber, 7 g pro. Daily Values: 3% vit. A, 5% vit. C, 6% iron

A hot roll mix makes easy work of these dim sum-inspired buns. Keep a stash on hand in your freezer and you'll always have a relaxing bite to linger over with friends.

To Make Ahead

Prepare and bake Mandarin Beef Buns as directed. Remove from baking sheet; cool on a wire rack for 30 minutes. Wrap buns in heavy foil, label, and freeze up to 1 month.

To Serve

Leave the frozen buns in foil wrap. Bake in a 325° oven about 40 minutes or until buns are heated through.

Serve these sports bar favorites the next time you have friends over to watch the big game. Make them up to a day ahead, and you'll be able to spend that much more time cheering for your favorite team.

To Make Ahead

Prepare Bacon and Tomato Potato Skins as directed through step 3. Cover and chill in refrigerator up to 24 hours.

To Serve

Bake and serve as directed.

Bacon and Tomato Potato Skins

Prep: 30 minutes **Bake:** 10 minutes **Makes:** 24 wedges

- 6 **large baking potatoes (such as russet or long white)**
- 2 **teaspoons cooking oil**
- 1 **teaspoon chili powder**
  Several dashes bottled hot pepper sauce
- ⅔ **cup chopped bacon, crisp cooked and drained**

- 2 **small tomatoes, seeded and finely chopped (about ⅔ cup)**
- 2 **tablespoons finely chopped green onion**
- 1 **cup shredded cheddar cheese (4 ounces)**
- ½ **cup dairy sour cream (optional)**

1 Scrub potatoes thoroughly and prick with a fork. Arrange on a microwave-safe plate. Micro-cook, uncovered, on 100% power (high) for 15 to 20 minutes or until almost tender, rearranging once. (Or bake potatoes in a 425° oven for 40 to 45 minutes or until almost tender.) Cool.

2 Halve each potato lengthwise. Scoop out the inside of each potato half, leaving about a ¼-inch-thick shell. (Cover and chill the leftover fluffy white part of potatoes for another use.) In a small bowl combine the oil, chili powder, and hot pepper sauce. Using a pastry brush, brush the insides of the potato shells with the oil mixture. Cut the potato shells in half lengthwise.

3 Place potato quarters on a baking sheet. Sprinkle evenly with bacon, tomatoes, and green onion. Top with cheese.

4 Bake in a 450° oven for 10 to 12 minutes or until cheese is melted and potato quarters are heated through. If desired, serve with sour cream.

Nutrition Facts per wedge: 70 cal., 3 g total fat (2 g sat. fat), 7 mg chol., 76 mg sodium, 8 g carbo., 1 g fiber, 3 g pro. Daily Values: 2% vit. A, 8% vit. C, 4% calcium, 3% iron

Don't be surprised if these neat-to-eat pinwheels—made rich with a buttery pastry and mushroom-studded filling—are the first nibbles to disappear from the appetizer tray. Look for self-rising flour, which has leavening incorporated, in 2- and 5-pound bags at most supermarkets.

To Make Ahead

Prepare Mushroom-Spinach Pinwheels as directed through step 3. Wrap rolls in moisture- and vaporproof wrap, label, and freeze up to 3 months.

To Store

Thaw rolls overnight in refrigerator. Slice, brush with egg white mixture, and bake as directed.

Mushroom-Spinach Pinwheels

Prep: 35 minutes   **Chill:** 1½ hours   **Bake:** 20 minutes   **Makes:** 28 slices

1 8-ounce package reduced-fat cream cheese (Neufchâtel), softened	1 tablespoon all-purpose flour
⅔ cup butter, softened	½ teaspoon salt
1 cup all-purpose flour	½ teaspoon dried oregano, crushed
1 cup self-rising flour*	½ teaspoon lemon juice
1 10-ounce package frozen chopped spinach	⅛ teaspoon garlic powder
2½ cups chopped fresh mushrooms	¼ cup grated Parmesan cheese (1 ounce)
1 cup chopped onion	1 egg white
2 tablespoons butter	1 tablespoon water

1 In a large bowl beat together cream cheese and the ⅔ cup butter. Add the 1 cup all-purpose flour and the self-rising flour; beat well. Divide dough in half; wrap in plastic wrap. Chill in refrigerator 30 to 60 minutes or until easy to handle. Cook spinach according to package directions; drain. Squeeze out excess liquid; set aside.

2 In a large skillet cook and stir mushrooms and onion in the 2 tablespoons butter over medium heat about 3 minutes or until onion is tender. Add spinach, the 1 tablespoon all-purpose flour, the salt, oregano, lemon juice, and garlic powder. Cook and stir until mixture thickens. Stir in Parmesan cheese; cool.

3 On a floured surface roll one dough portion into a 12×7-inch rectangle. Spread with half of the mushroom mixture to within ½ inch of edges. Starting with a short edge, roll up dough and filling into a spiral. Moisten edge with water; pinch to seal. Repeat with remaining dough and filling. Cover and chill in refrigerator for 1 hour.

4 Combine egg white and the water. Slice rolls into ½-inch slices. Place slices on an ungreased baking sheet; brush with egg white mixture. Bake in a 400° oven about 20 minutes or until golden. Transfer to wire racks; cool.

Nutrition Facts per pinwheel: 101 cal., 7 g total fat (4 g sat. fat), 19 mg chol., 190 mg sodium, 8 g carbo., 1 g fiber, 2 g pro. Daily Values: 11% vit. A, 2% vit. C, 2% calcium, 4% iron

*Note: If you can't find self-rising flour, substitute 1 cup all-purpose flour, 1 teaspoon baking powder, ½ teaspoon salt, and ¼ teaspoon baking soda for 1 cup self-rising flour.

Salmon-Dill Cheesecake

Prep: 30 minutes **Bake:** 30 minutes **Cool:** 1¾ hours **Chill:** 2 hours **Makes:** 16 servings

1½ cups finely crushed crispy rye or
     sesame crackers
 6 tablespoons butter or margarine,
     melted
 2 tablespoons grated Parmesan cheese
 1 8-ounce package cream cheese,
     softened
 2 eggs

 ½ of an 8-ounce tub cream cheese with
     salmon or plain tub cream cheese
 1 tablespoon white wine vinegar or
     lemon juice
 1 8-ounce carton dairy sour cream
 ¼ pound dry-smoked salmon, skin and
     bones removed and flaked
 1 tablespoon snipped fresh dill

1 For crust, in a medium bowl combine crushed crackers, melted butter, and Parmesan cheese. Press mixture evenly on the bottom and about 1 inch up the side of a 9-inch springform pan. Set aside.

2 For filling, in a large bowl beat softened cream cheese with an electric mixer on low to medium speed until smooth. Add eggs all at once. Beat on low speed just until combined. Add tub cream cheese and vinegar, beating on low speed just until combined. Stir in sour cream, smoked salmon, and snipped dill.

3 Pour into crust-lined springform pan. Place the springform pan on a shallow baking pan on the oven rack. Bake in a 350° oven for 30 to 35 minutes or until center appears nearly set when gently shaken.

4 Remove springform pan from baking pan. Cool cheesecake on a wire rack for 15 minutes. Use a small metal spatula to loosen crust from side of pan. Cool 30 minutes more. Remove side of the springform pan. Cool 1 hour; cover and chill in refrigerator at least 2 hours. If desired, garnish with fresh dill sprigs and salmon caviar.

Nutrition Facts per serving: 202 cal., 16 g total fat (10 g sat. fat), 72 mg chol., 210 mg sodium, 9 g carbo., 2 g fiber, 5 g pro. Daily Values: 12% vit. A, 5% calcium, 3% iron

Dessert cheesecakes top the list of great make-ahead party fare. It's no surprise, then, that savory appetizer cheesecakes make great do-ahead options too. Try serving this one in thin wedges over crisp greens for an elegant first course. Or set it alongside crackers on an appetizer buffet table.

To Make Ahead

Prepare Salmon-Dill Cheesecake as directed, except cover and chill in refrigerator up to 24 hours.

To Serve

Garnish cheesecake as directed.

If you like your shrimp hot, hot, hot, take a hint from Jamaican cooks. Instead of using a jalapeño chile pepper, substitute a Scotch bonnet pepper, one of the world's hottest chile peppers.

To Make Ahead

Prepare Jamaican Shrimp as directed through step 2. Seal the bag and chill in refrigerator up to 24 hours. Serve as directed.

Jamaican Shrimp

Prep: 30 minutes **Marinate:** 1 hour **Makes:** 10 to 12 appetizer servings

2 pounds fresh or frozen large shrimp in shells
¼ cup salad oil
3 tablespoons white wine vinegar
2 tablespoons lime juice
1 jalapeño pepper, seeded and finely chopped*
1 tablespoon honey

2 teaspoons homemade Jamaican Jerk Seasoning (below) or purchased Jamaican jerk seasoning
1 medium mango, peeled, seeded, sliced, and halved crosswise**
1 small lime, cut into small wedges
1 small red onion, quartered and thinly sliced

1 In a large saucepan cook fresh or frozen shrimp, uncovered, in lightly salted boiling water for 1 to 3 minutes or until shrimp turn pink. Drain immediately and cool. Peel shrimp, leaving tails intact; devein. Place shrimp in a heavy, self-sealing plastic bag.

2 For marinade, in a screw-top jar combine salad oil, white wine vinegar, lime juice, jalapeño pepper, honey, and the Jamaican Jerk Seasoning. Cover and shake well to mix; pour over shrimp in plastic bag. Seal and marinate in refrigerator 1 hour, turning bag occasionally.

3 To serve, drain shrimp, reserving marinade. Arrange shrimp, mango, lime wedges, and onion on a serving platter. Drizzle with reserved marinade.

Jamaican Jerk Seasoning: In a small bowl combine 2 teaspoons onion powder, 1 teaspoon sugar, 1 teaspoon salt, 1 teaspoon ground thyme, ½ teaspoon ground allspice, ¼ teaspoon ground cinnamon, and ¼ teaspoon ground red pepper.

Nutrition Facts per serving: 171 cal., 7 g total fat (1 g sat. fat), 138 mg chol., 201 mg sodium, 8 g carbo., 1 g fiber, 19 g pro. Daily Values: 20% vit. A, 19% vit. C, 5% calcium, 13% iron

*Note: Because chile peppers, such as jalapeños, contain volatile oils that can burn your skin and eyes, avoid direct contact with them as much as possible. When working with chile peppers, wear plastic bags over your hands or wear plastic or rubber gloves. If your bare hands do touch the chile peppers, wash your hands well with soap and warm water.

**Note: See tip on peeling and seeding mangos, page 100.

These fresh, puffy
homemade tortillas are
among the most versatile
on-call breads around. Fill
them with scrambled eggs
and salsa for breakfast
burritos, cold meats and
veggies for lunchtime
wraps, or grilled beef and
chicken for festive fajitas.

To Make Ahead

Prepare Herbed Flour
Tortillas as directed.
Cool. Stack cooled
tortillas with waxed
paper between layers.
To chill, wrap in plastic
wrap and store in the
refrigerator up to
5 days. To freeze, wrap
in plastic wrap and seal
in a self-sealing freezer
bag. Label and freeze up
to 6 months.

To Serve

Remove the number of
tortillas needed; return
remaining tortillas to
refrigerator or freezer.
Thaw frozen tortillas
in refrigerator or at
room temperature.

Herbed Flour Tortillas

Start to finish: 50 minutes **Makes:** 12 tortillas

1 cup whole wheat flour	½ teaspoon salt
1 cup all-purpose flour	½ teaspoon crushed red pepper
1 tablespoon snipped fresh cilantro	2 tablespoons shortening
1 teaspoon baking powder	½ cup warm water

1 In a medium bowl combine flours, cilantro, baking powder, salt, and crushed red pepper. Using a pastry blender, cut in shortening until mixture resembles fine crumbs. Add warm water, 1 tablespoon at a time, tossing until dough can be gathered into a ball. (If necessary, add additional water, 1 tablespoon at a time.) On a lightly floured surface, knead dough by gently folding and pressing dough 15 to 20 times. Cover and let rest 15 minutes.

2 Divide dough into 12 equal portions; shape into balls. Flatten one portion on a lightly floured surface. Roll from center to edges into an 8-inch circle. Repeat with remaining dough portions, layering dough circles between sheets of waxed paper as completed.

3 Heat a 10- or 12-inch ungreased skillet over medium-high heat. Remove top sheet of waxed paper from a dough circle and place the dough, paper side up, in the hot pan. As dough begins to heat, carefully peel off remaining waxed paper. Cook about 30 seconds or until puffy. Turn and cook about 30 seconds more or until edge curls up slightly. Wrap tortilla in foil. Repeat with remaining dough circles.

Nutrition Facts per tortilla: 91 cal., 2 g total fat (1 g sat. fat), 0 mg chol., 131 mg sodium, 15 g carbo., 2 g fiber, 2 g pro. Daily Values: 1% vit. A, 3% calcium, 5% iron

Easy Yeast Bread

Prep: 40 minutes **Chill:** 2 hours to 3 days **Rise:** 30 or 35 minutes
Bake: 10 minutes (rolls), 25 minutes (loaves) **Makes:** 24 rolls or 2 loaves (24 servings)

3¾ cups all-purpose flour*	¼ cup butter or shortening
1 package active dry yeast	2 to 4 tablespoons sugar
½ teaspoon dried dillweed, sage, or basil, crushed (optional)	½ teaspoon salt
1¼ cups milk	1 egg or 2 egg whites

1 In a large bowl mix 1½ cups of the all-purpose flour, the yeast, and, if desired, herb; set aside. In a medium saucepan heat and stir milk, butter, sugar, and salt just until warm (120° to 130°) and butter almost melts. Add milk mixture to flour mixture along with egg or egg whites. Beat with an electric mixer on low to medium speed for 30 seconds, scraping bowl. Beat on high speed for 3 minutes. Stir in the remaining flour.

2 Cover and refrigerate at least 2 hours or up to 3 days. Stir dough down. Divide dough in half. Cover; let rest 10 minutes. Shape into Butterhorns or Loaves (below), as desired. Let rise as directed. Bake in a 375° oven until done. (For rolls, allow 10 to 12 minutes or until golden. For loaves, allow 25 to 30 minutes or until bread sounds hollow when you tap tops. If necessary to prevent overbrowning, cover loaves with foil the last 10 minutes of baking.) Immediately remove from pans. Cool on wire racks.

Nutrition Facts per serving: 96 cal., 3 g total fat (1 g sat. fat), 15 mg chol., 73 mg sodium, 16 g carbo., 1 g fiber, 3 g pro. Daily Values: 2% vit. A, 1% calcium, 6% iron

Butterhorns: Divide each half of dough into 2 portions (4 portions total). On a lightly floured surface, roll each portion into an 8-inch circle. If desired, brush with melted butter. Cut each circle into 6 wedges. Starting at the wide end of each wedge, roll toward point. Place, point sides down, on greased baking sheets. Cover; let rise in warm place until nearly double in size (30 to 40 minutes). Bake rolls as directed above.

Loaves: On a lightly floured surface, roll each half of the dough into a 12×8-inch rectangle. Starting with a short side, roll up each rectangle into a spiral. Seal with your fingertips as you roll. Place in two greased 8×4×2-inch loaf pans. Cover; let rise in a warm place until nearly double in size (35 to 45 minutes). Bake as directed above.

*Note: If desired, substitute 2¾ cups all-purpose flour plus 1 cup whole wheat flour for the 3¾ cups all-purpose flour.

Name your pleasure— butterhorn rolls or simple loaves. You'll enjoy fresh bread in only a few minutes when you keep this no-knead dough on hand.

To Make Ahead

Prepare Easy Yeast Bread dough as directed through step 1. Divide the dough in half. Wrap in plastic wrap; place in self-sealing freezer bags. Seal, label, and freeze up to 3 months.

To Serve

Thaw frozen bread dough, covered, about 2½ hours at room temperature or overnight in refrigerator. Shape and bake as directed.

You will love the triple dose of apple flavor in these extra-large rolls. They bake up beautifully, whether baked immediately or chilled up to 24 hours. For easier cutting, use a serrated knife to cut the dough spiral into rolls.

To Make Ahead

Prepare Apple Harvest Cinnamon Rolls as directed through step 3. Cover with oiled waxed paper, then with plastic wrap. Chill at least 2 hours or up to 24 hours.

To Serve

Allow pan of rolls to stand, covered, at room temperature for 20 minutes. Uncover and puncture any surface bubbles with a greased wooden toothpick. Bake and glaze as directed.

Apple Harvest Cinnamon Rolls

Prep: 50 minutes **Rise:** 1¼ hours **Bake:** 35 minutes **Makes:** 12 rolls

6 to 6½ cups all-purpose flour	1 cup packed brown sugar
2 packages active dry yeast	2¼ teaspoons ground cinnamon
2 cups milk	2 cups chopped, peeled apple
¾ cup butter	¾ cup apple butter
¼ cup granulated sugar	1 cup sifted powdered sugar
1 egg	Apple juice

1 In a large bowl combine 3 cups of the flour and the yeast; set aside. In a medium saucepan heat and stir milk, ¼ cup of the butter, the granulated sugar, and 1½ teaspoons salt until warm (120° to 130°). Add to flour mixture. Add egg. Beat with an electric mixer on low to medium speed 30 seconds, scraping side of bowl. Beat on high speed 3 minutes. Using a wooden spoon, stir in as much of the remaining flour as you can. Turn dough out onto a lightly floured surface. Knead in enough of the remaining flour to make a moderately soft dough that is smooth and elastic (3 to 5 minutes total). Shape dough into a ball. Place dough in lightly greased very large bowl, turning once. Cover; let rise in warm place until double in size (45 to 60 minutes).

2 For filling, melt remaining butter; stir in brown sugar and 2 teaspoons of the cinnamon. Stir in chopped apple and apple butter. Set aside.

3 Punch dough down. Turn dough out onto a lightly floured surface. Divide dough in half. Cover and let rest 10 minutes. Roll each half of dough into a 16×12-inch rectangle. Spread half of the filling over each rectangle to within 1 inch of the short sides. Starting from one of the short sides, roll each rectangle into a spiral. Pinch seams to seal. Cut each roll into six 2-inch pieces. Place pieces, cut sides down, in greased 13×9×2-inch baking pan.

4 Cover; let rolls rise in a warm place until nearly double in size (30 to 40 minutes). Bake in a 350° oven 35 to 40 minutes or until golden. If necessary to prevent overbrowning, cover with foil the last 10 minutes of baking. Cool in pan on wire rack for 10 minutes. Meanwhile, combine powdered sugar and 1 tablespoon apple juice. Stir in additional apple juice, 1 teaspoon at a time, until of drizzling consistency. Drizzle half over rolls. Stir in remaining cinnamon; drizzle over rolls. Serve warm.

Nutrition Facts per roll: 582 cal., 13 g total fat (8 g sat. fat), 51 mg chol., 461 mg sodium, 107 g carbo., 3 g fiber, 9 g pro. Daily Values: 14% vit. A, 3% vit. C, 10% calcium, 22% iron

Overnight guests will appreciate a breakfast table graced with these fruit-studded gems, and you'll appreciate not having to get up extra early to mix the batter. If you find yourself close to the three-day deadline with batter left over, bake remaining batter. Cool muffins and transfer to self-sealing freezer bags. Label and freeze the muffins up to 3 months. Thaw muffins at room temperature or wrap in foil and reheat in a 300° oven until warm.

To Make Ahead

Prepare Refrigerator Bran Muffins as directed through step 1. Store batter in a covered container in refrigerator up to 3 days.

To Serve

Gently stir batter. Bake muffins as directed.

Refrigerator Bran Muffins

Prep: 15 minutes **Bake:** 18 minutes **Makes:** 12 muffins

1½ cups packaged reduced-fat biscuit mix
1 cup whole bran cereal
1 teaspoon ground cinnamon
1 cup fat-free milk

½ cup refrigerated or frozen egg product, thawed
⅓ cup packed brown sugar
2 tablespoons cooking oil
¾ cup dried fruit (such as cherries, raisins, or snipped apricots)

1 In a large bowl combine biscuit mix, cereal, and cinnamon. Make a well in the center. In a small bowl combine milk, egg product, brown sugar, and oil. Add milk mixture all at once to cereal mixture. Stir just until moistened. (The batter will be lumpy.) Fold in fruit.

2 Coat twelve 2½-inch muffin cups with nonstick cooking spray; fill cups ⅔ full. Bake in a 375° oven 18 to 20 minutes or until golden. Remove from pans; cool on wire rack.

Nutrition Facts per muffin: 150 cal., 3 g total fat (1 g sat. fat), 0 mg chol., 213 mg sodium, 27 g carbo., 2 g fiber, 4 g pro. Daily Values: 4% vit. A, 5% vit. C, 8% calcium, 9% iron

The Gift of Time

A nourishing, home-cooked meal ready and waiting in the freezer is a great gift for a friend. It will help solve the dinnertime dilemma on "one of those days." A few good freezer combinations follow; be sure to include thawing and cooking instructions with the gift.
● Penne with Meat Sauce (page 37), Focaccia Breadsticks (page 77), Custard Cream Gelato (page 230). Pick up a package of mixed salad greens to complete the meal.
● Parmesan Chicken and Broccoli (page 48), Bread Machine Buttermilk Rolls (page 76), and Giant Cherry-Oatmeal Cookies (page 226).
● Comforting Cassoulet-Style Stew (page 59), Biscuits Supreme (page 25), and Toasted Hazelnut Bars (page 225).

Biscuits Supreme

Prep: 20 minutes **Bake:** 10 minutes **Makes:** 10 biscuits

2 cups all-purpose flour	¼ teaspoon salt
1 tablespoon baking powder	½ cup butter or shortening
2 teaspoons sugar	⅔ cup milk
½ teaspoon cream of tartar	

1 In large bowl stir together flour, baking powder, sugar, cream of tartar, and salt. Using a pastry blender, cut in butter or shortening until mixture resembles coarse crumbs. Make a well in center. Add milk all at once; stir until moistened.

2 Turn dough out onto a lightly floured surface. Quickly knead dough by gently folding and pressing dough 10 to 12 strokes or until nearly smooth. Pat or lightly roll dough to ½-inch thickness. Cut dough with a floured 2½-inch biscuit cutter.

3 Place biscuits 1 inch apart on an ungreased baking sheet. Bake in a 450° oven for 10 to 12 minutes or until golden. Serve hot.

Nutrition Facts per biscuit: 189 cal., 10 g total fat (6 g sat. fat), 27 mg chol., 281 mg sodium. 21 g carbo., 1 g fiber, 3 g pro. Daily Values: 8% vit. A, 0% vit. C, 10% calcium, 7% iron

Tender, flaky, homemade biscuits ready to pop in the oven anytime—that's the idea here. Keep some on hand to bake and split, then top with creamed chicken, turkey, or ham for a home-style supper in minutes.

To Make Ahead

Prepare Biscuits Supreme as directed through step 2. Arrange biscuits in a single layer on a baking sheet. Cover and freeze until firm. Transfer to a self-sealing freezer bag. Seal, label, and freeze up to 1 month.

To Serve

Unwrap frozen biscuits. Place frozen biscuits on an ungreased baking sheet. Bake in a 400° oven for 15 to 17 minutes or until golden. Serve hot.

Salmon Pinwheel Salad

Prep: 20 minutes **Cook:** 6 minutes **Chill:** 2 hours **Makes:** 6 servings

1	1½-pound fresh or frozen skinless salmon fillet, ½ to ¾ inch thick	2	medium oranges, peeled and sectioned
½	cup dry white wine or water	1	cup thinly sliced cucumber
¼	teaspoon salt	¼	cup sliced almonds, toasted
¼	teaspoon pepper	1	recipe Fresh Orange Dressing (below)
1	bay leaf		
1	10-ounce package European-style torn mixed salad greens		

1 Thaw salmon, if frozen. Cut salmon fillet lengthwise into six even strips. Lightly season with salt and pepper. Starting with the thick end of each strip, roll into pinwheels. Secure each pinwheel with a wooden toothpick or wooden skewer.

2 In a large skillet combine white wine or water, the ¼ teaspoon salt, ¼ teaspoon pepper, and bay leaf; bring to boiling. Add salmon. Return to boiling; reduce heat. Cover and simmer for 6 to 8 minutes or until fish just flakes easily when tested with a fork; turn once. Using a slotted spoon, remove salmon from cooking liquid. Discard cooking liquid. Cover and chill salmon in refrigerator at least 2 hours.

3 To serve, arrange salad greens, orange sections, cucumber slices, and almonds on salad plates or in salad bowls. Top each salad with a salmon pinwheel. Spoon Fresh Orange Dressing over salads.

Fresh Orange Dressing: In a small bowl stir together ½ cup light dairy sour cream, ½ teaspoon finely shredded orange peel, 2 tablespoons orange juice, 2 teaspoons sugar, and ½ teaspoon poppy seed. Add additional orange juice, 1 teaspoon at a time, until desired consistency. Makes about ½ cup.

Nutrition Facts per serving: 244 cal., 9 g total fat (2 g sat. fat), 66 mg chol., 191 mg sodium, 11 g carbo., 3 g fiber, 26 g pro. Daily Values: 19% vit. A, 52% vit. C, 10% calcium, 9% iron

Here's an elegant salad that's perfect for a weekend lunch. Serve it with the shaped rolls made from the Easy Yeast Bread (page 21) and a simple dessert, and you're set.

To Make Ahead

Prepare salmon rolls for Salmon Pinwheel Salad as directed through step 2, except chill in refrigerator up to 24 hours.

To Serve

Arrange salad greens, orange sections, cucumber slices, and almonds as directed. Top each salad with a salmon pinwheel. Spoon the Fresh Orange Dressing over salads.

Make this refreshing salad some spring or summer morning. After work pick up a loaf of bakery fresh bread, and you'll come home to an instant (and relaxing) dinner on the deck.

To Make Ahead

Prepare Curried Chicken-Peanut Salad as directed through step 1, except chill in refrigerator up to 24 hours.

To Serve

Spoon chicken mixture onto lettuce-lined individual salad plates. Sprinkle with peanuts.

Curried Chicken-Peanut Salad

Prep: 20 minutes **Chill:** 2 hours **Makes:** 6 servings

- 2 cups chopped cooked chicken
- 1 8-ounce can pineapple tidbits, drained
- 2 stalks celery, chopped (1 cup)
- ⅓ cup light dairy sour cream
- ⅓ cup light mayonnaise dressing or salad dressing
- ½ teaspoon curry powder
- ⅛ teaspoon salt
  Lettuce leaves
- ½ cup chopped peanuts

1 In a large bowl stir together chicken, pineapple, and celery. In a small bowl combine sour cream, mayonnaise dressing, curry powder, and salt; stir into chicken mixture until evenly moistened. Cover and chill in refrigerator at least 2 hours.

2 To serve, spoon chicken mixture onto lettuce-lined individual salad plates. Sprinkle each serving with chopped peanuts.

Nutrition Facts per serving: 239 cal., 15 g total fat (3 g sat. fat), 47 mg chol., 246 mg sodium, 9 g carbo., 2 g fiber, 17 g pro. Daily Values: 3% vit. A, 8% vit. C, 4% calcium, 6% iron

Cooked Chicken on Call

Whenever you have a little extra chicken—whether from Friday's cookout or Sunday's roasted bird—simply freeze it in a freezer container for up to 3 months. You'll find that a little bit of chicken left over from here and there can add up in no time to just the right amount for a quick chicken salad, a satisfying casserole, or a hearty pot pie.

Three-Cheese Orzo Salad

Prep: 30 minutes **Chill:** 4 hours **Makes:** 8 servings

  2 cups sugar snap peas, ends trimmed
  1¼ cups dried orzo (rosamarina)
  1 6-ounce jar marinated artichoke
    hearts
  2 cups red or yellow cherry tomatoes
    and/or baby pear tomatoes, halved
  1 cup cubed mozzarella cheese
    (4 ounces)

  1 4-ounce package (1 cup) crumbled
    feta or peppercorn feta cheese
  ¼ cup shredded Parmesan cheese
    (1 ounce)
  ¼ cup white wine vinegar
  ¼ cup water
  2 teaspoons sugar
  1 tablespoon snipped fresh dill or
    1 teaspoon dried dillweed

Quick-cooking orzo makes this main dish salad speedy, fresh vegetables make it colorful, and three cheeses make it rich. All in all, it's a great make-ahead totable for your next picnic.

To Make Ahead

Prepare Three-Cheese Orzo Salad as directed, except chill in refrigerator up to 24 hours.

To Serve

Gently stir salad.

1 In a large saucepan cook sugar snap peas in boiling, lightly salted water for 1 minute. Using a slotted spoon, transfer peas to a colander. Rinse under cold water; drain and set aside.

2 Add orzo to the same saucepan. Boil for 8 to 10 minutes or until tender but firm; drain. Rinse with cold water; drain again.

3 Meanwhile, drain artichoke hearts, reserving marinade. Cut artichokes into bite size pieces. In a large bowl toss together artichokes, sugar snap peas, orzo, tomatoes, mozzarella cheese, feta cheese, and Parmesan cheese.

4 For dressing, in a screw-top jar combine reserved artichoke marinade, vinegar, water, sugar, and dill. Cover and shake well. Pour dressing over salad. Toss lightly to coat. Cover and chill in refrigerator at least 4 hours.

Nutrition Facts per serving: 233 cal., 8 g total fat (4 g sat. fat), 23 mg chol., 336 mg sodium, 28 g carbo., 1 g fiber, 12 g pro. Daily Values: 9% vit. A, 38% vit. C, 17% calcium, 13% iron

Nutty sesame oil adds intriguing flavor to this salad. It's sure to satisfy your family's craving for Asian food without waiting for takeout.

To Make Ahead

Prepare Pork and Noodle Salad as directed through step 3, except chill in refrigerator up to 24 hours.

To Serve

Toss salad with dressing as directed.

Pork and Noodle Salad

Prep: 30 minutes **Chill:** 2 hours **Makes:** 4 servings

4 ounces dried Chinese egg noodles or linguine, broken in half
¼ cup soy sauce
2 tablespoons rice vinegar or vinegar
1 tablespoon salad oil
1 tablespoon honey
1 teaspoon sesame oil

¾ pound fresh asparagus, trimmed and cut into 2-inch pieces, or one 10-ounce package frozen cut asparagus
½ pound cooked lean pork, cut into thin strips
1 large carrot, cut into thin strips
1 cup fresh bean sprouts

1 Cook noodles according to package directions; drain. Cover noodles with ice water and let stand until thoroughly chilled. Drain well.

2 Meanwhile, for dressing, in a screw-top jar combine soy sauce, rice vinegar, salad oil, honey, and sesame oil. Cover and shake to mix well. Chill.

3 If using fresh asparagus, cook in a covered saucepan in a small amount of boiling, lightly salted water 4 to 6 minutes or until crisp-tender. (Or if using frozen asparagus, cook according to package directions.) Drain. Combine noodles, asparagus, pork, carrot strips, and bean sprouts. Cover and chill in refrigerator at least 2 hours.

4 To serve, pour dressing over salad; toss lightly. If desired, garnish with toasted sesame seed and sliced green onions.

Nutrition Facts per serving: 328 cal., 12 g total fat (3 g sat. fat), 76 mg chol., 974 mg sodium, 31 g carbo., 2 g fiber, 24 g pro. Daily Values: 69% vit. A, 35% vit. C, 19% iron

Make this truly
impressive soup up
to two days before your
next sit-down dinner party
and you'll have a
sumptuous and stress-free
first course waiting for your
guests.

To Make Ahead

Prepare Roasted Garlic
and Sweet Pepper Soup
as directed through
step 3. Transfer to an
airtight container. Cover
and chill in refrigerator
up to 2 days.

To Serve

Stir in remaining broth
and the half-and-half;
heat as directed. Garnish
as directed.

Roasted Garlic and Sweet Pepper Soup

Start to finish: 1¼ hours **Makes:** 6 to 8 side-dish servings

2 whole heads garlic
1 large onion, sliced
1 tablespoon snipped fresh rosemary
   or 1 teaspoon dried rosemary,
   crushed
1 tablespoon olive oil
4 large red sweet peppers, stems,
   seeds, and membranes removed
   and quartered lengthwise

⅓ cup firmly packed fresh parsley
   sprigs with stems removed
⅓ cup firmly packed fresh basil leaves
1 fresh jalapeño pepper, seeded and
   chopped (1 tablespoon)
¼ teaspoon ground black pepper
¼ teaspoon crushed red pepper
   Dash bottled hot pepper sauce
4 cups chicken broth
½ cup half-and-half or light cream

1 Peel away the dry outer layers of skin from the garlic heads. Leave skins of the cloves intact. Cut ¼ inch off the pointed top portion of each head to expose the individual cloves. Place the garlic heads, cut sides up, and onion slices in a small baking dish. Sprinkle rosemary over the garlic and onion; drizzle with oil. Place sweet pepper quarters, cut sides down, on a foil-lined baking sheet. Roast the onion, garlic, and peppers in a 425° oven for 20 to 25 minutes or until garlic cloves feel soft when pressed and the pepper skins are bubbly and browned.

2 Wrap peppers in the foil; let stand for 20 to 30 minutes or until cool enough to handle. Using a paring knife, gently pull off and discard the skins. When the garlic is cool enough to handle, press garlic paste from individual cloves. Discard skins.

3 Place the garlic paste, sweet peppers, onion, parsley, basil, jalapeño pepper, black pepper, crushed red pepper, and hot pepper sauce in a blender container or food processor bowl. Blend or process until almost smooth. Add 1 cup of the broth; blend until smooth.

4 Transfer the mixture to a large saucepan. Stir in remaining broth and half-and-half. Heat over medium-low heat until warm. If desired, garnish each serving with a spoonful of dairy sour cream.

Nutrition Facts per serving: 114 cal., 6 g total fat (2 g sat. fat), 7 mg chol., 681 mg sodium, 12 g carbo., 3 g fiber, 4 g pro. Daily Values: 98% vit. A, 269% vit. C, 6% calcium, 5% iron

*Note: See tip on handling chile peppers, page 18.

Savory Bean Soup

Prep: 30 minutes **Stand:** 1 hour **Cook:** 1¾ hours **Makes:** 6 servings

1 pound dry navy or Great Northern
  beans, rinsed and drained
1 to 1½ pounds meaty ham bone or
  smoked pork hocks
1 teaspoon dried thyme or sage,
  crushed (optional)

1 large onion, chopped (1 cup)
½ teaspoon seasoned salt
½ teaspoon celery salt
½ teaspoon pepper
¼ teaspoon garlic powder

1 In a 4- to 6-quart Dutch oven combine beans and 6 cups water. Bring to boiling;
reduce heat. Simmer, uncovered, for 2 minutes. Remove from heat. Cover; let stand
1 hour. (Or in a covered 4- to 6-quart Dutch oven soak beans overnight in 6 cups water.)

2 Drain and rinse beans. In same Dutch oven combine beans, ham bone, and 6 cups
fresh water. Bring to boiling; reduce heat. Cover and simmer for 1 hour.

3 Remove ham bone. When cool enough to handle, cut meat off bone. Discard bone and
coarsely chop meat. Return meat to pan. If desired, add thyme or sage. Add onion,
seasoned salt, celery salt, pepper, and garlic powder.

4 Return to boiling; reduce heat. Cover and simmer for 45 to 60 minutes or until beans
are tender.

Nutrition Facts per serving: 290 cal., 2 g total fat (1 g sat. fat), 12 mg chol., 521 mg sodium,
48 g carbo., 6 g fiber, 20 g pro. Daily Values: 12% vit. C, 11% calcium, 32% iron

Veggies in Store

**Most good soups, stews, and casseroles call for onions; many call for
green peppers. So why not shave a little time off future prep work by
keeping a stash of these vegetables in the freezer? To do this, chop the
onions or green peppers, seal in freezer bags, label, and freeze up to
2 months. These tidbits thaw pretty quickly, so when you're ready to use
them they can be stirred directly into the recipe without thawing first.**

If it looks like your family
has a hectic week ahead,
keep a batch of this soup
in the refrigerator so that
everyone can heat up a bowl
of something warm and
satisfying on demand. South-
of-the-Border Corn Biscuits
(page 176) and Crackled
Sugar Cookies (page 227)
make perfect grab-and-go
accompaniments.

To Make Ahead

**Prepare Savory Bean
Soup as directed. Cool
soup slightly. Transfer
to an airtight container.
Cover and chill in
refrigerator up to
2 days.**

To Serve

**Transfer soup to a large
saucepan. Cover and
cook over medium heat
until heated through,
stirring occasionally.**

Mole—a flavorful
Mexican-Native
American sauce—varies
from cook to cook in
Mexico. The chocolate, a
traditional mole ingredient,
adds richness to this
intriguing chili without
adding sweetness.

To Make Ahead

Prepare Mole-Style Pork
and Squash Chili as
directed. Cool chili.
Transfer to an airtight
container. Cover and
chill in refrigerator up
to 2 days.

To Serve

Transfer chili to a Dutch
oven. Cover and cook
over medium heat until
heated through.

Mole-Style Pork and Squash Chili

Prep: 20 minutes **Cook:** 30 minutes **Makes:** 6 servings

¾ pound boneless pork sirloin chops or
   pork shoulder steaks, cut
   ½ inch thick
½ cup chopped onion
2 cloves garlic, minced
2 tablespoons olive oil or cooking oil
2 14½-ounce cans stewed tomatoes
8 ounces butternut squash, peeled and
   cut into ½-inch cubes (about
   1½ cups)
1 15-ounce can red kidney beans,
   rinsed and drained

1 15-ounce can black beans, rinsed
   and drained
1 cup loose-pack frozen whole kernel
   corn
1 cup water
1 tablespoon chili powder
1 tablespoon grated unsweetened
   chocolate
½ teaspoon ground cumin
¼ teaspoon ground cinnamon
¼ teaspoon dried oregano, crushed

1 Cut pork into ½-inch cubes. In a Dutch oven cook and stir the pork, onion, and garlic in hot oil until meat is browned. Stir in undrained tomatoes, squash, kidney beans, black beans, corn, water, chili powder, chocolate, cumin, cinnamon, and oregano. Bring to boiling; reduce heat. Cover and simmer about 30 minutes or until squash and pork are tender, stirring occasionally. To serve, ladle chili into bowls.

Nutrition Facts per serving: 289 cal., 9 g total fat (2 g sat. fat), 23 mg chol., 678 mg sodium, 41 g carbo., 11 g fiber, 20 g pro. Daily Values: 41% vit. A, 58% vit. C, 10% calcium, 24% iron

Spice Storage Smarts

While whole spices usually have a shelf life of two years, ground spices lose their flavor quickly after purchase—they tend to stay fresh up to six months. Purchase spices in small quantities and store tightly covered in a cool, dry place. Check their freshness periodically. If the color or the aroma seems weak, replace the spice. To prolong the shelf life of red spices, such as ground red pepper, paprika, and chili powder, store them in the refrigerator.

The strip of cheese hidden in each individual loaf makes these ground beef and sausage meat loaves extra special.

To Make Ahead

Prepare Two-Meat Meat Loaves as directed through step 2. Cover and freeze until firm. Wrap meat loaves in moisture- and vaporproof wrap. Label and freeze up to 3 months.

To Serve

Place desired number of frozen meat loaves in a shallow baking pan. Bake in a 325° oven, covered loosely with foil, for 1 hour. Uncover; bake 10 minutes more. Spoon the remaining ½ cup spaghetti sauce over the loaves and sprinkle each with 1 tablespoon of the shredded cheese. Bake about 5 minutes more or until an instant-read thermometer inserted in the thickest part of each loaf registers 160°.* Let stand for 5 minutes. Serve as directed.

Two-Meat Meat Loaves

Prep: 20 minutes **Bake:** 35 minutes **Makes:** 6 single-serving loaves

1 beaten egg
1 cup soft bread crumbs (about 1½ slices)
½ cup bottled spaghetti sauce or pasta sauce
1 or 2 cloves garlic, minced
½ teaspoon dried rosemary, crushed
1 pound lean ground beef

½ pound bulk Italian or pork sausage or lean ground beef
6 2½×½×½-inch sticks provolone or mozzarella cheese
½ cup bottled spaghetti sauce or pasta sauce
6 tablespoons shredded provolone or mozzarella cheese

1 In a large bowl combine egg, bread crumbs, ½ cup spaghetti sauce, the garlic, and dried rosemary. Add ground beef and sausage; mix well.

2 Divide meat mixture into 6 equal portions; form each into a 3½×2-inch loaf. Press a stick of cheese lengthwise into the center of each loaf, shaping so that meat completely covers the cheese. Place loaves in a 13×9×2-inch baking pan.

3 Bake, uncovered, in a 350° oven for 30 minutes. Spoon ½ cup spaghetti sauce over the meat loaves, and sprinkle each with 1 tablespoon of the shredded cheese. Bake about 5 minutes more or until an instant-read thermometer inserted in the thickest part of each loaf registers 160°.* Let stand for 5 minutes. Transfer meat loaves to a platter. If desired, garnish with fresh rosemary sprigs.

Nutrition Facts per serving: 369 cal., 26 g total fat (10 g sat. fat), 124 mg chol., 715 mg sodium, 8 g carbo., 2 g fiber, 26 g pro. Daily Values: 4% vit. A, 8% vit. C, 17% calcium, 15% iron

*Note: The internal color of a meat loaf is not a reliable doneness indicator. A ground meat loaf cooked to 160°, regardless of color, is safe. Use an instant-read thermometer to check the internal temperature. To measure the doneness of these meat loaves, insert an instant-read thermometer through one end of each loaf to a depth of 2 inches.

Penne with Meat Sauce

Prep: 30 minutes **Bake:** 25 minutes **Makes:** 4 to 6 servings

1	14½-ounce can whole Italian-style tomatoes	1	pound lean ground beef
1	8-ounce can tomato sauce	½	cup chopped onion (1 medium)
¼	cup dry red wine or beef broth	8	ounces dried penne pasta
1	tablespoon snipped fresh oregano or 1 teaspoon dried oregano, crushed	¼	cup sliced pitted ripe olives
½	teaspoon sugar	1	cup shredded mozzarella cheese (4 ounces)
¼	teaspoon pepper		

1 In a blender container or food processor bowl combine undrained tomatoes, tomato sauce, wine or beef broth, dried oregano (if using), sugar, and pepper. Cover and blend or process until smooth. Set aside.

2 In a large skillet cook ground beef and onion until meat is brown. Drain off fat. Stir in tomato mixture. Bring to boiling; reduce heat. Cover and simmer for 10 minutes.

3 Meanwhile, cook pasta according to package directions. Drain well. Toss sauce with cooked pasta, olives, and fresh oregano (if using).

4 Spoon pasta mixture into a 2-quart casserole. (Or divide pasta mixture among four to six 12- to 16-ounce individual casseroles.) Bake 2-quart casserole, covered, in a 350° oven for 20 minutes. (Or bake individual casseroles, covered, in a 350° oven for 15 minutes.) Sprinkle with mozzarella cheese. Bake, uncovered, about 5 minutes more or until cheese is melted and casserole is heated through.

Nutrition Facts per serving: 663 cal., 30 g total fat (12 g sat. fat), 98 mg chol., 891 mg sodium, 59 g carbo., 4 g fiber, 36 g pro. Daily Values: 18% vit. A, 36% vit. C, 29% calcium, 28% iron

There's something about this hearty and wholly satisfying dish that practically begs everyone to gather around and dig in. Serve it with a mixed green salad, Focaccia Breadsticks (page 77), and Chocolate-Raspberry Cheesecake (page 219).

To Make Ahead

Prepare sauce for Penne with Meat Sauce as directed through step 2. Cool about 30 minutes. Spoon into a freezer container. Seal, label, and freeze up to 3 months.

To Serve

Transfer frozen sauce to a large saucepan. Add 2 tablespoons water. Cover and cook over medium heat about 25 minutes or until heated through, stirring occasionally. Meanwhile, cook penne pasta according to package directions. Drain well. Assemble and bake as directed.

Consider this hearty casserole as comfort food with a Tex-Mex twist. The perfect dish to come home to after a busy day—it's a definite family-pleaser.

To Make Ahead

Prepare Bean-and-Beef Enchilada Casserole as directed through step 2. Cover with plastic wrap; chill in refrigerator up to 24 hours.

To Serve

Remove plastic wrap. Cover dish with foil. Bake in a 350° oven for 35 to 40 minutes or until nearly heated through. Uncover and sprinkle with cheese; bake 5 minutes more. Garnish as directed.

Bean-and-Beef Enchilada Casserole

Prep: 25 minutes **Bake**: 35 minutes **Makes**: 6 to 8 servings

½ pound lean ground beef
½ cup chopped onion
1 teaspoon chili powder
½ teaspoon ground cumin
1 15-ounce can pinto beans, rinsed and drained
1 4½-ounce can diced green chile peppers

1 8-ounce carton dairy sour cream or light dairy sour cream
2 tablespoons all-purpose flour
¼ teaspoon garlic powder
8 6-inch corn tortillas
1 10-ounce can enchilada sauce or one 10¾-ounce can tomato puree
1 cup shredded cheddar cheese (4 ounces)

1 In a large skillet cook the ground beef, onion, chili powder, and cumin until meat is brown and onion is tender. Drain off fat. Stir pinto beans and undrained chile peppers into meat mixture; set aside. In a small bowl stir together sour cream, flour, and garlic powder until combined; set aside.

2 Place half of the tortillas in the bottom of a lightly greased 2-quart rectangular baking dish, cutting to fit as necessary. Top with half of the meat mixture, half of the sour cream mixture, and half of the enchilada sauce. Repeat layers.

3 Bake, covered, in a 350° oven about 30 minutes or until nearly heated through. Uncover; sprinkle with cheese and bake 5 minutes more. If desired, garnish with chopped tomato.

Nutrition Facts per serving: 429 cal., 24 g total fat (12 g sat. fat), 64 mg chol., 632 mg sodium, 36 g carbo., 6 g fiber, 19 g pro. Daily Values: 23% vit. A, 10% vit. C, 30% calcium, 14% iron

These pinwheels, based on a much-loved Italian dish called braciola, are stress-free and company-special. The do-ahead instructions let you get most of the prep work out of the way long before anyone arrives, and the vegetables roast alongside the meat for a super-easy side dish.

To Store

Prepare Herbed Beef Pinwheels as directed through step 2. Wrap roll tightly in plastic wrap and chill in refrigerator up to 24 hours.

To Use

Unwrap meat roll and brown meat as directed in step 3. Continue as directed.

Herbed Beef Pinwheels

Prep: 30 minutes **Cook:** 1 hour **Makes:** 4 servings

- 1 1- to 1¼-pound beef flank steak
- 2 tablespoons olive oil or cooking oil
- 2 medium leeks, sliced (⅔ cup)
- 2 cloves garlic, minced
- 3 tablespoons snipped fresh basil
- ¼ teaspoon salt
- ⅛ teaspoon pepper
- 2 Yukon gold potatoes, cut into eighths
- 1 large onion, cut into thin wedges
- 1 14½-ounce can diced tomatoes with basil, oregano, and garlic

1 Score steak by making shallow diagonal cuts at 1-inch intervals in a diamond pattern on both sides. Place steak between 2 pieces of plastic wrap. Working from center to edges, use the flat side of a meat mallet to pound steak into a 12×8-inch rectangle. Remove plastic wrap; set steak aside.

2 In a large skillet heat 1 tablespoon of the oil over medium-high heat. Add leeks and garlic. Cook 3 to 5 minutes or until leeks are tender. Stir in basil, salt, and pepper. Remove from heat. Spread leek mixture evenly on one side of steak. Starting at a short end, tightly roll up meat into a spiral. Tie 100% cotton kitchen string around steak in four evenly spaced places.

3 In same large skillet heat remaining oil over medium-high heat. Brown meat on all sides in the hot oil. Transfer meat to a 2-quart rectangular baking dish.

4 Arrange potatoes and onion wedges around meat in dish. Pour undrained tomatoes over beef and vegetables. Bake, uncovered, in a 350° oven about 1 hour or until beef is medium doneness (160°). Transfer meat to a cutting board. Cut into serving-size slices. Remove string. Serve meat with vegetables.

Nutrition Facts per serving: 355 cal., 15 g total fat (4 g sat. fat), 53 mg chol., 722 mg sodium, 30 g carbo., 4 g fiber, 25 g pro. Daily Values: 7% vit. A, 49% vit. C, 6% calcium, 27% iron

Pot Roast with Basil Mashed Potatoes

Prep: 30 minutes **Cook:** 4 to 10 hours **Stand:** 10 minutes **Makes:** 6 servings

2 carrots, cut into ½-inch pieces	⅛ teaspoon pepper
1 medium turnip, peeled and cubed (about 1 cup)	1 1½- to 2-pound boneless beef chuck pot roast
1 small onion, chopped	1 cup water
½ cup snipped dried tomatoes (not oil-packed)	1 10-ounce package frozen lima beans or whole kernel corn
1 clove garlic, minced	1 cup frozen peas
1 teaspoon instant beef bouillon granules	1 20-ounce package refrigerated mashed potatoes
½ teaspoon dried basil, crushed	1 tablespoon finely snipped fresh basil
½ teaspoon dried oregano, crushed	

1 In a 3½- or 4-quart electric crockery cooker combine the carrots, turnip, onion, dried tomatoes, garlic, bouillon granules, dried basil, dried oregano, and pepper. Trim fat from roast. If necessary, cut roast to fit into cooker. Place roast on top of vegetables. Pour the water over all.

2 Cover; cook on low-heat setting for 8 to 10 hours or on high-heat setting for 4 to 5 hours. Stir in lima beans or corn and peas. Cover and let stand for 10 minutes.

3 Meanwhile, prepare mashed potatoes according to package directions, except stir the snipped basil into potatoes just before serving. Remove meat and vegetables from cooker with a slotted spoon. If desired, reserve cooking juices. Slice meat; serve meat and vegetables over hot mashed potatoes. If desired, serve cooking juices over meat.

Nutrition Facts per serving: 436 cal., 12 g total fat (5 g sat. fat), 87 mg chol., 497 mg sodium, 46 g carbo., 8 g fiber, 35 g pro. Daily Values: 55% vit. A, 12% vit. C, 4% calcium, 34% iron

On a cold winter day, you'll love coming home to a melt-in-your-mouth pot roast that has simmered to perfection all day in your crockery cooker. Herb-flecked mashed potatoes, an American bistro classic, lend a cosmopolitan yet comforting flair to this savory dish.

With spicy jerk
seasoning, sweet
mango, and tangy lime
dressing, the humble
pulled-pork sandwich gets
an eye-opening update. And
it all starts from a simple
crockery cooker recipe.

Jerk Porkwiches with Lime Mayo

Prep: 30 minutes **Cook:** 4 to 10 hours **Makes:** 6 to 8 servings

1 1½- to 2-pound boneless pork shoulder roast	6 to 8 kaiser rolls, split and toasted
1 tablespoon purchased or homemade Jamaican Jerk Seasoning (page 18)	6 to 8 lettuce leaves (optional)
¼ teaspoon dried thyme, crushed	6 thinly sliced red or green sweet pepper rings (optional)
1 cup water	1 medium mango, peeled, seeded, and thinly sliced (optional)
1 tablespoon lime juice	1 recipe Lime Mayo (below)

1 Trim fat from meat. Rub jerk seasoning evenly over roast. Place meat in a 3½- or 4-quart electric crockery cooker. Sprinkle with the thyme. Pour the water over meat.

2 Cover; cook on low-heat setting for 8 to 10 hours or on high-heat setting for 4 to 5 hours. Remove meat from cooker, reserving cooking juices. Shred meat, discarding any fat. Skim fat from cooking juices. Add enough of the cooking juices to moisten meat (about ½ cup). Stir lime juice into meat.

3 To serve, if desired, line roll bottoms with lettuce leaves. Use a slotted spoon to place pork mixture on roll bottoms. If desired, top with sweet pepper rings and mango slices. Spoon some of the Lime Mayo onto each sandwich; add roll tops.

Lime Mayo: In a small bowl stir together ½ cup light mayonnaise dressing or regular mayonnaise, ¼ cup finely chopped red onion, ¼ teaspoon finely shredded lime peel, 1 tablespoon lime juice, and 1 clove garlic, minced. Cover; chill in refrigerator until ready to serve or up to 1 week.

Nutrition Facts per serving: 430 cal., 21 g total fat (6 g sat. fat), 74 mg chol., 609 mg sodium. 34 g carbo., 0 g fiber, 26 g pro. Daily Values: 4% vit. A, 4% vit. C, 6% calcium, 22% iron

***Note:** See tip on peeling and seeding mangos, page 100.

Ragout (rah-GOO), the French term for a thick, rich stew, is derived from a verb that means "to stimulate the appetite." This crockery cooker version, whether for company or simply a special meal with your family, will do just that.

Lamb Ragoût with Couscous

Prep: 30 minutes **Cook:** 4½ to 10½ hours **Makes:** 6 servings

1½ to 2 pounds lamb stew meat, cut
    into 1-inch cubes
1 tablespoon cooking oil
2 cups coarsely chopped onions
2 medium tomatoes, chopped
2 medium carrots, cut into
    ½-inch slices
3 cloves garlic, minced
2 tablespoons quick-cooking tapioca
1 cup beef broth

¼ cup dry red wine or water
1 teaspoon dried Italian seasoning or
    oregano, crushed
½ teaspoon salt
¼ teaspoon pepper
2 small zucchini, halved lengthwise
    and cut into ¼-inch slices
1 9-ounce package frozen artichoke
    hearts, thawed and quartered
    Hot cooked couscous or rice

1 In a large skillet brown meat, half at a time, in hot oil. Drain off fat. Transfer meat to a 3½-, 4-, or 5-quart electric crockery cooker. Add the onions, tomatoes, carrots, and garlic. Sprinkle with tapioca. In a small bowl combine beef broth, wine or water, Italian seasoning, salt, and pepper. Pour over all. Stir to combine.

2 Cover and cook on low-heat setting for 8 to 10 hours or on high-heat setting for 4 to 5 hours.

3 If using low-heat setting, turn to high-heat setting. Stir in the zucchini and thawed artichoke hearts. Cover; cook for 30 minutes more. Serve over couscous.

Nutrition Facts per serving: 373 cal., 8 g total fat (3 g sat. fat), 61 mg chol., 456 mg sodium, 47 g carbo., 6 g fiber, 28 g pro. Daily Values: 59% vit. A, 37% vit. C, 6% calcium, 23% iron

A Little "Pearl"

Tapioca is a starch extracted from the root of the cassava plant. Though we think pudding when we think tapioca, the starch is used to thicken a variety of cooked dishes. In fact, it is the best choice for thickening a crockery cooker recipe because it withstands long cooking times without breaking down, and it doesn't need to be stirred during cooking to prevent settling. Make sure you purchase quick-cooking tapioca instead of regular pearl tapioca for this recipe.

Chicken and Shrimp with Orzo

Prep: 20 minutes **Cook:** 3 to 7 hours **Makes:** 4 or 5 servings

¾ pound skinless, boneless chicken thighs

1 large onion, chopped

3 cloves garlic, minced

1 14½-ounce can diced tomatoes with basil, oregano, and garlic or diced tomatoes with onion and garlic

½ cup port wine or chicken broth

2 tablespoons tomato paste

2 tablespoons lemon juice

2 bay leaves

½ teaspoon salt

¼ teaspoon crushed red pepper

1 9-ounce package frozen artichoke hearts, thawed and coarsely chopped

1 8-ounce package frozen, peeled, cooked shrimp, thawed and drained

Hot cooked orzo (rosamarina)

½ cup crumbled feta cheese (2 ounces)

1 Cut chicken thighs into quarters. Place onion and garlic in a 3½-, 4-, or 5-quart electric crockery cooker. Top with the chicken thighs. In a medium bowl combine the undrained tomatoes, wine or broth, tomato paste, lemon juice, bay leaves, salt, and crushed red pepper. Pour tomato mixture over chicken and vegetables in cooker.

2 Cover and cook on low-heat setting for 6 to 7 hours or on high-heat setting for 3 to 3½ hours.

3 If using low-heat setting, turn to high heat setting. Discard bay leaves. Stir in artichoke hearts and shrimp. Cover; cook for 5 minutes more. Serve chicken and shrimp mixture over hot cooked orzo. Sprinkle with feta cheese.

Nutrition Facts per serving: 615 cal., 21 g total fat (9 g sat. fat), 187 mg chol., 1,203 mg sodium, 56 g carbo., 4 g fiber, 46 g pro. Daily Values: 22% vit. A, 267% vit. C, 23% calcium, 40% iron

When it comes to the crockery cooker, it's easy to get into a pot roast rut. This recipe shows that the ultimate fix-and-forget appliance also works well for innovative, worldly dishes.

This oven-fried chicken is so easy it's ready to pop in the oven in 15 minutes. Or rather than waiting until you get home, get a head start on dinner by coating the chicken in the morning, then putting it in the oven as soon as you get home from work. Round out the meal with a packaged rice pilaf mix and a marinated cucumber salad—you'll have plenty of time to relax before dinner.

To Make Ahead

Prepare Mustard Crisp Chicken as directed through step 1, except place chicken in a covered container or in a baking dish covered with plastic wrap. Refrigerate up to 24 hours.

To Serve

Arrange chicken in a foil-lined 15×10×1-inch baking pan, making sure pieces do not touch. Drizzle with melted margarine and bake as directed.

Mustard Crisp Chicken

Prep: 15 minutes **Bake:** 40 minutes **Makes:** 4 to 6 servings

¼ cup Dijon-style mustard
2 tablespoons water
2 teaspoons snipped fresh thyme or
    ¾ teaspoon dried thyme, crushed
½ teaspoon bottled minced garlic or
    1 clove garlic, minced
¼ teaspoon pepper

¼ teaspoon paprika
¾ cup fine dry bread crumbs
2½ to 2¾ pounds meaty chicken pieces
    (breasts, thighs, and drumsticks),
    skin removed
2 tablespoons margarine or butter,
    melted

1 In a large bowl or shallow dish combine mustard, water, thyme, garlic, pepper, and paprika. In another bowl or plastic bag place bread crumbs. Coat chicken with mustard mixture, allowing excess to drip off; roll or shake in the bread crumbs. Arrange chicken in a foil-lined 15×10×1-inch baking pan, making sure pieces do not touch.

2 Drizzle chicken with melted margarine. Bake chicken, uncovered, in a 375° oven for 40 to 50 minutes or until golden and an instant-read thermometer inserted in chicken registers 170° for breasts or 180° for thighs or drumsticks. Do not turn chicken during baking.

Nutrition Facts per serving: 466 cal., 16 g total fat (4 g sat. fat), 198 mg chol., 725 mg sodium, 13 g carbo., 1 g fiber, 63 g pro. Daily Values: 10% vit. A, 9% vit. C, 9% calcium, 21% iron

A few flavorful touches, including toasted almonds, rich Parmesan cheese, and a little ham, turn a quick chicken-and-rice casserole into a dinner worth savoring.

To Make Ahead

Prepare Parmesan Chicken and Broccoli as directed through step 4, except don't sprinkle with almonds. Cover dish with heavy foil. Seal, label, and freeze up to 3 months.

To Serve

Place covered frozen casserole in the refrigerator overnight. (The casserole may still be icy at baking time.) Bake casserole, covered with foil, in a 350° oven for 1 hour. Uncover and bake for 20 to 25 minutes more or until heated through. Sprinkle with almonds.

Parmesan Chicken and Broccoli

Prep: 30 minutes **Bake:** 25 minutes **Makes:** 6 servings

1 cup converted rice	4 teaspoons cornstarch
½ cup sliced green onions	2¾ cups milk
1¼ pounds skinless, boneless chicken breast halves, cut into strips	½ of an 8-ounce package cream cheese, cut up
1 tablespoon cooking oil	1½ cups loose-pack frozen cut broccoli
1 teaspoon dried Italian seasoning, crushed	½ cup grated Parmesan cheese (2 ounces)
1 teaspoon bottled minced garlic or 2 cloves garlic, minced	⅓ cup diced cooked ham
	2 tablespoons toasted sliced almonds

1 Cook rice according to package directions; remove from heat and stir in half of the green onions. Spread in a greased 2-quart rectangular baking dish; set aside.

2 In a large skillet cook half the chicken strips in hot oil over medium heat about 6 minutes or until chicken is no longer pink. Remove from skillet. Add remaining chicken strips, the Italian seasoning, and garlic to skillet. Cook 6 minutes or until chicken is no longer pink. Remove from skillet; reserve drippings.

3 For sauce, cook remaining green onions in reserved skillet drippings until tender, adding more oil if necessary. Stir in cornstarch; add milk all at once. Cook and stir over medium heat until slightly thickened and bubbly. Reduce heat; stir in cream cheese until nearly smooth. Remove sauce from heat; stir in cooked chicken strips, broccoli, Parmesan cheese, and ham. Spoon chicken mixture over rice in baking dish; season with salt and pepper.

4 Bake the casserole, covered, in a 350° oven for 25 to 30 minutes or until heated through. Sprinkle with almonds.

Nutrition Facts per serving: 455 cal., 17 g total fat (8 g sat. fat), 95 mg chol., 537 mg sodium, 37 g carbo., 3 g fiber, 37 g pro. Daily Values: 30% vit. A, 37% vit. C, 34% calcium, 12% iron

Three-Cheese and Artichoke Lasagna

Prep: 40 minutes **Bake:** 40 minutes **Stand:** 10 minutes **Makes:** 8 servings

9 dried lasagna noodles

1 9-ounce package frozen artichoke hearts, thawed, or one 14-ounce can artichoke hearts, drained

1 tablespoon butter or olive oil

1 large red onion, finely chopped

4 cloves garlic, minced

½ cup dry white wine or chicken broth

2 cups milk

3 tablespoons all-purpose flour

2 teaspoons finely shredded lemon peel

¼ teaspoon salt

¼ teaspoon pepper

1 15-ounce container fat-free or part-skim ricotta cheese

¾ cup finely shredded Parmigiano-Reggiano, Asiago, or Parmesan cheese (3 ounces)

2 teaspoons snipped fresh tarragon or ½ teaspoon dried tarragon, crushed

1½ cups shredded Gruyère or Swiss cheese (6 ounces)

1 cup cubed smoked turkey or cooked ham (5 ounces)

1 Cook noodles according to package directions. Drain and set aside. Quarter artichoke hearts lengthwise and pat dry; set aside.

2 Meanwhile, for sauce, in a large saucepan heat butter or olive oil over medium heat. Add onion and garlic; cook and stir about 5 minutes or until tender. Add wine or broth; cook 3 minutes more. In a small bowl gradually stir milk into flour; stir into onion mixture. Cook and stir until thickened and bubbly. Stir in artichoke hearts, lemon peel, salt, and pepper; set aside.

3 In another small bowl stir together ricotta cheese, ¼ cup of the Parmigiano-Reggiano cheese, and the tarragon. Set aside. In a lightly greased 2-quart rectangular baking dish layer 1 cup of the sauce, 3 noodles, half of the Gruyère, and half of the smoked turkey. Spoon half of the ricotta mixture on top. Repeat layers. Top with the remaining noodles and sauce. Cover dish with foil.

4 Bake in a 375° oven for 20 minutes. Uncover and sprinkle with the remaining Parmigiano-Reggiano cheese. Bake, uncovered, about 20 minutes more or until bubbly and golden. Let stand 10 minutes before serving.

Nutrition Facts per serving: 360 cal., 13 g total fat (6 g sat. fat), 56 mg chol., 578 mg sodium, 32 g carbo., 3 g fiber, 29 g pro. Daily Values: 20% vit. A, 41% calcium, 11% iron

Lasagna almost always makes for easygoing make-ahead fare—but it's rarely thought of as particularly elegant. Here, artichokes, smoked meat, white wine, and garlic make the dish regal enough for a dinner party.

To Make Ahead

Prepare Three-Cheese and Artichoke Lasagna as directed through step 3. Store, covered, in refrigerator up to 24 hours.

To Serve

Allow lasagna to stand at room temperature for 30 minutes. Bake as directed.

Here's a hearty meatless casserole that's brimming with a variety of flavors, colors, and textures. The unbelievable thing is that it's low in fat too.

To Make Ahead

Prepare Red Bean Shepherd's Pie as directed through step 3. Cover tightly and chill in refrigerator up to 24 hours.

To Serve

Bake, covered, in a 350° oven about 1 hour or until heated through. Uncover and sprinkle with the cheese. Bake, uncovered, 10 minutes more or until the cheese melts.

Red Bean Shepherd's Pie

Prep: 25 minutes **Bake:** 45 minutes **Makes:** 5 servings

1 pound small round red potatoes	1 10¾-ounce can condensed cream of potato soup
1 cup chopped onion	1 cup frozen peas
½ cup sliced celery	1 cup chopped green sweet pepper
4 cloves garlic, minced	¼ cup fat-free milk
¼ teaspoon cracked black pepper	½ teaspoon ground cumin
1 tablespoon cooking oil	½ teaspoon ground coriander
1 15-ounce can chickpeas (garbanzo beans), rinsed and drained	½ cup shredded reduced-fat Monterey Jack cheese (2 ounces)
1 15-ounce can small red beans, rinsed and drained	

1 Scrub potatoes and thinly slice. In a covered medium saucepan cook potatoes in enough boiling water to cover for 4 to 5 minutes or until almost tender; drain in a colander. Run cold water over potatoes in colander. Drain and set aside.

2 In a large saucepan cook onion, celery, garlic, and black pepper in hot oil about 5 minutes or until vegetables are tender. Mash ½ cup of the chickpeas; add to vegetable mixture along with the remaining chickpeas, red beans, soup, peas, sweet pepper, milk, cumin, and coriander. Stir gently to combine.

3 In a greased 2-quart casserole place a single layer of the potato slices. Spoon bean mixture on top and cover with remaining potato slices, overlapping if necessary.

4 Bake, covered, in a 350° oven for 35 minutes. Uncover and sprinkle with cheese. Bake, uncovered, about 10 minutes more or until cheese melts.

Nutrition Facts per serving: 376 cal., 8 g total fat (2 g sat. fat), 11 mg chol., 1,073 mg sodium, 63 g carbo., 12 g fiber, 19 g pro. Daily Values: 6% vit. A, 41% vit. C, 16% calcium, 35% iron

Lahvosh Roll

Prep: 15 minutes **Stand:** 1 hour **Chill:** 2 hours **Makes:** 6 servings

1 15-inch sesame seed lahvosh
   (Armenian cracker bread) or two
   10-inch flour tortillas
1 4-ounce tub cream cheese with
   chives and onion
¼ cup chopped, drained marinated
   artichoke hearts

2 tablespoons chopped pimiento
1 teaspoon dried oregano, crushed
6 ounces thinly sliced prosciutto or
   cooked ham
4 ounces sliced provolone cheese
1 large romaine leaf, rib removed

1 Dampen both sides of lahvosh by holding it briefly under gently running cold water. Place lahvosh, sesame side down, between 2 damp clean kitchen towels. Let stand about 1 hour or until soft. (If using tortillas, omit this step.)

2 In a small bowl stir together cream cheese, artichoke hearts, pimiento, and oregano. Remove top towel from lahvosh. Spread lahvosh with cream cheese mixture. Arrange prosciutto over cream cheese. Place cheese slices in center and romaine leaf next to cheese. Starting from romaine edge, use the towel to lift and roll the bread into a spiral. (Or if using tortillas, spread tortillas with cream cheese mixture. Divide remaining ingredients between the tortillas. Roll up tortillas.)

3 Wrap roll in plastic wrap and chill in refrigerator, seam side down, for 2 hours. To serve, cut roll into 1-inch slices.

Nutrition Facts per serving: 327 cal., 20 g total fat (7 g sat. fat), 33 mg chol., 879 mg sodium, 21 g carbo., 16 g pro. Daily Values: 10% vit. C, 13% calcium

Wrap this colorful, varied sandwich in the morning. After work, pick it up and head to a nearby park for an instant picnic. Lahvosh, which looks like a giant crisp cracker, is softened before using. If you're able to find the presoftened variety, you can skip a step.

To Make Ahead
Prepare Lahvosh Roll as directed through step 2. Wrap roll in plastic wrap and chill in refrigerator, seam side down, up to 24 hours.

To Serve
To serve, cut roll into 1-inch-thick slices

Creamy Chicken Enchiladas (page 63)

Make a
Bonus Batch

Yes, you can have your cake and eat it too—and the same goes for soups, stews, enchiladas, and more. With these recipes, one tour of duty in the kitchen yields a batch to enjoy right away and extra helpings to savor later.

In This Chapter

The beloved season of fresh, home-grown tomatoes passes all too quickly! Next time it rolls around, preserve its magic by making this soup. You'll be able to savor summer's vine-ripened flavor even when autumn leaves begin to fall.

To Store

Seal, label, and freeze up to 2 months.

To Serve

Transfer frozen Two-Tomato Soup to a saucepan. Cook, covered, over medium heat for 15 to 20 minutes, stirring occasionally. Stir in ½ cup whipping cream. Cook and stir 5 to 10 minutes more or until heated through. Ladle into soup bowls and serve as directed.

Two-Tomato Soup

Prep: 15 minutes **Stand:** 30 minutes **Cook:** 65 minutes **Makes:** 8 side-dish servings total

1 3-ounce package dried tomatoes (not oil-packed)	8 medium fresh tomatoes, chopped (about 2½ pounds)
½ cup chopped onion	4 cups water
¼ teaspoon coarsely ground black pepper	1 teaspoon salt
1 tablespoon olive oil or cooking oil	½ cup whipping cream

1 Place the dried tomatoes in a small bowl. Add enough boiling water to cover. Soak for 30 minutes. Drain and rinse. Coarsely chop rehydrated tomatoes.

2 In a Dutch oven cook and stir rehydrated tomatoes, onion, and pepper in hot oil about 5 minutes or until onion is tender.

3 Reserve ¾ cup of the chopped fresh tomatoes; set aside. Add remaining fresh tomatoes to rehydrated tomato mixture. Cook, covered, over low heat about 20 minutes or until tomatoes are soft. Add water and salt. Cook, uncovered, over low heat for 40 minutes more, stirring often. Transfer one-fourth of mixture at a time to a blender container or food processor bowl. Cover and carefully blend or process until smooth. Return all of the mixture to Dutch oven. Heat to simmering.

4 Remove half of soup mixture; cool slightly. Transfer to freezer containers. Store as directed at left.

5 To serve remaining soup, stir cream into soup. Heat just until simmering. Ladle soup into bowls. Spoon some of the reserved fresh chopped tomatoes into each bowl.

Nutrition Facts per serving: 176 cal., 14 g total fat (7 g sat. fat), 41 mg chol., 540 mg sodium, 13 g carbo., 3 g fiber, 3 g pro. Daily Values: 21% vit. A, 47% vit. C, 4% calcium, 9% iron

Fresh Mushroom Soup

Start to finish: 40 minutes **Makes:** 12 side-dish servings total

1	pound fresh shiitake and/or button mushrooms
12	ounces small fresh oyster mushrooms
⅔	cup chopped shallots
3	tablespoons butter
¼	cup all-purpose flour
1	teaspoon salt
¼ to ½	teaspoon coarsely ground black pepper
2	14½-ounce cans vegetable broth or chicken broth
2	cups half-and-half or light cream
2	cups milk
⅛	teaspoon ground saffron or saffron threads

1 Remove any tough or woody stems from mushrooms. Coarsely chop the mushrooms. In a 4-quart Dutch oven cook mushrooms and shallots in hot butter over medium-high heat for 5 to 6 minutes or until tender, stirring occasionally. Stir in flour, salt, and pepper. Add broth. Cook and stir over medium heat until slightly thickened and bubbly. Cook and stir 1 minute more. Stir in half-and-half, milk, and saffron.

2 Remove half of the mixture (a scant 5 cups); cool slightly. Transfer to a 1½-quart freezer container. Store as directed at right.

3 To serve remaining soup, continue to cook until heated through. Ladle into soup bowls. If desired, garnish with additional saffron threads.

Nutrition Facts per serving: 141 cal., 9 g total fat (5 g sat. fat), 26 mg chol., 558 mg sodium, 11 g carbo., 1 g fiber, 6 g pro. Daily Values: 11% vit. A, 4% vit. C, 10% calcium, 7% iron

Make this flavorful soup as an elegant first course for a dinner party, then freeze the rest to serve with a salad or sandwich for an out-of-the-ordinary weekend lunch.

To Store

Seal, label, and freeze up to 2 months.

To Serve

Transfer frozen Fresh Mushroom Soup to a large saucepan. Cook, covered, over medium heat about 20 minutes or until heated through, stirring occasionally. Ladle into soup bowls and serve as directed.

A Little Goes a Long Way

The spice called saffron comes from the stigmas or threadlike filaments of the purple crocus flower. Each flower contains only three stigmas, which are hand-picked and dried. More than 14,000 stigmas are needed to make an ounce of saffron. Because of the labor-intensive process of harvesting the stigmas, saffron is very expensive. You need only a small amount to flavor your recipes. To release the flavor, crush the saffron threads by rubbing them between your fingers.

Remember this recipe
when you're looking
for something special to
serve on a crisp fall evening.
For an enticing contrast in
color and texture, sprinkle
each serving with finely
chopped pistachio nuts.

To Store

Seal, label, and freeze
up to 2 months.

To Serve

Transfer frozen Solid
Gold Squash Soup to a
medium saucepan. Cover
and cook over medium
heat for 20 to 25 minutes
or until heated through,
stirring occasionally.
Ladle into soup bowls
and serve as directed.

Solid Gold Squash Soup

Start to finish: 20 minutes **Makes:** 8 side-dish servings total

½ cup finely chopped onion
2 to 3 teaspoons curry powder
1 teaspoon ground ginger
1 tablespoon cooking oil

4 12-ounce packages frozen cooked
    winter squash, thawed
2¼ cups apple juice or apple cider
1 14½-ounce can chicken broth
¼ teaspoon salt

1 In a 4-quart Dutch oven cook and stir onion, curry powder, and ginger in hot oil for 2 minutes. Add the squash, apple juice, chicken broth, and salt. Remove half of the soup; cool slightly. Transfer to a 1½-quart freezer container. Store as directed at left.

2 To serve remaining soup, continue to cook soup until heated through. Ladle into soup bowls. If desired, sprinkle with finely chopped pistachio nuts.

Nutrition Facts per serving: 126 cal., 2 g total fat (0 g sat. fat), 0 mg chol., 293 mg sodium, 27 g carbo., 0 g fiber, 3 g pro. Daily Values: 114% vit. A, 12% vit. C, 4% calcium, 8% iron

Here's a family favorite that freezes well for up to 3 months, allowing you to bring a satisfying soup supper to the table in minutes. Maybe that's why it's a family favorite.

To Store

Seal, label, and freeze up to 3 months.

To Serve

Transfer frozen Minestrone to a large saucepan. Cover and cook over medium heat for 25 to 30 minutes or until heated through, stirring occasionally to break up mixture. Ladle into soup bowls and serve as directed.

Minestrone

Start to finish: 50 minutes **Makes:** 8 servings total

6 cups water	¼ teaspoon pepper
1 28-ounce can tomatoes, cut up	1 15-ounce can white kidney beans (cannellini) or Great Northern beans
1 8-ounce can tomato sauce	
1 large onion, chopped	
1 cup chopped cabbage	1 10-ounce package frozen lima beans or one 9-ounce package frozen Italian-style green beans
1 medium carrot, chopped	
1 stalk celery, chopped	
4 teaspoons instant beef bouillon granules	4 ounces dried linguini or spaghetti, broken
1 tablespoon dried Italian seasoning, crushed	1 small zucchini, halved lengthwise and sliced
2 cloves garlic, minced	Grated Parmesan cheese

1 In a 5- to 6-quart Dutch oven combine water, undrained tomatoes, tomato sauce, onion, cabbage, carrot, celery, bouillon granules, Italian seasoning, garlic, and pepper. Bring to boiling; reduce heat. Cover and simmer for 10 minutes.

2 Stir in undrained kidney beans, lima beans, linguini, and zucchini. Return to boiling; reduce heat. Simmer, uncovered, for 15 minutes. Remove half of the soup; cool slightly. Transfer to a 2-quart freezer container. Store as directed at left.

3 To serve remaining soup, continue to cook until heated through. Ladle into bowls. If desired, garnish each serving with 1 teaspoon purchased pesto. Pass the Parmesan.

Nutrition Facts per serving: 177 cal., 3 g total fat (1 g sat. fat), 5 mg chol., 992 mg sodium, 32 g carbo., 5 g fiber, 10 g pro. Daily Values: 33% vit. A, 41% vit. C, 14% calcium, 19% iron

A Spoonful of Pesto

Pesto is the perfect ingredient for adding a quick flavor boost to foods. Try these ideas to finish off that partial carton of pesto:
● **Spread a spoonful on top of grilled fish, chicken, or turkey.**
● **Stuff some under the skin of a whole chicken before roasting.**
● **Slather some on the toasted bun of a grilled burger or chicken sandwich.**

Comforting Cassoulet-Style Stew

Prep: 50 minutes **Stand:** 1 hour **Cook:** 1¾ hours **Makes:** 12 servings total

6 cups water
1 pound dry navy beans, rinsed and
  drained
1 meaty lamb shank (1 to
  1½ pounds)
1 tablespoon olive oil or cooking oil
2 cups chopped celery (include leaves)
2 medium potatoes, coarsely chopped
¾ cup coarsely chopped carrot
¾ cup coarsely chopped parsnip
3 cloves garlic, minced

7 cups water
3 cups sliced fresh mushrooms
1¼ cups dry black-eyed peas, rinsed
  and drained
½ cup dry red wine or beef broth
2 teaspoons salt
½ teaspoon pepper
1 28-ounce can diced tomatoes
2 tablespoons snipped fresh thyme
1 tablespoon snipped fresh rosemary

Instead of just white beans, the usual choice in a French-style cassoulet, this recipe calls on black-eyed peas for a little stateside Southern comfort. And, speaking of comforting, won't it be nice to know there's a batch of this waiting in the freezer for an on-call, one-dish warmer?

To Store

Seal, label, and freeze up to 3 months.

To Serve

Transfer frozen Comforting Cassoulet-Style Stew to a medium saucepan. Cover and cook over medium-low heat about 45 minutes or until heated through, stirring occasionally. Ladle into soup bowls and serve as directed.

1 In a saucepan combine the 6 cups water and the beans. Bring to boiling; reduce heat. Simmer, uncovered, for 2 minutes. Remove from heat. Cover and let stand for 1 hour. Drain and rinse beans.

2 In an 8- to 10-quart Dutch oven brown lamb shank in hot oil. Add celery, potatoes, carrot, parsnip, and garlic. Cook over medium-high heat for 5 minutes, stirring frequently. Add the 7 cups water, the mushrooms, black-eyed peas, wine or broth, salt, pepper, and navy beans. Bring to boiling; reduce heat. Cover and simmer about 1½ hours or until the beans and peas are tender. Remove shank; let cool.

3 Add the undrained tomatoes, thyme, and rosemary to stew. Remove meat from shank; chop meat and add to stew. Simmer, covered, for 15 minutes more.

4 Remove half of the stew; cool slightly. Transfer to a 2-quart freezer container. Store as directed at right.

5 To serve remaining cassoulet, continue to cook until heated through. Ladle into soup bowls. If desired, garnish with fresh rosemary sprigs.

Nutrition Facts per serving: 287 cal., 4 g total fat (1 g sat. fat), 14 mg chol., 553 mg sodium, 46 g carbo., 5 g fiber, 18 g pro. Daily Values: 24% vit. A, 29% vit. C, 36% iron

Allspice sounds like a kind of spice blend, but it's really a single spice that comes from the berry of the pimiento tree. It gets its name because it tastes like a combination of cinnamon, nutmeg, and cloves. Here, it adds a Caribbean touch to this savory stew.

To Store

Seal, label, and freeze up to 3 months.

To Serve

Transfer frozen Allspice Meatball Stew to a large saucepan. Cover and cook over medium heat about 30 minutes or until heated through, stirring occasionally. Ladle into soup bowls.

Allspice Meatball Stew

Start to finish: 30 minutes **Makes:** 8 servings total

1 16-ounce package frozen prepared Italian-style meatballs
3 cups fresh green beans cut into 1-inch pieces or loose-pack frozen cut green beans
2 cups packaged peeled baby carrots

1 14½-ounce can beef broth
2 teaspoons Worcestershire sauce
½ to ¾ teaspoon ground allspice
½ teaspoon ground cinnamon
2 14½-ounce cans stewed tomatoes

1 In a Dutch oven combine the meatballs, green beans, carrots, beef broth, Worcestershire sauce, allspice, and cinnamon. Bring to boiling; reduce heat. Cover and simmer for 10 minutes.

2 Stir in the undrained tomatoes. Return to boiling; reduce heat. Cover and simmer 5 minutes more.

3 Remove half of soup; cool slightly. Transfer to a 1½-quart freezer container. Store as directed at left.

4 To serve remaining stew, continue to cook stew until vegetables are crisp-tender and stew is heated through. Ladle into soup bowls.

Nutrition Facts per serving: 251 cal., 16 g total fat (7 g sat. fat), 44 mg chol., 829 mg sodium, 16 g carbo., 4 g fiber, 10 g pro. Daily Values: 35% vit. A, 12% vit. C, 8% calcium, 12% iron

Picadillo Chicken Loaves

Prep: 15 minutes **Bake:** 28 minutes **Makes:** 8 single-serving loaves

2   beaten eggs
½   cup fine dry bread crumbs
½   cup raisins
¼   cup thinly sliced pimiento-stuffed olives
¼   cup apple juice or milk
1   teaspoon ground cinnamon

1   teaspoon ground cumin
2   pounds ground raw chicken or turkey
½   cup toasted chopped almonds or pecans
¼   cup shredded cheddar or Monterey Jack cheese (1 ounce)

1 In a large bowl stir together the eggs, bread crumbs, raisins, olives, apple juice, cinnamon, and cumin. Add ground chicken and almonds; mix well.

2 Shape mixture into eight 4×2½×1-inch loaves. Place 4 loaves in a 2-quart baking dish. Place remaining loaves in a freezer container or in self-sealing freezer bags. Store as directed at right.

3 Bake loaves in baking dish, uncovered, in a 350° oven about 25 minutes or until done (165°).* Sprinkle each loaf with 1 tablespoon of the shredded cheese. Bake about 3 minutes more or until cheese melts.

Nutrition Facts per serving: 318 cal., 18 g total fat (2 g sat. fat), 61 mg chol., 552 mg sodium, 14 g carbo., 2 g fiber, 26 g pro. Daily Values: 3% vit. A, 1% vit. C, 13% calcium, 13% iron

***Note:** The internal color of a meat loaf is not a reliable doneness indicator. A ground chicken or turkey loaf cooked to 165°, regardless of color, is safe. Use an instant-read thermometer to check the internal temperature. To measure the doneness of each loaf, insert the thermometer through one end of the loaf to a depth of 2 inches.

Sweet and spicy! Two great tastes you don't expect to find in a meat loaf.

To Store

Seal, label, and freeze up to 3 months.

To Serve

Bake frozen Picadillo Chicken Loaves in individual casseroles, uncovered, in a 350° oven for 35 to 40 minutes or until done (165°).* Sprinkle each loaf with 1 tablespoon shredded cheddar or Monterey Jack cheese. Bake about 3 minutes more or until cheese melts.

I t will be easy to pass by the Mexican food drive-in when you know that these satisfying, homemade burritos await you at home.

To Store

Seal, label, and freeze up to 6 months.

To Serve

Wrap each of the frozen Make-Ahead Burritos in foil.* Place on a baking sheet and bake in a 350° oven about 50 minutes or until heated through. (Or thaw burritos in the refrigerator overnight. Wrap each burrito in foil.* Place on a baking sheet. Bake 30 minutes.) Remove foil. Bake about 10 minutes more or until tortillas are crisp and brown. If desired, serve with additional salsa and dairy sour cream.

Make-Ahead Burritos

Prep: 30 minutes **Bake:** 35 minutes **Makes:** 16 burritos

1 **pound cooked chicken, beef, or pork**	3 **to 4 tablespoons cooking oil**
1 **16-ounce jar salsa**	16 **8-inch flour tortillas**
1 **16-ounce can refried beans**	1 **pound Monterey Jack or cheddar**
1 **4½-ounce can diced green chile**	**cheese, cut into sixteen 5×½-inch**
peppers	**sticks**
1 **1½-ounce envelope burrito or taco**	
seasoning mix	

1 Using two forks, shred cooked chicken. (You should have about 3 cups shredded chicken.) In a large skillet combine shredded chicken, salsa, beans, undrained chile peppers, and seasoning mix. Cook and stir over medium heat until heated through.

2 In another skillet heat 1 tablespoon of the cooking oil over medium-low heat. Heat tortillas, one at a time, in the hot oil about 30 seconds per side or until brown, adding more oil as necessary. Set aside to cool. To assemble, place ⅓ cup of the meat mixture on each tortilla, near one edge. Top each with a cheese stick. Fold in the sides; roll up, starting from edge with the cheese. Secure with wooden toothpicks.

3 Place half of the burritos in a single layer in a freezer container. Store as directed at left. To serve remaining burritos,* wrap each of the burritos in foil. Place on a baking sheet. Bake in a 350° oven for 25 to 30 minutes or until heated through. Unwrap burritos. Bake about 10 minutes more or until tortillas are crisp and brown. If desired, serve with additional salsa and dairy sour cream.

Nutrition Facts per burrito: 316 cal., 16 g total fat (7 g sat. fat), 53 mg chol., 675 mg sodium, 23 g carbo., 3 g fiber, 19 g pro. Daily Values: 11% vit. A, 13% vit. C, 28% calcium, 13% iron

*Note: If you wish to make chimichangas, fry rather than bake the burritos. To fry, in a skillet heat about ¼ inch cooking oil over medium-low heat. Cook burritos in hot oil about 18 minutes (25 minutes, if frozen) or until golden brown, turning often.

Creamy Chicken Enchiladas

Prep: 35 minutes **Bake:** 25 minutes **Makes:** 12 servings total

- 1 pound skinless, boneless chicken breasts
- 1 14½-ounce can chicken broth
- ½ teaspoon ground black pepper
- 8 cups torn fresh spinach or one 10-ounce package frozen chopped spinach, thawed and well drained
- ¼ cup thinly sliced green onions
- 2 8-ounce cartons light dairy sour cream

- ½ cup plain low-fat yogurt
- ¼ cup all-purpose flour
- ½ teaspoon salt
- ½ teaspoon ground cumin
- 1 cup milk
- 2 4½-ounce cans diced green chile peppers, drained
- 12 7- to 8-inch flour tortillas
- ½ cup shredded cheddar or Monterey Jack cheese (2 ounces)

1 In a large skillet place chicken, chicken broth, and black pepper. Bring to boiling; reduce heat. Cover and simmer for 12 to 14 minutes or until chicken is no longer pink. Drain well. When cool enough to handle, use 2 forks to pull chicken into shreds. (You should have about 3 cups shredded chicken.) Set aside.

2 If using fresh spinach, cook in a small amount of boiling water, covered, for 3 to 5 minutes or until tender. Drain well. In a large bowl combine cooked or thawed spinach, chicken, and green onions; set aside.

3 In a bowl whisk together sour cream, yogurt, flour, salt, and cumin until smooth. Stir in milk and chile peppers. For filling, combine half of the sour cream mixture and the chicken mixture. Divide filling among tortillas. Roll up tortillas. Place, seam sides down, in two ungreased 2-quart rectangular baking dishes. Divide remaining sour cream mixture evenly between the two casseroles, spreading over tortillas. Wrap one of the casseroles with moisture- and vaporproof wrap or heavy foil. Store as directed at right.

4 To serve remaining casserole, bake casserole, uncovered, in a 350° oven about 25 minutes or until heated through. Sprinkle with cheese; let stand for 5 minutes. If desired, garnish with chopped tomato or salsa and additional green onion.

Nutrition Facts per enchilada: 287 cal., 15 g total fat (8 g sat. fat), 51 mg chol., 560 mg sodium, 21 g carbo., 3 g fiber, 17 g pro. Daily Values: 33% vit. A, 18% vit. C, 23% calcium, 17% iron

Because it yields two 6-serving casseroles, this recipe certainly taps into the "cook once, eat twice" philosophy. Served all at once, it's a great, crowd-pleasing choice for potlucks or an informal party of 12.

To Store

Seal, label, and freeze one of the casseroles up to 3 months.

To Serve

Thaw frozen Creamy Chicken Enchiladas overnight in refrigerator. Bake casserole, covered, in a 350° oven for 20 minutes. Uncover and bake about 20 minutes more or until heated through. Sprinkle with ½ cup shredded cheddar or Monterey Jack cheese; let stand for 5 minutes. Garnish and serve as directed.

Roasted Turkey Calzones

Prep: 30 minutes **Bake:** 18 minutes **Makes:** 8 calzones

1 pound roasted or cooked turkey
  breast, chopped (about 3 cups)
2½ cups chopped fresh spinach
1½ cups shredded four-cheese pizza
  cheese (6 ounces)

1 14- or 15-ounce jar pizza sauce
2 10-ounce packages refrigerated
  pizza dough
Milk

1 In a large bowl combine turkey, spinach, pizza cheese, and ½ cup of the pizza sauce. On a lightly floured surface, roll each package of pizza dough out to a 12×12-inch square. Cut each square into four 6×6-inch squares.

2 Spread about ⅔ cup of the turkey mixture onto half of each dough square to within about ½ inch of edge. Moisten edges of dough with water and fold over, forming triangles or rectangles. Pinch or press with a fork to seal edges. Prick tops of calzones with a fork; brush with milk and place on a greased large baking sheet.

3 If desired, sprinkle tops of calzones with grated Parmesan or Romano cheese. Bake calzones in a 375° oven about 18 minutes or until golden. Heat half of the remaining pizza sauce and serve with half of the calzones immediately. If desired, pass grated Parmesan or Romano cheese.

4 Transfer remaining calzones to an ungreased baking sheet. Cover loosely and freeze just until firm. Transfer to a self-sealing freezer bag or freezer container. Store calzones and remaining pizza sauce as directed at right.

Nutrition Facts per calzone: 295 cal., 9 g total fat (3 g sat. fat), 35 mg chol., 1,221 mg sodium, 31 g carbo., 1 g fiber, 22 g pro. Daily Values: 17% vit. A, 9% vit. C, 17% calcium, 17% iron

Keep a batch of these foldover pizzas on hand in the freezer. They'll make a soothing, satisfying supper for those days when saying you're overwhelmed is an understatement.

To Store

Seal, label, and freeze up to 3 months. Transfer remaining pizza sauce to a freezer container. Seal, label, and freeze up to 3 months.

To Serve

Thaw frozen Roasted Turkey Calzones and frozen pizza sauce in the refrigerator overnight. Unwrap calzones and place on a lightly greased large baking sheet. If desired, sprinkle with grated Parmesan or Romano cheese. Bake calzones, uncovered, in a 350° oven for 12 to 15 minutes or until heated through. Heat pizza sauce in a small saucepan. Serve with calzones.

Some kids could eat tacos and spaghetti night after night. Why fight it? Here these two kid-pleasing favorites get rolled into one great casserole. With the bonus batch, you have a repeat performance to serve on demand.

To Store

Seal, label, and freeze up to 3 months.

To Serve

Thaw frozen Taco Spaghetti in refrigerator overnight (mixture may still be icy at baking time). Bake, covered, in a 375° oven for 1 hour or until heated through, stirring once about halfway through baking time. Sprinkle with ½ cup shredded colby and Monterey Jack or cheddar cheese. Serve with 4 cups shredded lettuce and 1 medium tomato, chopped. If desired, pass broken tortilla chips and dairy sour cream.

Taco Spaghetti

Prep: 40 minutes **Bake:** 20 minutes **Makes:** 12 servings total

10 ounces dried spaghetti, linguine, or fettuccine, broken	1½ cups shredded colby and Monterey Jack, or cheddar cheese (6 ounces)
2 pounds ground beef or ground raw turkey	1 cup sliced, pitted ripe olives
2 large onions, chopped	1 cup salsa
1½ cups water	2 4½-ounce cans diced green chile peppers, drained
1 1¼-ounce envelope (2 tablespoons) taco seasoning mix	4 cups shredded lettuce
2 11-ounce cans whole kernel corn with sweet peppers, drained	1 medium tomato, chopped

1 Cook pasta according to package directions; drain. Meanwhile, in 4-quart Dutch oven cook ground meat and onion until meat is brown. Drain off fat. Stir in water and taco seasoning mix. Bring to boiling; reduce heat. Simmer, uncovered, for 2 minutes, stirring occasionally. Stir in cooked pasta, corn, 1 cup of the shredded cheese, the olives, salsa, and chile peppers.

2 Divide mixture evenly between two lightly greased 2-quart casseroles. Wrap one casserole with moisture- and vaporproof wrap. Store as directed at left.

3 To serve remaining casserole, cover and bake in a 350° oven for 20 to 25 minutes or until heated through. Sprinkle with remaining cheese. Top with lettuce and chopped tomato. If desired, pass broken tortilla chips and dairy sour cream as additional toppings.

Nutrition Facts per serving: 352 cal., 17 g total fat (7 g sat. fat), 66 mg chol., 772 mg sodium, 30 g carbo., 3 g fiber, 24 g pro. Daily Values: 11% vit. A, 26% vit. C, 19% calcium, 18% iron

Two-for-Six Pizza

Prep: 30 minutes **Bake:** 22 minutes **Makes:** 12 servings total (2 pizzas)

2¾ to 3¼ cups all-purpose flour
1 package active dry yeast
¼ teaspoon salt
1 cup warm water (120° to 130°)
2 tablespoons cooking oil
Cornmeal (optional)
1 15-ounce can pizza sauce
1 pound bulk Italian sausage, ground beef, or ground pork, cooked and drained; or 1 cup cubed cooked ham or Canadian-style bacon

½ cup sliced green onions or sliced pitted ripe olives
1 cup sliced fresh mushrooms or chopped green sweet pepper
2 to 3 cups shredded mozzarella cheese (8 to 12 ounces)

1 For crust, in a large bowl combine 1¼ cups of the flour, the yeast, and salt. Add water and oil. Beat with an electric mixer on low speed for 30 seconds, scraping side of bowl. Beat on high speed for 3 minutes. Stir in as much of the remaining flour as you can. Turn out onto a lightly floured surface. Knead in enough of the remaining flour to make a moderately stiff dough that is smooth and elastic (6 to 8 minutes total). Divide in half. Cover dough; let rest for 10 minutes. (If desired, store dough as directed at right.)

2 Grease two 12-inch pizza pans or baking sheets. If desired, sprinkle with cornmeal. On a lightly floured surface, roll each dough portion into a 13-inch circle. Transfer dough to prepared pans. Build up edges slightly. Bake in a 425° oven about 12 minutes or until golden.

3 Spread pizza sauce on hot crusts. Top with meat, vegetables, and cheese. Bake one pizza for 10 to 15 minutes more or until cheese is bubbly. Serve immediately.

4 Cover remaining assembled pizza with plastic wrap; freeze until firm. Wrap frozen pizza in moisture- and vaporproof wrap. Overwrap in heavy foil or place in a self-sealing freezer bag. Store as directed at right.

Nutrition Facts per serving: 324 cal., 18 g total fat (6 g sat. fat), 40 mg chol., 495 mg sodium, 26 g carbo., 2 g fiber, 13 g pro. Daily Values: 11% vit. A, 9% vit. C, 16% calcium, 14% iron

Pizza is all about choices, and this recipe offers two make-ahead options. Assemble the extra pizza and freeze, as directed. Or assemble and bake one pizza now (using half of the sauce, meat, vegetables, and cheese) and freeze the extra portion of dough.

To Store

Dough: Wrap in moisture- and vaporproof wrap or place in a self-sealing freezer bag. Seal, label, and freeze up to 1 month.

Pizza: Seal, label, and freeze assembled Two-for-Six Pizza up to 1 month.

To Serve

Dough: Thaw frozen dough overnight in the refrigerator. Roll out dough, assemble, and bake pizza as directed.

Pizza: Bake assembled frozen Two-for-Six Pizza in a 375° oven about 25 minutes or until cheese is bubbly.

Lots of old-fashioned casseroles started with a sauté of ground beef, onions, and celery. For a tasty update, this one starts with ground lamb and fennel. It's decidedly different, and equally easy and comforting.

To Store

Seal, label, and freeze up to 3 months.

To Serve

Remove frozen casseroles of Lamb & Polenta Bake from overwrap; remove plastic wrap. Return to the same four greased 10- to 12-ounce casseroles. Cover; let casseroles and tomato sauce thaw overnight in refrigerator. Bake casseroles, covered, in a 350° oven for 45 to 55 minutes or until heated through, uncovering the last 10 minutes of baking. Sprinkle ¼ cup crumbled feta cheese over casseroles. Let stand 10 minutes. Heat tomato sauce just to boiling; drizzle over.

Lamb & Polenta Bake

Prep: 40 minutes **Bake:** 35 minutes **Makes:** 8 servings total

1½	pounds ground lamb	2	14½-ounce cans whole Italian-style tomatoes, cut up
1	large onion, chopped		
2	small fennel bulbs, trimmed, cored, and chopped (about 1½ cups)	2	16-ounce tubes refrigerated cooked polenta
6	cloves garlic, minced (1 tablespoon)	¾	cup crumbled feta cheese (3 ounces)
2	teaspoons dried oregano, crushed	1	15-ounce can Italian-style tomato sauce
½	teaspoon pepper		

1 In a very large skillet cook lamb, onion, fennel, garlic, oregano, and pepper until lamb is brown. Drain. Add undrained tomatoes to skillet. Bring to boiling; reduce heat. Simmer, uncovered, 10 to 15 minutes or until most of the liquid has evaporated, stirring occasionally. Meanwhile, coat a 1½-quart casserole with nonstick cooking spray. Line four 10- to 12-ounce casseroles with large pieces of plastic wrap, allowing excess to extend over edges; coat the wrap lightly with cooking spray. Set aside.

2 Slice each polenta tube in half lengthwise; slice ¼ inch thick. Press one-fourth of the slices into bottom of prepared 1½-quart casserole, overlapping slices as necessary. Press another one-fourth of the slices into the bottoms of prepared individual casseroles.

3 Spoon half of the lamb mixture over polenta in 1½-quart casserole. Spoon remaining lamb mixture over polenta in individual casseroles. Sprinkle ¼ cup of the cheese over mixture in 1½-quart casserole. Sprinkle another ¼ cup cheese over mixture in individual casseroles. Arrange half of the remaining polenta slices around edge of 1½-quart casserole. Place remaining polenta slices around edges of individual casseroles.

4 Bring the plastic wrap together over mixture in individual casseroles. Seal. Freeze just until firm. Remove from the dishes. Overwrap each with heavy foil. Pour half of the tomato sauce into freezer container. Store as directed at left.

5 To serve remaining casserole, bake the 1½-quart casserole, covered, in a 375° oven for 35 to 40 minutes or until hot in center; uncover the last 10 minutes. Top with remaining cheese. Let stand 10 minutes. Heat remaining tomato sauce; drizzle over.

Nutrition Facts per serving: 405 cal., 20 g total fat (10 g sat. fat), 75 mg chol., 1,165 mg sodium, 34 g carbo., 10 g fiber, 21 g pro. Daily Values: 2% vit. A, 28% vit. C, 14% calcium, 14% iron

With a bonus batch of this full-flavored meat sauce ready and waiting in the freezer, you can serve an Italian-style meal for six even on the busiest days.

To Store

Seal, label, and freeze up to 2 months.

To Serve

Thaw the frozen sausage mixture for the Baked Cavatelli in refrigerator overnight (mixture may still be icy). Transfer mixture to a medium saucepan. Cover; cook over medium-low heat for 15 to 20 minutes or until bubbly, stirring often. Meanwhile, cook 2½ cups dried cavatelli or wagon wheel pasta according to package directions. Drain; return to pot. Gently stir heated sausage mixture and ½ cup shredded mozzarella cheese into pasta. Spoon into 2-quart casserole. Sprinkle with ½ cup shredded mozzarella cheese. Bake, uncovered, in a 375° oven for 5 to 10 minutes or until cheese is melted.

Baked Cavatelli

Prep: 35 minutes **Bake:** 30 minutes **Makes:** 12 servings total

2½ cups dried cavatelli or wagon wheel pasta (7 ounces)
1¼ pounds Italian sausage links, sliced ½ inch thick
1½ cups chopped onion
4 cloves garlic, minced

2 26- to 28-ounce cans or jars spaghetti sauce
¼ to ½ teaspoon pepper
1 cup shredded mozzarella cheese (4 ounces)

1 Cook pasta according to package directions. Drain; set aside. Meanwhile, cook sausage in a large skillet until brown. Drain sausage on paper towels, reserving 1 tablespoon drippings in skillet. Cook onion and garlic in the reserved drippings until tender; drain.

2 In a large bowl combine sausage, onion mixture, spaghetti sauce, and pepper. Transfer half of the sausage-sauce mixture to a freezer container. Store as directed at left.

3 Add the cooked pasta and ½ cup of the cheese to the remaining sausage-sauce mixture. Stir gently to combine. Spoon into a 2-quart casserole.

4 Bake, covered, in a 375° oven for 25 to 30 minutes or until nearly heated through. Uncover and sprinkle with the remaining cheese. Bake, uncovered, about 5 minutes more or until cheese is melted and mixture is heated through.

Nutrition Facts per serving: 350 cal., 15 g total fat (6 g sat. fat), 43 mg chol., 643 mg sodium, 36 g carbo., 3 g fiber, 17 g pro. Daily Values: 2% vit. A, 11% vit. C, 16% calcium, 11% iron

Slow-Simmering Pork Sandwiches

Prep: 15 minutes **Cook:** 5½ to 12½ hours **Makes:** 12 servings total

1 2½- to 3-pound pork shoulder roast
½ cup water
3 tablespoons vinegar
2 tablespoons Worcestershire sauce

1 teaspoon ground cumin or chili
   powder
1 recipe Homemade Barbecue Sauce
   (below) or 3 cups bottled barbecue
   sauce
6 kaiser rolls or hamburger buns, split

1 Trim fat from roast. Cut roast, if necessary, to fit in a 3½- to 4-quart electric crockery cooker. Add water, vinegar, Worcestershire sauce, and cumin. Cover and cook on low-heat setting for 10 to 12 hours or on high-heat setting for 5 to 6 hours.

2 Remove meat from the cooker; discard cooking liquid. Using two forks, pull meat apart and return it to the cooker. Stir in Homemade Barbecue Sauce or bottled barbecue sauce. Cover and cook on high-heat setting for 30 to 45 minutes or until heated through. Slightly cool half of the meat mixture; transfer to 1½-quart freezer container. Store as directed at right.

3 Serve the remaining meat mixture in kaiser rolls. If desired, serve with sliced red onion and dill pickles.

Homemade Barbecue Sauce: In large saucepan combine 2½ cups reduced-sodium catsup; 1 cup finely chopped onion; ¼ cup packed brown sugar; ¼ cup vinegar; 3 tablespoons bottled Pickapeppa or Worcestershire sauce; 3 cloves garlic, minced; and ¼ teaspoon bottled hot pepper sauce. Bring mixture to boiling; reduce heat. Cover and simmer for 15 minutes, stirring occasionally. Use the sauce immediately or let it cool slightly, transfer to a storage container, cover, and chill up to 3 days. Makes 3 cups.

Nutrition Facts per sandwich: 404 cal., 12 g total fat (4 g sat. fat), 57 mg chol., 727 mg sodium, 44 g carbo., 0 g fiber, 29 g pro. Daily Values: 31% vit. C, 34% iron

A crockery cooker makes the pork for these pulled-pork sandwiches, a convenient fix-and-forget choice for a casual supper for friends. Freeze the extra pork to enjoy up to 2 months down the road.

To Store

Seal, label, and freeze up to 2 months.

To Serve

Transfer the frozen meat mixture for Slow-Simmering Pork Sandwiches to a medium saucepan. Cover and cook over medium heat 30 to 35 minutes or until heated through, stirring occasionally. Serve in 6 split kaiser rolls or hamburger buns. If desired, serve with sliced red onion and dill pickles.

These meals-in-a-pocket freeze individually so you can take them to the table one at a time, two at a time—as many as needed—depending on how many are coming to dinner.

To Store

Seal, label, and freeze up to 2 months.

To Serve

Line a baking sheet with foil; coat with nonstick cooking spray. Place frozen, unbaked Pork Pocket Pies on prepared baking sheet. Bake, uncovered, in a 350° oven for 50 to 55 minutes or until golden.

Pork Pocket Pies

Prep: 1 hour **Bake:** 45 minutes **Makes:** 8 pocket pies

1 recipe Pocket Pie Pastry (below)
1 recipe Skillet Gravy (below)
½ pound boneless pork sirloin, cut into ½-inch cubes

1½ cups peeled, chopped turnip
1 cup peeled, cubed sweet potato
¾ cup chopped onion
¼ teaspoon salt

1 Prepare Pocket Pie Pastry. Divide dough in half; divide each half into 4 portions. Form each portion into a ball. Cover and set aside.

2 For filling, prepare Skillet Gravy. In a large bowl combine pork, turnip, sweet potato, onion, and salt. Stir in Skillet Gravy.

3 On a lightly floured surface, flatten one portion of dough. (Keep remaining dough covered until ready to use.) Roll from center to edge into a 7-inch circle. Place about ½ cup filling on half of the circle. Brush edge with water. Fold pastry over filling. Seal edge by crimping with a fork. Prick top of pastry several times with a fork. Repeat with remaining dough and filling.

4 Place four pies in a single layer on a baking sheet; freeze until firm. Transfer to a self-sealing freezer bag or freezer containers. Store as directed at left.

5 To serve remaining pies, line a baking sheet with foil; coat with nonstick cooking spray. Place remaining pies 1 inch apart on baking sheet. Bake in a 375° oven about 45 minutes or until golden.

Pocket Pie Pastry: In medium bowl combine 3 cups all-purpose flour, ¾ teaspoon baking powder, and ½ teaspoon salt. Using a pastry blender, cut in ½ cup shortening until the pieces are pea-size. Sprinkle 1 tablespoon ice water over part of mixture; gently toss with a fork. Push moistened dough to side. Repeat, using 1 tablespoon ice water at a time, until all dough is moistened (10 to 12 tablespoons water total).

Skillet Gravy: In a medium skillet melt 2 tablespoons margarine or butter. Stir in 3 tablespoons all-purpose flour and 1 teaspoon curry powder. Carefully add 1 cup canned vegetable or chicken broth all at once. Cook and stir over medium heat until thickened and bubbly. Makes about 1 cup.

Nutrition Facts per pie: 359 cal., 18 g total fat (4 g sat. fat), 12 mg chol., 405 mg sodium, 42 g carbo., 3 g fiber, 9 g pro. Daily Values: 35% vit. A, 12% vit. C, 4% calcium, 17% iron

I f family members occasionally miss dinner, freeze the fish rolls in the individual casseroles (and bake the rolls in the baking dish immediately). You can reheat as many servings as you need on those nights when one or more of the family is gone. The reheating time stays the same.

To Store

Seal, label, and freeze up to 3 months.

To Serve

Cover baking dishes of Mediterranean-Style Fish Rolls with foil. Bake in a 350° oven for 60 to 70 minutes or until fish is nearly done. Uncover and sprinkle each fish roll with 2 tablespoons shredded Monterey Jack cheese. Bake, uncovered, for 3 to 5 minutes more or just until fish begins to flake easily when tested with a fork and cheese is melted. If desired, garnish with lemon slices and sliced pitted ripe olives.

Mediterranean-Style Fish Rolls

Prep: 25 minutes **Bake:** 23 minutes **Makes:** 8 servings total

8 **4-ounce fresh or frozen flounder, sole, or other fish fillets**	1 **teaspoon dried basil, crushed**
1½ **pounds fresh asparagus spears or two 10-ounce packages frozen asparagus spears**	½ **teaspoon dried oregano, crushed**
	2 **8-ounce cans tomato sauce**
	2 **4½-ounce cans diced green chile peppers, drained**
½ **cup finely chopped onion**	2 **tablespoons lemon juice**
4 **teaspoons olive oil or cooking oil**	½ **cup shredded Monterey Jack cheese (2 ounces)**
4 **teaspoons cornstarch**	

1 Thaw fish, if frozen. If using fresh asparagus, cut into 6-inch spears; discard woody stems. Cook the fresh asparagus, covered, in a small amount of boiling water for 8 to 10 minutes or until crisp-tender. (If using frozen asparagus, cook according to package directions.) Drain well.

2 Grease four 10- to 12-ounce individual casseroles and a 2-quart square or rectangular baking dish; set aside. Place 4 or 5 asparagus spears crosswise on each fillet. Roll each into a spiral starting from a narrow end. Place 4 rolls, seam sides down, in prepared individual casseroles. Place remaining 4 rolls in prepared baking dish.

3 For sauce, in small saucepan cook onion in oil until tender. Stir in cornstarch, basil, and oregano. Add tomato sauce, chile peppers, and lemon juice. Cook and stir until thickened and bubbly. Cook and stir for 2 minutes more. Spoon sauce over fish rolls.

4 Wrap baking dish of fish rolls in moisture- and vaporproof wrap. Store as directed at left.

5 To serve remaining fish rolls, bake the individual casseroles in a 350° oven about 20 minutes or until fish is nearly done. Sprinkle fish rolls with cheese. Bake 3 minutes more or just until fish begins to flake easily when tested with a fork and cheese is melted. If desired, garnish with lemon slices and sliced pitted ripe olives.

Nutrition Facts per serving: 219 cal., 9 g total fat (3 g sat. fat), 67 mg chol., 514 mg sodium, 7 g carbo., 1 g fiber, 27 g pro. Daily Values: 5% vit. A, 42% vit. C, 17% calcium, 8% iron

Shrimp-Stuffed Buns

Prep: 40 minutes. **Rise:** 15 minutes **Bake:** 15 minutes **Makes:** 16 buns

1 16-ounce package hot roll mix	2 tablespoons snipped fresh parsley
½ of an 8-ounce package cream cheese, softened	1 tablespoon snipped fresh chives
½ cup shredded Monterey Jack or Swiss cheese (2 ounces)	½ teaspoon dried dillweed
⅓ cup finely shredded carrot	⅛ teaspoon pepper
	1 pound frozen, peeled, cooked shrimp, thawed and chopped

1 Prepare hot roll mix according to package directions through the kneading step. Cover and let rest while preparing filling. For filling, in a medium bowl stir together cream cheese, shredded cheese, carrot, parsley, chives, dillweed, and pepper. Stir in shrimp.

2 Divide dough into 16 portions; shape each into a ball. On a lightly floured surface roll each ball into a 4½-inch circle. Place about 2 tablespoons filling on each dough circle. Bring up sides of dough around filling; pinch edges of dough to seal well.

3 Place buns, seam sides down, on greased baking sheets. Cover and let rise in a warm place for 15 minutes. Bake in a 375° oven for 15 to 18 minutes or until brown. Cool half of the buns slightly on wire racks before serving.

4 Cool remaining buns completely on the baking sheet. Freeze on the baking sheet, uncovered, about 1 hour or until firm. Transfer buns to self-sealing freezer bags. Store as directed at right.

Nutrition Facts per bun: 199 cal., 6 g total fat (2 g sat. fat), 80 mg chol., 281 mg sodium, 22 g carbo., 13 g pro. Daily Values: 19% vit. A, 3% vit. C, 5% calcium, 10% iron

Bite into one of these golden buns, and the creamy goodness of the shrimp-and-cheese filling will have you asking for more. Team the rolls with a favorite soup or a crisp tossed salad.

To Store

Seal, label, and freeze up to 3 months.

To Serve

Remove desired number of frozen Shrimp-Stuffed Buns from freezer bag. Wrap buns in foil. Bake in a 350° oven about 35 minutes or until heated through.

This weekend, use your bread machine to make the dough for this batch of rolls. Bake some for Sunday dinner, and put the rest of the dough in the freezer to bring home-baked goodness to future meals.

To Store

Seal, label, and freeze up to 1 month.

To Serve

Thaw desired number of Bread Machine Buttermilk Rolls, covered, overnight in the refrigerator in muffin cups or on a baking sheet. Cover; let rise in a warm place until double in size (about 45 minutes). Bake as directed.

Bread Machine Buttermilk Rolls

Prep: 20 minutes **Rise:** 30 minutes **Bake:** 10 minutes **Makes:** 12 to 16 rolls

¾ cup buttermilk or sour milk*	2 tablespoons sugar
1 egg	¾ teaspoon salt
¼ cup butter, cut up	1 teaspoon active dry yeast or bread
3 cups bread flour	machine yeast

1 Add the ingredients to a bread machine according to the manufacturer's directions. Select the dough cycle. When the cycle is complete, remove dough from machine. Punch down. Cover and let rest for 10 minutes. Shape dough into Basic Rolls, Rosettes, or Cloverleaf Rolls.

2 For Basic Rolls: Divide dough into 12 pieces. Shape each piece into a smooth ball. Place each ball in a greased 2½-inch muffin cup, smooth side up.

3 For Rosettes: Divide dough into 16 pieces. On lightly floured surface, roll each piece into a 12-inch rope. Tie each rope in a loose knot, leaving 2 long ends. Tuck top end under roll. Bring bottom end up and tuck into center of roll. Place 2 to 3 inches apart on greased baking sheets.

4 For Cloverleaf Rolls: Divide dough into 36 pieces. Shape each piece into a ball, pulling edges under to make smooth top. Place 3 balls in each greased 2½-inch muffin cup, smooth sides up.

5 Cover half of the rolls with plastic wrap. Freeze until firm. Transfer to a self-sealing freezer bag. Store as directed at left.

6 To serve remaining rolls, cover and let rise in a warm place until nearly double (about 30 minutes). Bake in a 375° oven for 10 to 12 minutes or until golden. Immediately remove rolls from pans. Cool slightly on wire racks. Serve warm.

Nutrition Facts per roll: 179 cal., 5 g total fat (3 g sat. fat), 28 mg chol., 212 mg sodium, 28 g carbo., 1 g fiber, 5 g pro. Daily Values: 4% vit. A, 3% calcium, 9% iron

*Note: To make ¾ cup sour milk, place 2 teaspoons lemon juice or vinegar in glass measuring cup. Add enough milk to make ¾ cup liquid; stir. Let the mixture stand for 5 minutes before using it.

Focaccia Breadsticks

Prep: 20 minutes **Bake:** 12 minutes **Makes:** 20 breadsticks

½ cup oil-packed dried tomatoes
½ cup grated Romano or Parmesan
    cheese
2 teaspoons snipped fresh rosemary or
    ¾ teaspoon dried rosemary,
    crushed

¼ teaspoon cracked black pepper
4 teaspoons water
2 10-ounce packages refrigerated
    pizza dough

1 Drain tomatoes, reserving 4 teaspoons of the oil. Finely snip tomatoes. In a small bowl combine tomatoes, cheese, rosemary, and pepper; stir in the reserved oil and the water. Set aside.

2 Unroll pizza dough. On a lightly floured surface roll each dough portion into a 10×8-inch rectangle. Spread tomato mixture crosswise over half of each rectangle. Cut each rectangle lengthwise into ½-inch-wide strips. Fold each strip in half and twist two or three times. Place 1 inch apart on lightly greased baking sheets.

3 Bake in a 350° oven for 12 to 15 minutes or until golden brown. Serve half of the breadsticks immediately.

4 Transfer remaining breadsticks to a wire rack. Cool completely. Wrap cooled breadsticks in a single layer in heavy foil. (Or place breadsticks in freezer container, separating layers with waxed paper.) Store as directed at right.

Nutrition Facts per breadstick: 84 cal., 2 g total fat (1 g sat. fat), 2 mg chol., 209 mg sodium, 14 g carbo., 1 g fiber, 3 g pro. Daily Values: 1% vit. A, 1% vit. C, 2% calcium, 4% iron

Wait! Don't turn the page because you think homemade breadsticks are a lot of work! These breadsticks start with convenient refrigerated pizza dough and feature the traditional focaccia flavors of tomato, rosemary, and cheese.

To Store

Seal, label, and freeze up to 1 month.

To Serve

Wrap desired number of frozen Focaccia Breadsticks in foil. Heat in a 350° oven about 15 minutes or until warm.

Yeast Bread Storage

To have a little home-baked goodness on hand, keep these tips in mind. Wrap yeast breads in foil or plastic wrap, or place in plastic bags, and store in a cool, dry place (not in the refrigerator) for 2 to 3 days. For longer storage, place completely cool, unfrosted breads in a freezer bag, or tightly wrap in heavy foil. freeze up to 3 months. Thaw at room temperature for 1 hour. Frost sweet breads after thawing.

Crumb-Topped Cherry Coffee Cakes

Prep: 30 minutes **Bake:** 40 minutes **Makes:** 18 servings (2 coffee cakes)

⅔ cup butter, softened
⅔ cup packed brown sugar
⅔ cup granulated sugar
4 eggs
4 cups all-purpose flour
1 tablespoon baking powder
1 teaspoon ground cardamom

½ teaspoon baking soda
½ teaspoon salt
1½ cups buttermilk or sour milk*
2 cups dried tart red cherries or cranberries
1 recipe Crumb Topping (below)

1 Line one 8×8×2-inch baking pan or 9×1½-inch round baking pan with foil, extending foil over edges slightly. Grease foil. Grease another 8×8×2-inch baking pan or 9×1½-inch round baking pan. Set both pans aside. In a large bowl beat butter with an electric mixer on low to medium speed for 30 seconds. Add sugars and beat until light and fluffy. Add eggs, one at a time, beating well after each.

2 Combine flour, baking powder, cardamom, baking soda, and salt. Add flour mixture and buttermilk alternately to beaten mixture, beating on low speed after each addition just until combined. Fold in dried cherries. Divide evenly between the prepared baking pans. Sprinkle each pan with half of the Crumb Topping.

3 Bake in a 350° oven about 40 minutes or until a wooden toothpick inserted near the centers comes out clean. Cool in pans on wire rack at least 30 minutes. Serve the coffee cake from unlined pan warm or at room temperature.

4 Let remaining coffee cake cool completely. Use foil to lift coffee cake from pan. Place in a self-sealing freezer bag or wrap in moisture- and vaporproof wrap.

Crumb Topping: In a medium bowl combine 1 cup all-purpose flour, 1 cup packed brown sugar, and ½ cup softened butter. Stir with a fork until mixture is crumbly.

Nutrition Facts per serving: 410 cal., 14 g total fat (8 g sat. fat), 82 mg chol., 338 mg sodium, 65 g carbo., 2 g fiber, 6 g pro. Daily Values: 11% vit. A, 10% calcium, 12% iron

*Note: To make 1½ cups sour milk, place 4 teaspoons lemon juice or vinegar in glass measuring cup. Add enough milk to make 1½ cups liquid; stir. Let the mixture stand for 5 minutes before using it.

How sweet it is! Hiding underneath a buttery crumb topping is a fruit-studded cake flavored with a hint of cardamom.

To Store

Seal, label, and freeze up to 3 months.

To Serve

Remove frozen Crumb-Topped Cherry Coffee Cake from freezer bag or wrap. Wrap in foil and bake in a 325° oven about 1 hour or until warm. (Or thaw wrapped coffee cake overnight in refrigerator. Remove from freezer bag or wrap. Wrap in foil and bake in a 325° oven about 30 minutes or until warm.)

To Store

Seal, label, and freeze
up to 3 months.

To Serve

Thaw wrapped frozen
Bread Machine
Choco-Nut Loaf at room
temperature. Unwrap
loaf. In a microwave-
safe bowl combine
2 tablespoons semisweet
chocolate pieces and
½ teaspoon shortening.
Heat on 100% power
(high) for 30 to
45 seconds or until
chocolate is softened
enough to stir smooth.
Drizzle chocolate
mixture over loaf.

Bread Machine Choco-Nut Loaves

Prep: 25 minutes **Rise:** 30 minutes **Bake:** 30 minutes **Makes:** 32 servings (2 loaves)

½ cup milk	½ teaspoon ground cinnamon
2 eggs	1½ teaspoons active dry yeast or bread
¼ cup water	machine yeast
2 tablespoons butter, cut up	½ cup semisweet chocolate pieces
½ teaspoon vanilla	¼ cup semisweet chocolate pieces
2 cups bread flour	¼ cup chopped walnuts
1 cup whole wheat flour	2 tablespoons semisweet chocolate
⅓ cup sugar	pieces
½ teaspoon salt	½ teaspoon shortening

1 Add milk, eggs, water, butter, vanilla, flours, sugar, salt, cinnamon, yeast, and ½ cup of the chocolate pieces to the bread machine according to manufacturer's directions. Select the dough cycle. When cycle is complete, remove dough from machine. Punch down. Cover and let rest for 10 minutes.

2 Divide the dough in half. On a lightly floured surface, roll each portion into a 10×7-inch rectangle. Divide the ¼ cup chocolate pieces and the walnuts between rectangles, sprinkling evenly and pressing in lightly.

3 Starting from a short side, roll up each rectangle into a spiral; seal seams and ends. Place loaves, seam sides down, in two greased 8×4×2-inch loaf pans. Cover and let rise in a warm place until nearly double (30 to 45 minutes).

4 Bake in a 350° oven about 30 minutes or until bread sounds hollow when lightly tapped. If necessary to prevent overbrowning, loosely cover with foil the last 10 minutes. Remove from pans; cool 1 loaf slightly on a wire rack.

5 In a microwave-safe bowl combine the 2 tablespoons chocolate pieces and the shortening. Heat on 100% power (high) for 30 to 45 seconds or until chocolate is softened enough to stir smooth. Drizzle chocolate mixture over slightly cooled loaf.

6 Cool remaining loaf completely on a wire rack. Wrap cooled loaf in moisture- and vaporproof wrap or a self-sealing freezer bag. Store as directed at left.

Nutrition Facts per serving: 99 cal., 4 g total fat (2 g sat. fat), 16 mg chol., 50 mg sodium, 13 g carbo., 2 g fiber, 2 g pro. Daily Values: 1% vit. A, 1% calcium, 4% iron

Rhubarb Bread

Prep: 20 minutes **Bake:** 50 minutes **Makes:** 32 servings (2 loaves)

2¾ cups all-purpose flour	1 8-ounce carton plain low-fat yogurt
1 teaspoon baking soda	½ cup bran cereal flakes
1 teaspoon salt	⅓ cup applesauce
1 teaspoon ground cinnamon	¼ cup cooking oil
1 slightly beaten egg	2 cups finely chopped fresh rhubarb
1⅓ cups packed brown sugar	1 recipe Streusel Topping (below)

1 Grease the bottom and ½ inch up the sides of two 8×4×2-inch loaf pans: set aside. In a large bowl stir together the flour, baking soda, salt, and cinnamon; set aside.

2 In a medium bowl stir together the egg, brown sugar, yogurt, cereal flakes, applesauce, and oil. Add egg mixture all at once to flour mixture. Stir just until combined. Gently stir in rhubarb.

3 Spread batter into prepared pans. Sprinkle with Streusel Topping. Bake in a 350° oven about 50 minutes or until a wooden toothpick inserted near centers comes out clean. Cool in pans on a wire rack for 10 minutes. Remove from pans. Cool completely on wire racks. Wrap and store one loaf overnight for easier slicing.

4 Wrap remaining loaf in moisture- and vaporproof wrap or place in a self-sealing freezer bag. Store as directed at right.

Streusel Topping: In a small bowl stir together ¼ cup packed brown sugar, ¼ cup rolled oats, 1 tablespoon all-purpose flour, and ¼ teaspoon ground cinnamon. Stir in 2 tablespoons melted butter.

Nutrition Facts per serving: 115 cal., 3 g total fat (1 g sat. fat), 8 mg chol., 130 mg sodium, 21 g carbo., 1 g fiber, 2 g pro. Daily Values: 1% vit. A, 1% vit. C, 2% calcium, 8% iron

Next time you see rhubarb in abundance at the farmers' market, buy some to tuck into this easy-to-make bread. The bread keeps in the freezer up to 3 months so you can savor the sweet-tart treat long after rhubarb season is over.

To Store

Seal, label, and freeze up to 3 months.

To Serve

Thaw frozen wrapped Rhubarb Bread at room temperature.

Baked Ham with Cherry Relish (page 102)

Leftover
Transformations

Sunday's hearty pot roast becomes Tuesday's refreshing beef salad, and Friday's cassoulet makes a terrific stew for the next rainy day. Each master recipe in this chapter yields one or two splendid spin-offs, giving a whole new meaning to the word leftovers.

In This Chapter

Fire up the grill for a lovely dinner for four tonight featuring a fruit-basted chicken and a mellow, three-onion side dish. The extra barbecued chicken and onion medley become tasteful toppings for another night's pizza.

To Store

Tangy Apricot Barbecue Sauce: Transfer half of the barbecue sauce to an airtight container or freezer container. Cover; refrigerate up to 3 days or freeze up to 3 months. For Barbecued Chicken and Roasted Onions: Transfer remaining onion mixture and 2 grilled chicken breasts to separate self-sealing plastic bags or freezer bags. Seal and refrigerate up to 3 days or freeze up to 3 months.

To Use

Before using, thaw sauce, chicken, and roasted onions overnight in the refrigerator, if frozen. Use to make Chicken, Onion, and Nectarine Pizza (page 85).

Barbecued Chicken with Roasted Onions

Prep: 30 minutes **Grill:** 30 minutes **Makes:** 4 servings

1 recipe Tangy Apricot Barbecue Sauce (below)
2 medium sweet white or yellow onions, cut into thin wedges
1 medium red onion, cut into thin wedges
2 leeks, quartered lengthwise and cut into 2-inch pieces (white part only)
4 green onions, cut into 1-inch pieces

2 cloves garlic, cut into thin slivers
2 teaspoons olive oil
2 teaspoons snipped fresh thyme or ½ teaspoon dried thyme, crushed
⅛ teaspoon salt
⅛ teaspoon pepper
6 medium skinless, boneless chicken breast halves (about 1½ pounds total)

1 Prepare Tangy Apricot Barbecue Sauce. Reserve half and store remaining half as directed at left. For onion medley, fold a 48×18-inch piece of heavy foil in half to make a double thickness of foil that measures 24×18 inches. Coat foil with nonstick cooking spray. Place onions, leeks, green onions, and garlic in center of foil. Drizzle with oil; sprinkle with thyme, salt, and pepper. Bring up two opposite edges of foil; seal with a double fold. Fold remaining ends to enclose vegetables, leaving space for steam to build.

2 Grill foil packet with onion mixture on rack of an uncovered grill directly over medium coals about 30 minutes or until onions are tender. Halfway through grilling time, add chicken to grill rack. Grill 12 to 15 minutes or until chicken is tender and no longer pink (170°), turning once halfway through grilling and brushing with some of the reserved Tangy Apricot Barbecue Sauce the last 5 minutes.

3 To serve, divide half of the onion mixture among 4 dinner plates. Slice 4 of the chicken breasts; serve over the onion mixture on plates. Heat remaining reserved Tangy Apricot Barbecue Sauce; serve with chicken. Store remaining Barbecued Chicken and Roasted Onions as directed at left.

Tangy Apricot Barbecue Sauce: In a medium saucepan cook ⅓ cup finely chopped onion and 1 teaspoon grated fresh ginger in 2 teaspoons hot oil until tender, stirring occasionally. Stir in 1 cup catsup, ⅓ cup apricot preserves, ⅓ cup orange juice, 1 tablespoon Worcestershire sauce, and dash pepper. Bring to boiling; reduce heat. Simmer, uncovered, about 10 minutes or until slightly thickened. Makes 1½ cups.

Nutrition Facts per serving: 252 cal., 4 g total fat (1 g sat. fat), 66 mg chol., 481 mg sodium, 26 g carbo., 2 g fiber, 28 g pro. Daily Values: 8% vit. A, 38% vit. C, 5% calcium, 9% iron

Chicken, Onion, and Nectarine Pizza

Prep: 15 minutes **Bake:** 15 minutes **Makes:** 6 servings

1 10-ounce thin Italian bread shell
   (Boboli)
½ recipe Tangy Apricot Barbecue
   Sauce (page 84)
1 cup shredded reduced-fat
   mozzarella cheese (4 ounces)

½ recipe Roasted Onions (page 84)
⅓ recipe Barbecued Chicken
   (2 chicken breast halves)
   (page 84), sliced diagonally into
   strips
2 medium nectarines or 3 apricots,
   pitted and thinly sliced

Create this gourmet pizza with chicken and vegetables you've grilled a day or more in advance. Add a touch of summer-fresh fruit, and you have a pizza with pizazz.

1 Place bread shell on a pizza pan or baking sheet. Spread Tangy Apricot Barbecue Sauce over shell to within ½ inch of edge. Sprinkle with half of the mozzarella cheese. Sprinkle Roasted Onions over cheese. Arrange Barbecued Chicken strips and nectarine slices over onions. Sprinkle with remaining cheese.

2 Bake in a 400° oven about 15 minutes or until pizza is heated through. Cut pizza into wedges. If desired, garnish with fresh thyme leaves. Serve immediately.

Nutrition Facts per serving: 317 cal., 7 g total fat (2 g sat. fat), 31 mg chol., 653 mg sodium, 42 g carbo., 3 g fiber, 21 g pro. Daily Values: 20% vit. A, 23% vit. C, 21% calcium, 10% iron

Why wait for the holidays to roast a turkey? Here you'll find that roasting a breast is quicker and easier than a whole bird. As for the leftovers, great, up-to-date options follow, but no one will be too disappointed if you serve turkey sandwiches instead.

To Store

Divide remaining turkey breast in half. Cube half (about 2 cups); shred the other half (about 2 cups). Place cubed and shredded turkey in separate self-sealing plastic bags or freezer bags. Seal and refrigerate up to 3 days or label and freeze up to 3 months.

To Serve

Use cubed turkey to make Turkey Tortilla Soup (page 87) and shredded turkey to make Turkey Taco Salad (page 89). Before using, thaw turkey overnight in refrigerator, if frozen.

Margarita Roast Turkey Breast

Prep: 20 minutes **Marinate:** 8 to 24 hours **Roast:** 2¼ hours **Stand:** 10 minutes
Makes: 4 servings

2 teaspoons finely shredded lime peel	¼ teaspoon salt
½ cup fresh lime juice	¼ teaspoon pepper
⅓ cup tequila or orange juice	1 6-pound whole turkey breast
3 tablespoons orange juice	2 teaspoons cornstarch
1 tablespoon olive oil	

1 For marinade, combine lime peel, lime juice, tequila, the 3 tablespoons orange juice, the oil, salt, and pepper. Place turkey breast in self-sealing plastic bag set in a large bowl. Pour marinade over turkey. Seal bag; turn to coat breast. Marinate in refrigerator at least 8 hours or up to 24 hours, turning bag occasionally. Lift turkey breast from bag, reserving 1 cup of the marinade; cover reserved marinade and refrigerate until ready to make sauce. Discard any remaining marinade.

2 Place turkey, skin side up, on a rack in a shallow roasting pan. Insert a meat thermometer into thickest part of the breast, without touching bone. Roast, uncovered, in a 325° oven for 2¼ to 2½ hours or until thermometer registers 170°. Transfer turkey to a cutting board; cover with foil. Let stand 10 to 15 minutes before carving.

3 Meanwhile, for margarita sauce, in a small saucepan stir the reserved marinade into cornstarch. Cook and stir until thickened and bubbly; cook and stir 2 minutes more.

4 To serve, thinly slice one-third of the turkey breast. Serve with the margarita sauce. Cut up and store remaining turkey as directed at left.

Nutrition Facts per serving: 219 cal., 8 g total fat (2 g sat. fat), 73 mg chol., 111 mg sodium, 2 g carbo., 0 g fiber, 29 g pro. Daily Values: 9% vit. C, 2% calcium, 8% iron

Turkey Tortilla Soup

Prep: 10 minutes **Cook:** 20 minutes **Makes:** 4 servings

1   cup coarsely chopped onion
¾   cup coarsely chopped green sweet
       pepper
2   cloves garlic, minced
2   tablespoons cooking oil
1   14½-ounce can diced tomatoes
3   6-inch corn tortillas, torn into pieces
2   tablespoons tomato paste
½   teaspoon ground cumin
⅛   to ¼ teaspoon ground red pepper

2   14½-ounce cans chicken broth
       (3½ cups)
1   medium fresh jalapeño pepper,
       seeded and finely chopped*
⅓   recipe Margarita Roast Turkey
       Breast (page 86), cubed
1   15-ounce can black beans, rinsed
       and drained
     Fried tortilla strips,** chopped
       avocado, and/or snipped fresh
       cilantro (optional)

1 In a large saucepan cook onion, green pepper, and garlic in hot oil over medium heat about 5 minutes or until tender. Meanwhile, place undrained tomatoes, torn tortillas, tomato paste, cumin, and ground red pepper in a blender container or food processor bowl. Add ½ cup of the chicken broth to container or bowl. Cover and blend or process until nearly smooth.

2 Add tomato mixture to onion mixture in the saucepan. Stir in the remaining chicken broth and the jalapeño pepper. Bring to boiling; reduce heat. Cover and simmer for 15 minutes.

3 Stir in cubed Margarita Roast Turkey Breast and the beans; heat through. If desired, serve soup with fried tortilla strips, avocado, and/or cilantro.

Nutrition Facts per serving: 493 cal., 17 g total fat (4 g sat. fat), 73 mg chol., 1,204 mg sodium, 40 g carbo., 8 g fiber, 42 g pro. Daily Values: 4% vit. A, 83% vit. C, 14% calcium, 27% iron

***Note:** See tip on handling chile peppers, page 18.

****Note:** To make fried tortilla strips, cut 6-inch corn tortillas into thin strips. Cover the bottom of a skillet with a thin layer of cooking oil, and heat over medium-high heat. Add a single layer of tortilla strips; fry for 1½ to 2 minutes or until crisp. Drain on paper towels. Repeat with remaining tortilla strips. Store cooled strips in an airtight container up to 3 days.

Some folks can't imagine this soup without fresh cilantro—others shy away from the distinctive herb. When serving this Tex-Mex specialty, set the optional toppings on a platter in the center of the table and let your guests add as many as they wish.

Turkey Taco Salad

Start to finish: 30 minutes **Makes:** 4 servings

1 5.6-ounce package refrigerated taco salad shells	1 cup loose-pack frozen whole kernel corn, thawed
1 6.75- or 7-ounce package Spanish rice pilaf mix or Spanish rice mix	½ cup sliced green onions
⅓ **recipe Margarita Roast Turkey Breast (page 86), shredded**	2 tablespoons lime juice
	1 tablespoon olive oil
4 medium plum tomatoes, seeded and chopped (about 1⅓ cups)	¼ teaspoon salt
	¼ teaspoon ground cumin
	Dash ground red pepper
	2 cups shredded lettuce

1 Prepare taco shells and rice according to package directions. Meanwhile, in a large bowl combine shredded Margarita Roast Turkey Breast, tomatoes, corn, and green onions. In a small bowl stir together the lime juice, oil, salt, cumin, and ground red pepper. Drizzle over turkey mixture, tossing lightly to coat.

2 To serve, divide rice equally among taco shells. Top with shredded lettuce. Spoon turkey mixture over lettuce. If desired, garnish with a spoonful of dairy sour cream; pass salsa.

Nutrition Facts per serving: 644 cal., 24 g total fat (5 g sat. fat), 73 mg chol., 1,159 mg sodium, 70 g carbo., 6 g fiber, 38 g pro. Daily Values: 23% vit. A, 57% vit. C, 8% calcium, 18% iron

It's hard to believe that two cups of leftover turkey can make a full-meal salad for four. The secret is the Spanish rice pilaf mix, which helps stretch the turkey in a satisfying way.

Make sure you serve good French or Italian bread to sop up every bit of the pan juices. They're extra aromatic thanks to the fresh herbs and extra flavorful thanks to the red wine. These delicious influences help flavor the meat, making the transformation recipes that follow all the better too!

To Store

Shred remaining meat. (You should have about 6 cups.) Divide shredded meat in half. Place each half in a self-sealing plastic bag or freezer bag. Seal and refrigerate up to 3 days or label and freeze up to 3 months.

To Serve

Use one portion of shredded meat to make Beef and Fennel Salad (page 91) and the other to make Open-Face Beef Sandwiches (page 92). Before using, thaw meat overnight in the refrigerator, if frozen.

Chuck Roast with Wine-Herb Sauce

Prep: 35 minutes **Marinate:** 12 to 24 hours **Cook:** 2 hours **Makes:** 4 servings

1	5-pound boneless beef chuck roast*	1	tablespoon cooking oil
2	cups dry red wine	½	cup beef broth
1	stalk celery, coarsely chopped	2	teaspoons snipped fresh thyme or
1	medium onion, coarsely chopped		½ teaspoon dried thyme, crushed
2	tablespoons red wine vinegar	2	teaspoons snipped fresh Italian
2	cloves garlic, minced		flat-leaf parsley
2	sprigs fresh Italian flat-leaf parsley	¼	teaspoon salt
1	sprig fresh thyme	2	cups sliced carrots
1	sprig fresh rosemary	1	large onion, coarsely chopped
1	bay leaf		
½	teaspoon pepper		

1 Trim fat from meat. Place in a self-sealing plastic bag set in a large shallow dish. For marinade, combine wine, celery, the medium onion, red wine vinegar, garlic, parsley sprigs, thyme sprig, rosemary sprig, bay leaf, and ¼ teaspoon of the pepper. Pour over meat. Seal bag. Marinate in refrigerator for at least 12 hours or up to 24 hours, turning bag occasionally.

2 Drain meat, reserving marinade. Pat meat dry with paper towels. In a 6-quart Dutch oven brown meat on all sides in hot oil. Drain off fat. Strain reserved marinade, discarding solids. Measure 1 cup of the marinade liquid and discard remainder. Combine the 1 cup marinade liquid, the beef broth, snipped thyme, snipped parsley, salt, and remaining pepper. Pour over meat in Dutch oven. Bring to boiling; reduce heat. Cover and simmer 2 to 2½ hours or until meat is tender. Add carrots and the large onion the last 45 minutes of cooking. Remove meat from cooking liquid.

3 To serve, thinly slice about one-third of the meat. Skim fat from pan juices. Serve pan juices and vegetables with sliced meat. Shred and store remaining meat as directed at left.

Nutrition Facts per serving: 373 cal., 20 g total fat (7 g sat. fat), 85 mg chol., 325 mg sodium, 11 g carbo., 3 g fiber, 26 g pro. Daily Values: 308% vit. A, 11% vit. C, 4% calcium, 21% iron

*****Note:** If you can't find a 5-pound roast, use two 2½-pound roasts.

Beef and Fennel Salad

Start to finish: 20 minutes **Makes:** 6 servings

⅓ recipe Chuck Roast with Wine-
   Herb Sauce (page 90), shredded
2 medium fennel bulbs, trimmed,
   cored, and thinly sliced (about
   3 cups)
1 medium red sweet pepper, cut into
   thin bite-size strips
¼ cup olive oil
¼ cup white wine vinegar

1 tablespoon snipped fresh chives
1 tablespoon snipped fresh Italian
   flat-leaf parsley
1 tablespoon Dijon-style mustard
¼ teaspoon salt
¼ teaspoon ground black pepper
6 cups torn red leaf lettuce

1 In a large bowl combine shredded Chuck Roast with Wine-Herb Sauce, fennel, and red pepper strips; set aside.

2 In a screw-top jar combine oil, vinegar, chives, parsley, mustard, salt, and black pepper. Shake well. Pour over beef mixture; toss to coat. Let stand 5 minutes to blend flavors. To serve, arrange beef mixture over leaf lettuce.

Nutrition Facts per serving: 292 cal., 21 g total fat (6 g sat. fat), 57 mg chol., 174 mg sodium, 7 g carbo., 13 g fiber, 18 g pro. Daily Values: 44% vit. A, 86% vit. C, 7% calcium, 16% iron

This refreshing salad mixture easily doubles as the perfect filling for a tortilla wrap-style sandwich. It will tame even the heartiest appetite.

Fennel Facts

At first crunch, fennel may be mistaken for its more slender cousin, celery, but with each bite fennel's distinctive slightly sweet, licoricelike flavor begins to build. Add fennel to soups, stir fries, vegetable medleys, and salads to give new life to old favorites. Fennel is available September through April. Look for firm, smooth bulbs without cracks or brown spots. The stalks should be crisp, the leaves fresh and green. Store fennel in a plastic bag in the refrigerator for up to 4 days.

A little heat from the jalapeño, some sweetness from the honey, and the distinct peppery spark of arugula—it's hard to believe that such a cleverly combined gourmet sandwich starts with a few humble slices of leftover pot roast.

Open-Face Beef Sandwiches

Start to finish: 20 minutes **Makes:** 4 servings

1 fresh jalapeño pepper, seeded and
    finely chopped*
1 medium shallot, thinly sliced
1 teaspoon cooking oil
⅓ recipe Chuck Roast with
    Wine-Herb Sauce (page 90),
    shredded
2 cups grape or cherry tomatoes, halved

2 tablespoons tomato paste
2 tablespoons white balsamic vinegar
    or white wine vinegar
1 tablespoon honey
½ teaspoon salt
¼ teaspoon pepper
4 slices sourdough bread
12 to 16 arugula leaves

1 In a large skillet cook jalapeño and shallot in hot oil over medium heat for 1 minute. Add shredded Chuck Roast with Wine-Herb Sauce, tomatoes, tomato paste, vinegar, honey, salt, and pepper. Cook over medium-high heat about 5 minutes or until tomatoes have softened and beef is heated through.

2 To serve, place a bread slice on each of 4 plates. Arrange 3 or 4 arugula leaves on each bread slice. Top each serving with some of the beef mixture.

Nutrition Facts per serving: 440 cal., 20 g total fat (7 g sat. fat), 85 mg chol., 675 mg sodium, 33 g carbo., 3 g fiber, 29 g pro. Daily Values: 16% vit. A, 38% vit. C, 5% calcium, 26% iron

*Note: See tip on handling chile peppers, page 18.

Luscious lamb for your every mood! Start by making this entrée for a special weekend dinner, and save some to enjoy in Lambwiches for a weeknight supper. Also stash some away for the Lamb-Stuffed Poblanos, a terrific recipe when you're craving something different.

To Store

Divide remaining lamb in half. Cube half (about 2 cups); thinly slice other half. Place cubed and sliced lamb in separate self-sealing plastic bags or freezer bags. Seal and refrigerate up to 3 days or label and freeze up to 3 months.

To Serve

Use cubed meat to make Lamb-Stuffed Poblanos (page 95) and sliced meat to make Lambwiches (page 97). Before using, thaw meat overnight in refrigerator, if frozen.

Balsamic-Marinated Leg of Lamb

Prep: 25 minutes **Marinate:** 8 to 24 hours **Roast:** 2 hours **Stand:** 15 minutes
Makes: 4 servings

1 5- to 6-pound leg of lamb, boned, rolled, and tied	1 tablespoon sugar
4 to 6 cloves garlic, sliced	2 teaspoons dried basil, crushed
⅔ cup balsamic vinegar	4 cloves garlic, minced
½ cup olive oil	1 teaspoon salt
2 tablespoons Dijon-style mustard	½ teaspoon pepper

1 Trim fat from lamb. Cut 1-inch-long pockets into lamb at 3-inch intervals. Place a slice of garlic in each of the pockets. For marinade, combine balsamic vinegar, oil, mustard, sugar, basil, minced garlic, salt, and pepper. Place leg of lamb in a self-sealing plastic bag set in a large bowl. Pour marinade over lamb; seal bag. Marinate in refrigerator for at least 8 hours or up to 24 hours, turning bag occasionally. Drain and discard marinade.

2 Place lamb on a rack in a shallow roasting pan. Insert a meat thermometer into the thickest portion of the meat. Roast in a 325° oven 2 to 2½ hours or until thermometer registers 140°. Cover and let stand for 15 minutes before carving. (The temperature of the meat will rise 5° during standing.)

3 To serve, remove strings from roasted leg of lamb. Thinly slice one-third of the roasted leg of lamb. Cut up and store remaining lamb as directed at left.

Nutrition Facts per serving: 237 cal., 10 g total fat (3 g sat. fat), 101 mg chol., 116 mg sodium, 1 g carbo., 0 g fiber, 32 g pro. Daily Values: 1% vit. C, 1% calcium, 14% iron

Lamb-Stuffed Poblanos

Prep: 50 minutes **Bake:** 20 minutes **Makes:** 6 servings

6 large fresh poblano chile peppers*
   (5 to 6 inches long)
1 5.8-ounce package toasted pine-nut
   or garlic-flavored couscous mix
⅓ **recipe Balsamic-Marinated Leg of**
   Lamb (page 94), cubed

2 medium plum tomatoes, seeded and
   chopped
¼ cup chopped pitted kalamata olives
1 teaspoon dried oregano, crushed
1 teaspoon finely shredded lemon peel
½ teaspoon freshly ground black
   pepper
½ cup crumbled feta cheese (2 ounces)

Here, the familiar stuffed pepper travels the globe and comes back with worldly, interesting accents. Couscous, lamb, olives, lemon, and feta cheese suggest a Mediterranean influence, while the poblano chile peppers leave a southwestern mark.

1 To roast chile peppers, cut a 3- to 4-inch lengthwise slit on one side of each pepper. Remove and discard seeds and membranes. Leave stems intact. Place peppers on a foil-lined baking sheet; roast in a 425° oven about 20 minutes or until skins are blistered. Wrap chile peppers in the foil and let stand for 20 to 30 minutes. If desired, carefully remove skin from chile peppers.

2 Meanwhile, prepare couscous according to package directions. Cool slightly. In a medium bowl combine couscous, cubed Balsamic-Marinated Leg of Lamb, tomatoes, olives, oregano, lemon peel, and black pepper. Carefully pack mixture into roasted chile peppers. (The chile peppers will be overstuffed.)

3 Lightly coat a foil-lined baking sheet with nonstick cooking spray. Place stuffed chile peppers on prepared baking sheet. Bake in a 350° oven for 20 to 25 minutes or until heated through. Sprinkle chile peppers with feta cheese. Use a spatula to transfer peppers to serving plates, being careful not to break peppers apart.

Nutrition Facts per serving: 295 cal., 10 g total fat (3 g sat. fat), 56 mg chol., 455 mg sodium, 32 g carbo., 4 g fiber, 23 g pro. Daily Values: 21% vit. A, 471% vit. C, 9% calcium, 27% iron

*Note: Green or red sweet peppers may be substituted for the poblano chile peppers.

Lambwiches

Start to finish: 40 minutes **Makes:** 4 sandwiches

1 medium cucumber, halved
    lengthwise, seeded, and thinly
    sliced

¼ cup white vinegar

1 tablespoon sugar

½ cup chopped onion

1 clove garlic, minced

1 tablespoon olive oil

½ cup dry red wine

2 tablespoons Dijon-style mustard

2 tablespoons tomato paste

1 teaspoon dried thyme, crushed

½ teaspoon salt

⅛ teaspoon ground red pepper

⅓ recipe Balsamic-Marinated Leg of
    Lamb (page 94), thinly sliced

4 onion buns, split and toasted; 4 pita
    rounds, halved and split; or one
    12-inch focaccia round, quartered,
    split and toasted

¼ cup bottled garlic ranch salad
    dressing

1 In a small bowl combine cucumber, vinegar, and sugar. Season to taste with salt and black pepper. Cover; refrigerate for 30 minutes, stirring occasionally. (If desired, cover and store in refrigerator up to 3 days.)

2 Meanwhile, in a medium saucepan cook onion and garlic in hot oil over medium heat about 5 minutes or just until tender. Stir in wine, mustard, tomato paste, thyme, salt, and red pepper. Bring to boiling; reduce heat. Simmer, uncovered, for 5 minutes. Stir in sliced Balsamic-Marinated Leg of Lamb; heat through.

3 To serve, divide meat mixture among buns. Using a slotted spoon, top with cucumber; drizzle with garlic ranch dressing.

Nutrition Facts per sandwich: 530 cal., 25 g total fat (6 g sat. fat), 102 mg chol., 875 mg sodium, 33 g carbo., 2 g fiber, 37 g pro. Daily Values: 4% vit. A, 8% vit. C, 10% calcium, 26% iron

With cool and crunchy marinated cucumbers topping the flavorful meat mixture, this sandwich might remind you of the classic Greek gyro sandwich. It's perfect casual supper fare.

Tidbits of Tomato Paste

The bad news: Recipes have a way of calling for a tablespoon or two of tomato paste at a time, leaving cooks with most of a can left over. The good news: Tomato paste can be frozen. Spoon 1-tablespoon portions onto a piece of plastic wrap; freeze until firm. Place into a freezer bag. Seal, label, and freeze until the next time you need a tablespoon or two.

Get ready for a week of eye-opening eats! For the weekend, give your meat-and-potatoes roast a Caribbean kick. Then, continue the food fest with a clever Caribbean Pork and Pepper Pizza one night and an anything-but-ordinary Jerk Pork Pilaf another.

To Store

Cut remaining pork into bite-size strips. Divide pork strips in half. Place each half in a self-sealing plastic bag or freezer bag. Seal and refrigerate up to 3 days or label and freeze up to 3 months.

To Serve

Use one portion of the pork strips to make Caribbean Pork and Pepper Pizza (page 100) and the other to make Jerk Pork Pilaf (page 101). Before using, thaw meat overnight in refrigerator, if frozen.

Caribbean Pork with Sweet Potatoes

Prep: 25 minutes **Chill:** 30 minutes **Roast:** 1½ hours **Stand:** 15 minutes **Makes:** 4 servings

1 3-pound boneless pork top loin roast (single loin)	½ teaspoon dried thyme, crushed
⅓ cup Pickapeppa sauce, or ⅓ cup Worcestershire sauce plus dash bottled hot pepper sauce	2 large sweet potatoes, peeled and cut into 1- to 2-inch pieces (1 to 1¼ pounds)
3 cloves garlic, minced	1 green onion, slivered
	1 recipe Mango-Jicama Salsa (below)

1 Trim fat from pork. Combine 3 tablespoons of the Pickapeppa sauce, the garlic, and thyme. Brush sauce mixture on all sides of pork. Cover and refrigerate 30 minutes.

2 Place pork on a rack in a shallow roasting pan. Insert a meat thermometer. Roast in a 325° oven for 45 minutes.

3 Meanwhile, cook sweet potato pieces in boiling, lightly salted water about 8 minutes or just until tender; drain. Toss with remaining Pickapeppa sauce.

4 Place sweet potatoes around pork in pan. Continue roasting about 45 minutes or until thermometer registers 155°. Remove pork from oven; cover with foil and let stand for 15 minutes before carving. (The temperature of the meat will rise 5° during standing.) Sprinkle green onion over sweet potatoes.

5 To serve, slice one-third of the pork. Serve sliced pork with the sweet potatoes and Mango-Jicama Salsa. Cut up and store remaining pork as directed at left.

Mango-Jicama Salsa: In a medium bowl combine 1 cup chopped fresh pineapple; 1 cup peeled, finely diced jicama; 1 medium mango, peeled, seeded, and chopped;* 1 large tomato, seeded and diced; 1 green onion, sliced; 1 or 2 fresh jalapeño peppers, seeded and finely chopped;** 1 tablespoon lime juice; and ⅛ teaspoon salt. Cover and refrigerate up to 24 hours.

Nutrition Facts per serving: 374 cal., 6 g total fat (2 g sat. fat), 71 mg chol., 273 mg sodium, 51 g carbo., 5 g fiber, 28 g pro. Daily Values: 479% vit. A, 99% vit. C, 7% calcium, 14% iron

*Note: See tip on peeling and seeding mangos, page 100.
**Note: See tip on handling chile peppers, page 18.

Although sausage and mushrooms are long-standing topping favorites, contemporary pizzerias across the country have shown us that virtually anything tastes good on top of pizza. Here, you'll find chutney, pork, and mango are no exceptions.

Caribbean Pork and Pepper Pizza

Prep: 15 minutes **Bake:** 10 minutes **Makes:** 6 servings

1 16-ounce Italian bread shell (Boboli)	1 tablespoon olive oil
½ cup mango chutney	⅛ teaspoon ground red pepper
⅓ recipe Caribbean Pork (page 98), cut into bite-size strips	1 large mango, peeled, seeded, and cut into bite-size pieces
¾ cup red and/or green sweet pepper cut into ¾-inch squares	1 cup shredded Monterey Jack cheese (4 ounces)
½ of a small red onion, cut into very thin wedges	

1 Place bread shell on a baking sheet or pizza pan. Cut up any large pieces in chutney; spread over bread shell. Top with Caribbean Pork strips.

2 In a large bowl combine sweet pepper, onion wedges, oil, and ground red pepper; toss to coat. Top pizza with vegetable mixture and mango. Sprinkle with cheese. Bake in a 425° oven for 10 to 12 minutes or until cheese is melted.

Nutrition Facts per serving: 518 cal., 18 g total fat (6 g sat. fat), 56 mg chol., 585 mg sodium, 61 g carbo., 3 g fiber, 30 g pro. Daily Values: 77% vit. A, 98% vit. C, 24% calcium, 14% iron

Managing a Mango

Because the meat from the mango holds tightly to the seed, it takes a little effort to free the fragrant spicy-peach flesh. An easy way to remove the meat is to make a cut through the mango, sliding a sharp knife next to the seed along one side. Repeat on other side of seed, resulting in two large pieces. Cut away all of the meat that remains around the oval seed. Remove peel on all pieces; cut the flesh into pieces as directed. If fresh mangos are unavailable, look for jars of chilled sliced mango in the produce aisle of your supermarket.

Jerk Pork Pilaf

Start to finish: 25 minutes **Makes:** 4 servings

- 1 14½-ounce can reduced-sodium chicken broth
- 1 cup chopped onion
- 1 cup chopped green or red sweet pepper
- 1 cup very thinly sliced carrots
- ¾ cup quick-cooking barley
- ¼ teaspoon bottled hot pepper sauce
- ⅓ **recipe Caribbean Pork (page 98), cut into bite-size strips**
- ⅓ **cup bottled Caesar salad dressing Romaine leaves**

1 In a large saucepan combine broth, onion, sweet pepper, and carrots. Bring to boiling; reduce heat. Cover and simmer for 5 minutes. Stir in barley and hot pepper sauce. Cover and simmer about 10 minutes or until liquid is absorbed.

2 Stir in Caribbean Pork strips; heat through. Remove from heat; stir in dressing. Serve warm or chilled over romaine leaves. If desired, garnish with fresh parsley and serve with additional bottled hot pepper sauce.

Nutrition Facts per serving: 409 cal., 18 g total fat (4 g sat. fat), 67 mg chol., 575 mg sodium. 32 g carbo., 5 g fiber, 30 g pro. Daily Values: 159% vit. A, 56% vit. C, 5% calcium, 11% iron

Serve this veggie-and-pork-studded barley pilaf warm for a quick and satisfying supper. Have some extra time? Chill it for a refreshing main-dish salad.

Start with this lovely ham that's perfect for a party of six. Dress up the leftovers with Brie for a sophisticated sandwich, or jazz 'em up in a lively jambalaya. And of course there's always the traditional ham-on-rye option—no recipe needed.

To Store

Remove remaining ham from the bone. Thinly slice half; cube the other half (about 3 cups). Place sliced and cubed ham in separate self-sealing plastic bags or freezer bags. Seal and refrigerate up to 3 days or label and freeze up to 3 months.

To Serve

Use cubed ham to make Cajun Ham Jambalaya (page 103) and thinly sliced ham to make Ham-and-Brie Sandwich Round (page 104). Before using, thaw ham overnight in refrigerator, if frozen.

Baked Ham with Cherry Relish

Prep: 20 minutes **Bake:** 1¼ hours **Makes:** 6 servings

1 5- to 6-pound cooked ham (rump half or shank portion)	24 whole cloves 1 recipe Cherry Relish (below)

1 Score ham by making diagonal cuts in a diamond pattern. Stud with cloves. Place ham on a rack in a shallow roasting pan. Insert a meat thermometer, making sure thermometer does not touch bone. Bake in a 325° oven for 1¼ to 2 hours or until thermometer registers 135°. Let stand 15 minutes before carving. (The temperature of the meat will rise 5° during standing.)

2 To serve, thinly slice one-third of the ham. Serve with the Cherry Relish. Cut up and store remaining ham as directed at left.

Cherry Relish: In a saucepan combine ¼ cup sugar, ¼ cup orange juice, 2 tablespoons cherry brandy or orange juice, and 2 tablespoons water. Cook and stir over medium heat until sugar dissolves. Add 1 cup dried tart red cherries. Bring to boiling; reduce heat. Cook and stir about 5 minutes or until cherries have softened. Remove from heat. Stir in ¼ cup chopped toasted pecans and 1 teaspoon finely shredded orange peel. Cover and refrigerate at least 2 hours or up to 24 hours. Makes about 1½ cups.

Nutrition Facts per serving: 321 cal., 13 g total fat (3 g sat. fat), 54 mg chol., 1,245 mg sodium, 30 g carbo., 1 g fiber, 18 g pro. Daily Values: 1% vit. A, 10% vit. C, 1% calcium, 6% iron

Cajun Ham Jambalaya

Start to finish: 40 minutes   **Makes:** 4 servings

6	ounces fresh or frozen medium shrimp in shells	1	14½-ounce can stewed tomatoes
½	cup chopped onion	1	14½-ounce can beef broth
⅓	cup chopped celery	⅔	cup long grain rice
⅓	cup chopped green sweet pepper	1	teaspoon Cajun seasoning
2	cloves garlic, minced	¼	to ½ teaspoon bottled hot pepper sauce
2	tablespoons olive oil	⅓	**recipe Baked Ham (page 102), cubed**

1 Thaw shrimp, if frozen. Peel and devein shrimp. Rinse shrimp; pat dry with paper towels. Set aside. In a large skillet cook onion, celery, green pepper, and garlic in hot oil about 5 minutes or until tender. Stir in undrained tomatoes, beef broth, uncooked rice, Cajun seasoning, and hot pepper sauce.

2 Bring to boiling; reduce heat. Cover and simmer 15 to 20 minutes or until rice is nearly tender. Stir in shrimp and cubed Baked Ham. Return to boiling; reduce heat. Cover and cook 2 to 3 minutes more or until shrimp are opaque and rice is tender, stirring once.

Nutrition Facts per serving: 509 cal., 23 g total fat (6 g sat. fat), 80 mg chol., 2,480 mg sodium, 41 g carbo., 2 g fiber, 32 g pro. Daily Values: 3% vit. A, 26% vit. C, 7% calcium, 22% iron

Why not time the Baked Ham recipe so you can freeze leftovers and thaw them in time to serve up this spirited New Orleans specialty for Mardi Gras? Remember, the ham can be stored in the freezer up to 3 months.

Leftover Rice is Nice

Cooking rice ahead of time (or storing leftover rice for another meal) is definitely in the doable category. Keep these tips in mind:
● Store cooked rice in an airtight container in the refrigerator up to 1 week or in the freezer up to 6 months.
● To reheat refrigerated or frozen rice, in a saucepan, add 2 tablespoons water or broth for each cup of rice. Cover and heat on top of the range about 5 minutes or until heated through.

Tender colorful peppers, meltingly smooth Brie, sweet slices of ham, and a lively spread make for a moist, oozy, and irresistible twist on the usual ham and cheese sandwich.

Ham-and-Brie Sandwich Round

Prep: 30 minutes   **Bake:** 40 minutes   **Stand:** 10 minutes   **Makes:** 8 servings

1   large onion, thinly sliced
1   medium green sweet pepper, cut into
      thin bite-size strips
1   medium red sweet pepper, cut into
      thin bite-size strips
1   tablespoon olive oil
1   16-ounce round loaf sourdough
      bread (about 7-inch diameter)

1   recipe Mustard-Mayonnaise Spread
      (below)
⅓   recipe Baked Ham (page 102),
      thinly sliced
1   4½-ounce round Brie cheese, rind
      removed, and thinly sliced

1 In a large skillet cook onion, green pepper, and red pepper in hot olive oil until tender; set aside.

2 Cut off the top third of the sourdough bread loaf; set top aside. Hollow out bottom, leaving a ½-inch-thick shell. Spread inside of bread shell with half of the Mustard-Mayonnaise Spread. Arrange half of the thinly sliced Baked Ham in bread shell. Top with half of the vegetable mixture and half of the Brie slices. Spread remaining Mustard-Mayonnaise Spread over Brie. Repeat layers of ham, vegetable mixture, and Brie. Replace bread top. Press down gently.

3 Wrap sandwich round in foil. Place on a baking sheet. Heat in a 400° oven about 40 minutes or until heated through. Let stand in foil 10 minutes before serving. To serve, cut into wedges.

Mustard-Mayonnaise Spread: In a small bowl combine ¼ cup mayonnaise or salad dressing, 2 tablespoons peppercorn or sweet-hot mustard, 1 teaspoon prepared horseradish, and ½ teaspoon Worcestershire sauce.

Nutrition Facts per serving: 425 cal., 21 g total fat (6 g sat. fat), 60 mg chol., 1,447 mg sodium, 37 g carbo., 3 g fiber, 21 g pro. Daily Values: 6% vit. A, 47% vit. C, 9% calcium, 14% iron

During the summer, when the garden or farmers' markets offer lush, ripe tomatoes, make and freeze a few batches of this pesto. For the rest of the summer, enjoy it as a starring ingredient in a garden-fresh gazpacho and an enticing take on chicken casserole.

To Store

Place 1 cup of the pesto in each of two 1-cup airtight storage or freezer containers or self-sealing plastic bags or freezer bags. Place 2 cups of the pesto in a 2-cup airtight storage or freezer container or self-sealing plastic bag or freezer bag. Seal and refrigerate up to 3 days or label and freeze up to 3 months.

To Serve

Use the 1-cup portions to make Roasted Tomato and Mushroom Chicken (page 107) and the 2-cup portion to make Roasted Tomato Gazpacho (page 108). Before using, thaw pesto overnight in refrigerator, if frozen.

Roasted Tomato Pesto

Prep: 45 minutes **Stand:** 30 minutes **Roast:** 20 minutes **Makes:** 4 cups

16 to 20 plum tomatoes, halved lengthwise and seeded (3 pounds)
1 teaspoon salt
2 small onions, cut into thin wedges

4 cloves garlic, quartered
6 tablespoons olive oil
2 tablespoons balsamic vinegar
¼ teaspoon pepper

1 Place tomatoes, cut sides up, in a shallow roasting pan. Sprinkle with salt. Let stand 30 minutes. Add onions and garlic to pan. Drizzle with 4 tablespoons of the olive oil, tossing gently to coat. Roast, uncovered, in a 450° oven about 20 minutes or until tomatoes have softened, stirring occasionally. Cool in pan on wire rack for 20 minutes.

2 Place half of the tomato mixture in a large food processor bowl. Add 1 tablespoon of the remaining olive oil, 1 tablespoon of the balsamic vinegar, and ⅛ teaspoon of the pepper. Cover and process with 4 or 5 on/off turns until coarsely chopped and mixture just begins to form a paste. Transfer to a bowl; repeat with remaining ingredients. (Or place one-fourth of the tomato mixture in a blender container. Add 1½ teaspoons oil, 1½ teaspoons balsamic vinegar, and a dash of pepper. Cover and blend with 4 or 5 on/off turns until coarsely chopped and mixture just begins to form a paste. Transfer to a bowl; repeat with remaining ingredients.) Store pesto and use as directed at left. For additional serving suggestions, see tip below.

Nutrition Facts per ¼ cup: 68 cal., 5 g total fat (1 g sat. fat), 0 mg chol., 153 mg sodium, 5 g carbo., 1 g fiber, 1 g pro. Daily Values: 11% vit. A, 28% vit. C, 1% calcium, 2% iron

Roasted Tomato Pesto Possibilities

Roasting vine-ripened, homegrown tomatoes yields a wonderfully sweet, flavorful pesto. It's a treat to set aside and savor in those winter months when summer tomatoes are scarce. Try one of the following suggestions for using any remaining Roasted Tomato Pesto:
● Toss 1 cup Roasted Tomato Pesto with 3 cups hot cooked pasta; sprinkle with grated Parmesan cheese.
● Spoon warm Roasted Tomato Pesto onto toasted baguette slices.
● Substitute Roasted Tomato Pesto for the pizza sauce in your favorite pizza recipe. Use 1 scant cup of pesto in place of one 8-ounce can of pizza sauce.
● Use as a stuffing for broiled mushroom caps

Roasted Tomato and Mushroom Chicken

Prep: 30 minutes **Bake:** 30 minutes **Makes:** 6 servings

2 tablespoons olive oil

4 ounces assorted sliced fresh mushrooms (such as crimini, shiitake, porcini, and/or button) (1½ cups)

6 medium skinless, boneless chicken breast halves (about 1½ pounds total)

1 cup Roasted Tomato Pesto (page 106)

6 ounces fresh mozzarella cheese, sliced

2 shallots, finely chopped

2 cloves garlic, minced

1 10-ounce package torn fresh spinach

¼ teaspoon salt

1 In a medium skillet heat 1 tablespoon of the olive oil. Add mushrooms; cook and stir for 3 to 5 minutes or until tender. Remove skillet from heat.

2 Season chicken breasts lightly with salt and pepper. Place in a 3-quart rectangular baking dish. Spread a scant 3 tablespoons of the Roasted Tomato Pesto on top of each breast half. Layer mushrooms and cheese slices over pesto. Bake, uncovered, in a 350° oven for 30 to 35 minutes or until chicken is tender and no longer pink.

3 Meanwhile, in a large skillet cook shallots and garlic in remaining hot olive oil until tender. Stir in spinach and the ¼ teaspoon salt. Cook and stir about 2 minutes more or just until spinach is wilted and heated through.

4 To serve, spoon wilted spinach onto each of 6 dinner plates. Bias-slice chicken breast halves. Arrange chicken slices on spinach.

Nutrition Facts per serving: 297 cal., 16 g total fat (5 g sat. fat), 75 mg chol., 429 mg sodium, 8 g carbo., 2 g fiber, 31 g pro. Daily Values: 45% vit. A, 43% vit. C, 20% calcium, 18% iron

The mild, woodsy flavor of mushrooms blends deliciously with the robust fresh flavor of pesto in this company-special chicken masterpiece. If you like, complete the menu with garlic mashed potatoes, steamed zucchini slices, and crusty bread.

Chickpeas add a little heartiness, and the Roasted Tomato Pesto contributes sweetness to one of summer's favorite soups.

Roasted Tomato Gazpacho

Prep: 20 minutes **Chill:** 2 to 24 hours **Makes:** 4 to 6 servings

2 cups Roasted Tomato Pesto (page 106)
1 large cucumber, halved, seeded, and chopped (about 1½ cups)
1 small yellow summer squash, chopped (about 1 cup)
1 cup chicken or vegetable broth
2 green onions, sliced

½ of a 15-ounce can chickpeas (garbanzo beans), rinsed and drained
2 tablespoons lime juice
½ teaspoon ground cumin
¼ teaspoon bottled hot pepper sauce
1 recipe Sour Cream Topper (optional) (below)

1 In a large bowl combine Roasted Tomato Pesto, cucumber, squash, broth, and green onions. Place half of the mixture in a food processor bowl or blender container. Cover and process or blend until nearly smooth. Add pureed mixture to remaining mixture in bowl. Stir in chickpeas, lime juice, cumin, and hot pepper sauce. Cover and chill in refrigerator at least 2 hours or up to 24 hours.

2 To serve, spoon the chilled vegetable mixture into soup bowls. If desired, pass the Sour Cream Topper.

Nutrition Facts per serving: 207 cal., 12 g total fat (2 g sat. fat), 0 mg chol., 649 mg sodium, 22 g carbo., 6 g fiber, 6 g pro. Daily Values: 27% vit. A, 75% vit. C, 6% calcium, 10% iron

Sour Cream Topper: In a small bowl stir 1 teaspoon finely shredded lime peel and 1 tablespoon lime juice into ¼ cup dairy sour cream; cover and chill in refrigerator at least 2 hours or up to 24 hours.

Vegetarians take note! This filling, bean-packed cassoulet satisfies six to eight hungry souls one night, then transforms into a new stew another night. Enjoy what's left on a delightfully hearty bruschetta.

To Store

Place 2 cups of the reserved bean mixture in a 2-cup airtight storage or freezer container or a self-sealing plastic bag or freezer bag. Place 3 cups of the reserved bean mixture in a 3-cup airtight storage or freezer container or a self-sealing plastic bag or freezer bag. Seal and refrigerate up to 3 days or label and freeze up to 3 months.

To Serve

Use the 2-cup portion to make Tuscan Bean Bruschetta (page 111) and the 3-cup portion to make Sausage, Kale, and Bean Stew (page 112). Before using, thaw bean mixture overnight in the refrigerator, if frozen.

Vegetarian Cassoulet

Prep: 20 minutes **Stand:** 1 hour **Cook:** 1½ hours **Bake:** 15 minutes **Makes:** 6 to 8 servings

1½ cups dry Great Northern beans
1½ cups dry pinto beans
 1 cup dry chickpeas (garbanzo beans)
 1 cup chopped celery
 1 cup chopped onion
 1 cup chopped carrot
 2 tablespoons olive oil
 4 14½-ounce cans vegetable broth
 1 0.75-ounce package dried porcini
      mushrooms (about 1 cup)
½ cup bottled roasted red pepper,
      chopped

½ cup oil-packed dried tomatoes,
      drained and snipped
¼ cup roasted garlic puree
½ teaspoon salt
½ teaspoon dried oregano, crushed
½ teaspoon dried thyme, crushed
½ teaspoon ground black pepper
 1 bay leaf
 2 cups soft sourdough bread crumbs
 2 tablespoons butter, melted
 1 clove garlic, minced

1 Rinse beans and chickpeas. In a 6-quart Dutch oven combine beans, chickpeas, and 12 cups water. Bring to boiling; reduce heat. Simmer 2 minutes. Remove from heat. Let stand 1 hour. Drain soaked beans and chickpeas; rinse in a colander and set aside.

2 In the same Dutch oven cook celery, onion, and carrot in hot oil for 5 minutes. Add beans, chickpeas, broth, and mushrooms. Bring to boiling; reduce heat. Cover and simmer for 1 hour.

3 Add roasted red pepper, tomatoes, garlic puree, salt, oregano, thyme, black pepper, and bay leaf. Return to boiling; reduce heat. Cover and simmer for 30 minutes more or until beans are tender and most of the liquid is absorbed. Discard bay leaf.

4 To serve, set aside 5 cups of the bean mixture. Transfer remaining bean mixture to a 2-quart casserole. In a small bowl combine bread crumbs, butter, and garlic. Sprinkle bread crumb mixture over bean mixture in casserole. Bake, uncovered, in a 350° oven for 15 to 20 minutes or until bread crumbs are lightly toasted. Store and use the reserved 5 cups bean mixture as directed at left.

Nutrition Facts per serving: 423 cal., 13 g total fat (4 g sat. fat), 11 mg chol., 963 mg sodium, 65 g carbo., 18 g fiber, 19 g pro. Daily Values: 69% vit. A, 57% vit. C, 12% calcium, 26% iron

Tuscan Bean Bruschetta

Prep: 15 minutes **Bake:** 18 minutes **Makes:** 12 servings

At its simplest, bruschetta is an Italian version of garlic bread. A topping of hearty beans, Parmesan cheese, and shredded prosciutto boosts the classic appetizer into main dish status.

2 cups Vegetarian Cassoulet beans
   (page 110)
½ teaspoon snipped fresh rosemary or
   ¼ teaspoon dried rosemary,
   crushed
1 16-ounce loaf sourdough or Italian
   bread, cut into 12 thick, bias-cut
   slices

¾ cup grated Parmesan cheese
   (3 ounces)
   Freshly ground black pepper
12 thin slices prosciutto (about
   9 ounces), shredded

1 In a food processor bowl or blender container combine Vegetarian Cassoulet beans and rosemary. Cover and process or blend until nearly smooth.

2 Divide bread slices among 2 baking sheets. Bake in a 350° oven for 5 minutes. Turn the bread slices; bake 5 minutes more. Divide bean-rosemary mixture among bread slices, spreading evenly over each slice. Sprinkle 1 tablespoon of the Parmesan cheese and some of the pepper over each bread slice.

3 Bake 8 to 10 minutes more or until cheese is melted and bean mixture is heated through. Arrange shredded prosciutto on top of cheese.

Nutrition Facts per bruschetta: 220 cal., 5 g total fat (2 g sat. fat), 20 mg chol., 1,013 mg sodium, 29 g carbo., 2 g fiber, 14 g pro. Daily Values: 8% vit. A, 6% vit. C, 10% calcium, 10% iron

Prosciutto from Parma

What's the Italian word for ham? Prosciutto, of course! Prosciutto is a ham that has been seasoned, salt-cured, and air-dried. Although the ham from Parma, Italy, is considered the true prosciutto, prosciutto is made in the United States as well. Traditionally, it is sliced paper-thin and served with fresh figs and melon slices as a first course. Look for packaged, sliced prosciutto in the deli section of your supermarket or seek out the "really good stuff" at any Italian market.

Meatball and bean soup becomes a whole new stew thanks to colorful, curly-leafed kale and the meaty intrigue of fresh shiitake mushrooms.

Sausage, Kale, and Bean Stew

Prep: 20 minutes **Cook:** 30 minutes **Makes:** 4 servings

1 pound bulk mild Italian sausage	¼ teaspoon ground black pepper
12 ounces kale	¼ teaspoon crushed red pepper
2 tablespoons water	3 cups Vegetarian Cassoulet beans
1 cup fresh shiitake mushrooms, sliced	(page 110)
1 clove garlic, minced	1 14½-ounce can vegetable broth
½ teaspoon salt	

1 Shape sausage into 1-inch balls. Arrange sausage balls in a single layer in a 12-inch nonstick skillet. Cook over medium heat until brown on all sides. Remove sausage from skillet and drain on paper towels. Wipe out skillet with paper towels.

2 Meanwhile, remove center stalks from kale; discard stalks. Coarsely chop kale. (You should have about 10 cups.) Add kale and the water to the skillet. Cover and cook about 10 minutes or just until kale is tender, stirring occasionally. Add mushrooms, garlic, salt, black pepper, and red pepper. Cook, uncovered, over medium heat for 5 minutes more. Add sausage balls, Vegetarian Cassoulet beans, and broth. Bring to boiling; reduce heat. Cover and simmer about 15 minutes or until kale is very tender.

Nutrition Facts per serving: 569 cal., 31 g total fat (10 g sat. fat), 76 mg chol., 1,823 mg sodium, 43 g carbo., 12 g fiber, 29 g pro. Daily Values: 179% vit. A, 135% vit. C, 19% calcium, 29% iron

Burgers Borracho (page 121)

Marinate Now, Grill Later

Go ahead, go about your business. First, get these lively marinades working their magic on your favorite meats, poultry, and fish. Tonight, for a relaxing dinner on the deck simply fire up the grill, pour a cool drink, and let the good times roll.

In This Chapter

With its intriguing mint, honey, and mustard-sparked marinade and a fresh fruit-studded relish, this recipe will make for a steak-fry that your friends will never forget.

Tropical Fiesta Steak

Prep: 20 minutes **Marinate:** 12 to 24 hours **Grill:** 14 minutes **Makes:** 6 servings

⅓ cup frozen orange juice concentrate, thawed	Few drops bottled hot pepper sauce
3 tablespoons cooking oil	1 1½-pound boneless beef sirloin steak, cut 1 to 1¼ inches thick
3 tablespoons honey	½ cup chopped red sweet pepper
1 tablespoon sliced green onion	½ cup chopped red apple
2 teaspoons spicy brown or Dijon-style mustard	½ cup chopped pear
1 teaspoon snipped fresh mint or ¼ teaspoon dried mint, crushed	½ cup chopped, peeled peach
	¼ cup chopped celery
	2 tablespoons sliced green onion
	2 teaspoons lemon juice

1 For marinade, stir together the orange juice concentrate, oil, honey, 1 tablespoon green onion, the mustard, mint, and hot pepper sauce. Remove ¼ cup of the mixture for the relish; cover and refrigerate until needed.

2 Trim fat from steak. Place the steak in a self-sealing plastic bag set in a shallow dish. Pour remaining marinade over steak; seal bag. Marinate in refrigerator at least 12 hours or up to 24 hours, turning bag occasionally.

3 For fruit relish, in a bowl combine the reserved marinade, the sweet pepper, apple, pear, peach, celery, the 2 tablespoons green onion, and the lemon juice. Cover; refrigerate until serving time or up to 24 hours.

4 Drain steak, reserving marinade. Grill steak on the rack of an uncovered grill directly over medium coals until desired doneness, turning once halfway through grilling, and brushing occasionally with marinade up to the last 5 minutes of grilling. Discard any remaining marinade. [Allow 14 to 20 minutes for medium-rare (145°) or 18 to 22 minutes for medium (160°).] Season to taste with salt and pepper. To serve, thinly slice steak across the grain. Serve with the fruit relish.

Nutrition Facts per serving: 344 cal., 17 g total fat (5 g sat. fat), 76 mg chol., 107 mg sodium, 21 g carbo., 1 g fiber, 27 g pro. Daily Values: 33% vit. C, 10% calcium, 13% iron

Jerk London Broil

Prep: 15 minutes **Marinate:** 30 minutes to 24 hours **Grill:** 12 minutes **Makes:** 6 servings

1 1¼ - to 1½-pound beef flank steak
4 green onions, sliced
¼ cup lime juice
2 tablespoons cooking oil
1 fresh Scotch bonnet pepper,* stem
   and seeds removed (optional)

2 teaspoons purchased or homemade
   Jamaican Jerk Seasoning (page 18)
1 1-inch piece fresh ginger, sliced
3 cloves garlic

1 Trim fat from steak. Score both sides of steak in a diamond pattern by making shallow diagonal cuts at 1-inch intervals. Place steak in a shallow glass dish. For marinade, in a blender container combine green onions, lime juice, oil, Scotch bonnet pepper (if desired), jerk seasoning, ginger, and garlic. Cover and blend until smooth. Spread the marinade over steak. Cover and marinate at room temperature 30 minutes or in refrigerator at least 6 hours or up to 24 hours.

2 Drain steak, discarding marinade. Grill steak on the rack of an uncovered grill directly over medium coals until desired doneness, turning once halfway through grilling. [Allow 12 to 14 minutes for medium (160°).] To serve, cut steak diagonally across the grain into ⅛- to ¼-inch-thick slices.

Nutrition Facts per serving: 187 cal., 11 g total fat (3 g sat. fat), 44 mg chol., 117 mg sodium, 2 g carbo., 0 g fiber, 18 g pro. Daily Values: 4% vit. A, 8% vit. C, 1% calcium, 13% iron

*Note: See tip on handling chile peppers, page 18.

Think one little pepper won't bring enough heat for six servings? Think again! The tiny Scotch bonnet ranks among the hottest chile peppers on the planet and packs a powerful punch. If you can't find this variety—or prefer fewer fireworks—substitute a jalapeño pepper.

Hot Advice

Do you have a burning question about food safety? The United States Department of Agriculture Meat and Poultry Hotline is ready to help. A registered dietitian or other food professional can answer your questions from 10 a.m. to 4 p.m. (EST) weekdays. Call 800-535-4555.

If you've never tried jicama, here's a great introduction to this one-of-a-kind root vegetable. It looks a little like a potato, crunches like a carrot, and has a sweet, nutty flavor all its own.

Steak Salad with Cilantro Dressing

Prep: 30 minutes **Marinate:** 2 to 24 hours **Grill:** 12 minutes **Makes:** 4 servings

¾ pound beef flank steak or boneless
    beef sirloin steak, cut 1 inch thick
⅛ teaspoon salt
⅛ teaspoon pepper
¼ cup olive oil
1½ teaspoons finely shredded lime peel
¼ cup lime juice

¼ cup snipped fresh cilantro
6 cups torn romaine
5 ounces jicama, peeled and cut into
    thin bite-size sticks (1 cup)
1 medium mango, peeled, seeded, and
    sliced*
1 small red onion, cut in thin wedges
2 teaspoons honey

1 Season meat with salt and pepper. Place in a self-sealing plastic bag set in a shallow bowl. In a screw-top jar combine oil, lime peel, lime juice, and cilantro. Pour half of the lime mixture over meat. Seal bag. Marinate in refrigerator at least 2 hours or up to 24 hours, turning bag occasionally. Cover and chill remaining lime mixture for dressing.

2 Drain meat, discarding marinade. Grill meat on rack of an uncovered grill directly over medium coals until desired doneness, turning once. [Allow 12 to 15 minutes for medium doneness (160°).] Remove from grill. Thinly slice the meat across the grain.

3 To serve, divide romaine among 4 dinner plates. Top with meat, jicama, mango, and onion. For dressing, add honey to reserved lime mixture; cover and shake well. Drizzle over salads.

Nutrition Facts per serving: 333 cal., 16 g total fat (5 g sat. fat), 47 mg chol., 136 mg sodium, 19 g carbo., 3 g fiber, 29 g pro. Daily Values: 87% vit. A, 77% vit. C, 4% calcium, 18% iron

***Note:** See tip on peeling and seeding mangos, page 100.

If you want your onion relish to take on sweet tones, seek out a sweet variety of onion, such as the Vidalia (available in May and June) or the Maui onion (available April to July).

Onion-Marinated Beef Eye Roast

Prep: 30 minutes **Marinate:** 6 to 24 hours **Grill:** 1½ hours **Makes:** 12 servings

½ cup dry white wine	2 medium onions, thinly sliced and separated into rings
¼ cup olive oil or cooking oil	⅔ cup mayonnaise or salad dressing
1 tablespoon dried dillweed	⅓ cup dairy sour cream
2 teaspoons coarsely ground black pepper	2 tablespoons prepared horseradish
½ teaspoon salt	⅛ teaspoon salt
1 2- to 3-pound beef eye of round roast	⅛ teaspoon ground black pepper

1 For marinade, combine white wine, oil, 2 teaspoons of the dillweed, the 2 teaspoons pepper, and the ½ teaspoon salt.

2 Trim fat from roast. Place roast and onions in a heavy self-sealing plastic bag set in a deep bowl. Pour marinade over roast. Seal bag; turn to coat meat well. Marinate in refrigerator at least 6 hours or up to 24 hours, turning bag occasionally.

3 Drain roast, reserving marinade and onions. Chill marinade and onions while grilling roast. Insert a meat thermometer near center of the roast.

4 Arrange medium coals on both sides of a covered grill. Test for medium-low heat above where the roast will cook. Place roast on a rack in a roasting pan. Place pan on grill rack not directly over the coals. Cover and grill to desired doneness. [Allow 1½ to 2 hours for medium (160°).] Add coals every 20 to 30 minutes or as necessary to maintain medium-low heat.

5 Meanwhile, for sauce, combine mayonnaise, sour cream, horseradish, remaining dillweed, the ⅛ teaspoon salt, and the ⅛ teaspoon pepper. Cover; chill until serving time.

6 In a small saucepan bring reserved marinade and onions to boiling; reduce heat. Cover and simmer about 12 minutes or until onions are tender. Thinly slice the roast; serve with the onion mixture and the sauce.

Nutrition Facts per serving: 297 cal., 20 g total fat (5 g sat. fat), 66 mg chol., 263 mg sodium, 2 g carbo., 0 g fiber, 24 g pro. Daily Values: 13% iron

Burgers Borracho

Prep: 20 minutes **Marinate:** 6 to 24 hours **Grill:** 14 minutes **Makes:** 6 servings

¼ cup finely chopped onion	1½ pounds lean ground beef
2 tablespoons tomato paste	1½ cups beer
4 cloves garlic, minced	6 hamburger buns, split and toasted
½ teaspoon salt	1 recipe Mustard Sauce (below)
½ teaspoon dried rosemary, crushed	Spinach leaves (optional)
½ teaspoon pepper	Tomato slices (optional)
¼ teaspoon ground allspice	Onion slices (optional)

1 In a medium bowl combine onion, tomato paste, garlic, salt, rosemary, pepper, and allspice. Add ground beef; mix well. Shape mixture into six ¾-inch-thick patties. Place in a single layer in a shallow dish. Set aside 1 tablespoon of the beer for the Mustard Sauce; pour remaining beer over burgers. Cover; marinate in refrigerator at least 6 hours or up to 24 hours, turning burgers once.

2 Drain burgers, discarding beer. Grill burgers on the rack of an uncovered grill directly over medium coals for 14 to 18 minutes or until done (160°),* turning once halfway through grilling. Serve burgers on buns with Mustard Sauce. If desired, garnish with spinach leaves, tomato slices, and onion slices.

Mustard Sauce: In a small bowl combine 3 tablespoons stone-ground mustard, ¾ teaspoon Worcestershire sauce, and the reserved 1 tablespoon beer. Cover; chill until needed or up to 24 hours.

Nutrition Facts per serving: 324 cal., 13 g total fat (5 g sat. fat), 71 mg chol., 547 mg sodium, 24 g carbo., 1 g fiber, 24 g pro. Daily Values: 1% vit. A, 8% vit. C, 4% calcium, 23% iron

*Note: The internal color of a ground beef patty is not a reliable doneness indicator. A beef patty cooked to 160°, regardless of color, is safe. Use an instant-read thermometer to check the internal temperature. To measure the doneness of a patty, insert the thermometer through the side of the patty to a depth of 2 to 3 inches.

Borracho means "drunk" in Spanish. True to their name, these big-flavored burgers—studded with rosemary, garlic, and allspice and emboldened by a little beer—are anything but mild-mannered.

The white wine and sage marinade adds depth to the flavor of tender veal chops, while the grilled apples bring an unexpected touch. All in all, it's a great combination for an early-autumn cookout.

Veal Chops with Apples

Prep: 10 minutes **Marinate:** 6 to 24 hours **Grill:** 15 minutes **Makes:** 4 servings

4 boneless veal top loin chops, cut ¾ inch thick	2 teaspoons dried sage, crushed
½ cup dry white wine	½ teaspoon salt
2 tablespoons cooking oil	½ teaspoon pepper
	2 medium tart cooking apples

1 Trim fat from chops. Place chops in a self-sealing plastic bag set in a shallow dish. For marinade, combine wine, oil, sage, salt, and pepper. Pour over chops. Seal bag. Marinate in refrigerator at least 6 hours or up to 24 hours, turning bag occasionally.

2 Drain chops, reserving marinade. Just before grilling, core apples. Cut crosswise into 1-inch-thick slices. Grill chops and apple slices on the rack of an uncovered grill directly over medium coals until desired doneness, turning and brushing once with marinade halfway through grilling. Discard any remaining marinade. [Allow 15 to 17 minutes for medium (160°).] Serve chops with apple slices.

Nutrition Facts per serving: 271 cal., 13 g total fat (3 g sat. fat), 95 mg chol., 354 mg sodium, 9 g carbo., 1 g fiber, 24 g pro. Daily Values: 5% vit. C, 2% calcium, 7% iron

How Hot Is It?

The grilling times in recipes depend on cooking the food over the proper coal temperatures, as specified. To determine coal temperature, remember that briquettes reach cooking temperature when they are covered in gray ash, usually 30 to 40 minutes after lighting. To test the coals, hold your hand just above where the food will cook. Count "one thousand one, one thousand two," etc. for as long as your hand can comfortably remain there. Two seconds means the coals are hot, three is medium-hot, four is medium, five is medium-low, and six is low. To reduce the temperature of a fire, arrange the coals in thinner layers and let them burn down 5 to 10 minutes longer. To build a hotter fire, use more coals and don't let them burn down as much. If you want more heat from the coals while they're burning, gently tap them with long-handled tongs to shake off the excess ash, then move them closer together.

Indonesian Satay

Prep: 25 minutes **Marinate:** 2 to 24 hours **Grill:** 12 minutes **Makes:** 10 servings

Meat-lovers, take note! Lamb, beef, and turkey combine for one all-out hearty dish that's anything but familiar, thanks to exotic peanut sauce. Serve with rice and steamed green beans—both can be cooked while the kabobs sizzle.

1 pound boneless leg of lamb, cut into 1½-inch cubes
1 1-pound boneless beef sirloin steak, cut into 1½-inch cubes
½ pound skinless, boneless turkey breast, cut into 1½-inch cubes
1 cup purchased unsweetened coconut milk
⅓ cup finely chopped onion
2 cloves garlic, minced

2 teaspoons dry mustard
2 teaspoons ground coriander
½ teaspoon ground turmeric
¼ teaspoon salt
¼ teaspoon ground cumin
10 green onions, trimmed and each cut into 4 pieces
1 recipe Peanut Sauce (below)
Hot cooked rice (optional)

1 Place the lamb, beef, and turkey cubes in a self-sealing plastic bag set in a shallow dish. For marinade, combine coconut milk, onion, garlic, mustard, coriander, turmeric, salt, and cumin. Pour over cubes. Seal bag. Marinate in refrigerator at least 2 hours or up to 24 hours, turning bag occasionally.

2 Drain cubes, reserving marinade. On twenty 8-inch metal skewers, alternately thread lamb, beef, turkey, and green onions leaving a ¼-inch space between pieces.

3 Grill kabobs on the rack of an uncovered grill directly over medium coals for 12 to 16 minutes or until turkey is no longer pink and lamb and beef are medium (160°), turning once and brushing occasionally with marinade during the first half of grilling. Discard any remaining marinade. Serve kabobs with Peanut Sauce. If desired, serve with rice.

Peanut Sauce: In a small saucepan combine ¾ cup reduced-sodium chicken broth, 2 tablespoons sliced green onion, and 1 clove garlic, minced. Bring to boiling; reduce heat. Cover and cook for 2 minutes. Add 1 tablespoon reduced-sodium soy sauce, ½ teaspoon finely shredded lemon peel, 1 tablespoon lemon juice, 1 to 1½ teaspoons chili powder, and ½ teaspoon brown sugar. Return to boiling; reduce heat. Boil gently, uncovered, for 5 minutes. Stir in ⅓ cup peanut butter and ¾ teaspoon ground ginger; heat through over low heat, stirring until smooth. If desired, thin with a little unsweetened coconut milk. Serve warm or at room temperature. Makes about 1 cup.

Nutrition Facts per serving: 224 cal., 12 g total fat (7 g sat. fat), 62 mg chol., 198 mg sodium, 4 g carbo., 0 g fiber, 25 g pro. Daily Values: 2% vit. A, 5% vit. C, 1% calcium, 15% iron

This is the recipe you'll want to turn to for a kick-back-and-relax dinner. The lamb takes about 1 hour to grill, which allows plenty of time for appetizers and drinks before sitting down to eat. Couscous and a marinated vegetable salad from a gourmet deli make carefree side dishes.

Lamb with Herb-Dijon Sauce

Prep: 20 minutes **Marinate:** 1 to 24 hours **Grill:** 1 hour **Stand:** 15 minutes
Makes: 12 servings

1 5- to 6-pound leg of lamb, boned and butterflied*	2 cloves garlic, minced
1 8-ounce jar (¾ cup) Dijon-style mustard	1 teaspoon dried rosemary, crushed
⅓ cup dry white wine	1 teaspoon dried basil, crushed
¼ cup cooking oil	½ teaspoon dried oregano, crushed
	½ teaspoon dried thyme, crushed
	¼ teaspoon pepper

1 Trim fat from meat. For marinade, combine mustard, wine, oil, garlic, rosemary, basil, oregano, thyme, and pepper. Place lamb in a shallow glass dish. Spread lamb with mustard mixture. Cover and marinate at room temperature 1 hour or in refrigerator for at least 4 hours or up to 24 hours.

2 Drain meat, reserving marinade. Chill marinade while grilling meat. Thread two 12- to 14-inch metal skewers diagonally through the meat to keep it flat during cooking. Insert a meat thermometer into the center of meat.

3 Arrange medium coals around a drip pan. Test for medium-low heat above pan. Place meat on the grill rack over drip pan. Cover and grill to desired doneness. [Allow about 1 hour for medium-rare (140°) or about 1½ hours for medium (155°).]

4 Remove meat from grill. Cover with foil; let stand for 15 minutes. (The temperature of the meat will rise 5° during standing.) To serve, remove skewers and thinly slice meat. Heat the chilled marinade until bubbly; serve with meat.

Nutrition Facts per serving: 251 cal., 15 g total fat (4 g sat. fat), 85 mg chol., 530 mg sodium, 6 g carbo., 0 g fiber, 29 g pro. Daily Values: 12% iron

*Note: If unavailable at the meat counter, ask your butcher to bone and butterfly a leg of lamb.

Smoked and Spiced Ribs

Prep: 20 minutes Chill: 6 to 24 hours Grill: 1 hour 20 minutes Makes: 6 servings

 4 pounds pork loin back ribs or pork
     spareribs
 ¼ cup packed brown sugar
 2 teaspoons seasoned salt
 2 teaspoons chili powder

 ¼ cup yellow mustard
 4 cups hickory or fruitwood chips
 ¼ cup bottled barbecue sauce
     Bottled barbecue sauce

1 Trim fat from ribs. Place ribs in a shallow glass dish. Combine brown sugar, seasoned salt, and chili powder. Brush ribs with mustard. Sprinkle brown sugar mixture on ribs. Cover and refrigerate for at least 6 hours or up to 24 hours. At least 1 hour before grilling, soak wood chips in enough water to cover. Drain.

2 Arrange medium-hot coals around a drip pan. Test for medium heat above the pan. Sprinkle some of the drained wood chips over the coals. Pour 1 inch of water into the drip pan. Place ribs, bone sides down, on grill rack over drip pan. (Or, place ribs in a rib rack; place on grill rack.) Cover and grill for 1¼ to 1½ hours or until ribs are tender, adding more coals and wood chips as necessary.

3 Brush with the ¼ cup barbecue sauce. Grill ribs for 5 minutes more. Serve with additional barbecue sauce.

Nutrition Facts per serving: 244 cal., 9 g total fat (3 g sat. fat), 57 mg chol., 810 mg sodium, 11 g carbo., 1 g fiber, 27 g pro. Daily Values: 4% vit. A, 3% vit. C, 3% calcium, 7% iron

Smoking on the Grill

You don't have to own a smoker to achieve mouthwatering smoked flavor. Smoking food on a charcoal grill is simple. Follow these guidelines:
1. Set up your grill for indirect grilling. (See tip, page 136.)
2. Soak hardwood chips in water for at least one hour before smoking. Use aromatic hardwood chips such as apple, hickory, maple, or mesquite.
3. Drain wood chips and sprinkle them directly over hot coals just before placing meat on the grill. (4 cups of wood chips will last about 2 hours.)
4. Add additional chips as needed to maintain a steady source of smoke. Avoid lifting the grill lid too often as this may lengthen the cooking time.

Coating the ribs with yellow mustard—a trick borrowed from barbecue champions—helps the spice rub stay on and gives the meat a distinctive flavor. Coleslaw, whether purchased or homemade, is a cooling accompaniment.

Gingery Apricot-Glazed Pork Ribs

Prep: 20 minutes **Marinate:** 6 to 24 hours **Grill:** 1¼ hours **Makes:** 4 servings

4 pounds pork loin back ribs	2 tablespoons minced garlic
1 cup finely chopped onion	(about 12 cloves)
⅓ cup dry sherry	½ teaspoon ground black pepper
¼ cup finely grated fresh ginger	⅔ cup apricot preserves
¼ cup rice vinegar	3 tablespoons spicy brown mustard
¼ cup soy sauce	1 tablespoon toasted sesame oil
	¼ teaspoon ground red pepper

1 Trim fat from ribs. Place ribs in a self-sealing plastic bag set in a shallow dish. For marinade, combine onion, sherry, ginger, vinegar, soy sauce, garlic, and black pepper. Pour over ribs. Seal bag. Marinate in refrigerator at least 6 hours or up to 24 hours, turning bag occasionally. Drain, reserving ¼ cup of the marinade.

2 For sauce, in a small saucepan combine apricot preserves, mustard, oil, and ground red pepper. Stir in reserved marinade. Bring to boiling; reduce heat. Simmer, uncovered, about 3 minutes or until slightly thickened.

3 Arrange medium-hot coals around a drip pan. Test for medium heat above the pan. Place ribs, bone sides down, on grill rack over drip pan. (Or place ribs in a rib rack; place on grill rack.) Cover and grill for 1¼ to 1½ hours or until ribs are tender, brushing occasionally with sauce during the last 15 minutes of grilling.

Nutrition Facts per serving: 740 cal., 42 g total fat (14 g sat. fat), 176 mg chol., 637 mg sodium, 42 g carbo., 1 g fiber, 45 g pro. Daily Values: 1% vit. A, 5% vit. C, 4% calcium, 19% iron

Hot and sour, sweet and nutty—you name it! A little bit of Asian-inspired this-and-that adds up to intriguing tastes that satisfy any flavor craving.

Oyster sauce is a thick, concentrated mixture of oysters, brine, and soy sauce. Asian cooks enjoy the way it adds richness to recipes, yet doesn't compete with other natural flavors in a dish.

Skewered Five-Spice Pork and Vegetables

Prep: 30 minutes **Marinate:** 8 to 24 hours **Grill:** 10 minutes **Makes:** 4 servings

1 pound boneless pork loin, cut into
   bite-size strips
¼ cup salsa
2 tablespoons soy sauce
2 tablespoons oyster sauce
1 tablespoon sugar
1 teaspoon five-spice powder

⅛ to ¼ teaspoon ground red pepper
1 medium red sweet pepper, cut into
   1-inch pieces
8 large fresh mushrooms
4 green onions, cut diagonally into
   1½-inch pieces
1 tablespoon cooking oil

1 Place pork in a self-sealing plastic bag set in a large bowl. For marinade, combine salsa, soy sauce, oyster sauce, sugar, five-spice powder, and ground red pepper. Pour over meat in bag. Seal bag. Turn to coat meat. Marinate in refrigerator at least 8 hours or up to 24 hours, turning bag occasionally. Drain meat, reserving marinade.

2 Brush vegetables lightly with oil. Alternately thread pork, sweet pepper, mushrooms, and green onions onto four 12- to 14-inch metal skewers leaving a ¼-inch space between pieces.

3 Grill kabobs on the rack of an uncovered grill directly over medium coals for 10 to 12 minutes or until juices run clear and vegetables are tender, turning and brushing with marinade halfway through grilling. Discard any remaining marinade.

Nutrition Facts per serving: 318 cal., 19 g total fat (6 g sat. fat), 67 mg chol., 829 mg sodium, 11 g carbo., 2 g fiber, 26 g pro. Daily Values: 37% vit. A, 101% vit. C, 3% calcium, 10% iron

Adobo Pork Chops

Prep: 15 minutes **Marinate:** 2 to 24 hours **Grill:** 8 minutes **Makes:** 6 servings

6 **boneless pork loin chops, cut**	2 **teaspoons hot chili powder**
¾ inch thick	1 **teaspoon ground cumin**
2 **tablespoons brown sugar**	1 **teaspoon dried oregano, crushed**
2 **tablespoons olive oil**	½ **teaspoon salt**
2 **tablespoons orange juice**	¼ **teaspoon ground cinnamon**
2 **tablespoons snipped fresh cilantro**	3 **cloves garlic, minced**
1 **tablespoon red wine vinegar or cider**	
vinegar	

1 Trim fat from chops. Place chops in a self-sealing plastic bag set in a shallow dish. For marinade, combine brown sugar, oil, orange juice, cilantro, vinegar, chili powder, cumin, oregano, salt, cinnamon, and garlic. Pour over chops. Seal bag. Marinate in refrigerator at least 2 hours or up to 24 hours, turning bag occasionally. Drain chops, discarding marinade.

2 Grill chops on the rack of an uncovered grill directly over medium coals for 8 to 11 minutes or until juices run clear (160°), turning once halfway through grilling.

Nutrition Facts per serving: 180 cal., 11 g total fat (3 g sat. fat), 51 mg chol., 166 mg sodium, 4 g carbo., 0 g fiber, 16 g pro. Daily Values: 2% vit. A, 4% vit. C, 1% calcium, 7% iron

A Thermometer Is a Must

A thermometer is a grilling essential—using one is the only way to tell whether food is cooked to a safe internal temperature as specified for the doneness given in the recipe. To use a thermometer, insert it into the thickest part of the food, making sure it isn't touching bone, fat, or gristle.

● **A meat thermometer works well for longer-cooking meats, such as a roast or whole poultry. It can be left in the food while it cooks.**

● **An instant-read thermometer is used for checking the internal temperature of food at the end of cooking and gives a reading in less than 20 seconds. It must be inserted at least 2 inches into the food.**

● **A digital thermometer gives digital readings in 10 seconds. Because the probe is inserted only ½ inch deep, it is perfect for thin foods.**

The marinade in this piquant recipe is inspired by adobo sauce, which hails from Mexico. Adobo sauce is usually made from ground chile peppers, vinegar, and herbs; for the sake of convenience, this version calls on hot chili powder rather than ground chile peppers. If you want additional heat, add ¼ teaspoon ground red pepper to the marinade.

No scurrying indoors and out to prepare this perfect side dish. The sweet potatoes and onions cook alongside the meat. You'll love the way grilling these perfect partners brings out their mellow, irresistible sweetness.

Sage-Marinated Chops with Sweet Potatoes

Prep: 25 minutes **Marinate:** 8 to 24 hours **Grill:** 25 minutes **Makes:** 4 servings

4 pork rib or loin chops, cut 1¼ inches thick	½ teaspoon salt
⅔ cup cider vinegar	¼ teaspoon pepper
⅓ cup balsamic vinegar	2 sweet potatoes, quartered lengthwise (about 1 pound)
2 tablespoons olive oil	1 medium sweet onion (such as Vidalia), cut into ¾-inch slices
2 teaspoons dried sage, crushed	

1 Trim fat from chops. Place chops in a self-sealing plastic bag set in a shallow dish. For marinade, in a small saucepan combine cider vinegar and balsamic vinegar. Bring to boiling; reduce heat. Boil gently, uncovered, about 8 minutes or until reduced to about ⅔ cup. Cool slightly. Stir in oil, sage, salt, and pepper. Set aside ¼ cup marinade.

2 Pour remaining marinade over chops. Seal bag. Marinate in refrigerator at least 8 hours or up to 24 hours, turning bag occasionally. Drain chops, discarding marinade. Brush potatoes and onion with the reserved marinade.

3 Place chops, sweet potatoes, and onion on the grill rack directly over medium coals. Cover and grill for 25 to 30 minutes or until juices from chops run clear (160°) and vegetables are tender, turning chops once and vegetables occasionally.

Nutrition Facts per serving: 354 cal., 16 g total fat (4 g sat. fat), 77 mg chol., 249 mg sodium, 28 g carbo., 4 g fiber, 26 g pro. Daily Values: 193% vit. A, 41% vit. C, 3% calcium, 13% iron

Zesty Curried Lime Chicken Kabobs

Prep: 20 minutes **Marinate:** 4 to 24 hours **Grill:** 18 minutes **Makes:** 4 servings

- 1 pound skinless, boneless chicken breast halves, cut into 1½-inch pieces
- ½ cup plain yogurt
- ¼ cup snipped fresh cilantro
- 1 teaspoon finely shredded lime peel
- 2 tablespoons lime juice
- 2 tablespoons olive oil or cooking oil
- 1 tablespoon honey
- 1 tablespoon Dijon-style mustard

- 2 cloves garlic, minced
- ½ teaspoon curry powder
- ¼ teaspoon salt
- ¼ teaspoon ground black pepper
- 2 medium green and/or red sweet peppers, cut into 1-inch pieces
- 1 medium zucchini, sliced ½ inch thick
- 8 cherry tomatoes

1 Place chicken in a self-sealing plastic bag set in a large bowl. For marinade, combine yogurt, cilantro, lime peel, lime juice, oil, honey, mustard, garlic, curry powder, salt, and black pepper. Pour over chicken; seal bag. Turn to coat chicken. Marinate in refrigerator at least 4 hours or up to 24 hours, turning bag occasionally. Drain chicken, reserving marinade.

2 Alternately thread chicken, sweet peppers, and zucchini on eight 10- to 12-inch metal skewers, leaving ¼-inch space between pieces. Brush vegetables with reserved marinade. Discard any remaining marinade.

3 Arrange medium-hot coals around a drip pan. Test for medium heat above pan. Place kabobs on the grill rack over drip pan. Cover and grill for 18 to 20 minutes or until chicken is tender and no longer pink, turning once. Place a cherry tomato on the end of each skewer during the last 1 minute of grilling.

Nutrition Facts per serving: 261 cal., 9 g total fat (2 g sat. fat), 68 mg chol., 256 mg sodium, 15 g carbo., 2 g fiber, 30 g pro. Daily Values: 11% vit. A, 103% vit. C, 97% calcium, 10% iron

Curry powder—which can blend as many as 20 spices, herbs, and seeds—contributes lots of flavor to this marinade. As if that's not enough, we've added some other distinctive flavors, including honey, mustard, and garlic. Lime peel brings a light fresh spark, and yogurt adds a creamy tang; both complement the curry's depth and intrigue.

Bean threads are clear, thin, delicate noodles made from the starch of mung beans. Also called cellophane noodles, they're often found in Southeast Asian specialties, including egg rolls. For variety, add them to this Thai-inspired salad. Soak 4 ounces of bean threads in enough water to cover for 30 minutes. Drain well; squeeze out excess moisture. Cut into 2-inch lengths. Place over the shredded cabbage before adding the remaining ingredients.

Thai Chicken Salad

Prep: 30 minutes **Marinate:** 2 to 24 hours **Grill:** 8 minutes **Makes:** 4 servings

¼ cup snipped fresh cilantro
¼ cup water
3 tablespoons soy sauce
2 large cloves garlic, minced
¼ to ½ teaspoon pepper
4 medium skinless, boneless chicken breast halves, cut into ½-inch-wide strips (about 1 pound total)
3 tablespoons lime juice

1½ teaspoons sugar
Romaine leaves (optional)
4 cups shredded Chinese cabbage
2 medium tomatoes, cut into wedges
1 medium cucumber, seeded and chopped
3 green onions, sliced
1 tablespoon chopped honey roasted or dry roasted peanuts

1 In a shallow baking dish combine 2 tablespoons of the cilantro, 3 tablespoons of the water, 2 tablespoons of the soy sauce, the garlic, and pepper. Thread chicken strips accordion-style on eight 6-inch skewers; place in baking dish, turning to coat. Cover and marinate in refrigerator at least 2 hours or up to 24 hours, turning occasionally.

2 For dressing, in a small screw-top jar combine lime juice, sugar, remaining water, and remaining soy sauce. Cover and refrigerate until serving time.

3 Remove chicken kabobs from marinade, discarding marinade. Grill chicken kabobs on the rack of an uncovered grill directly over medium coals for 8 to 10 minutes or until chicken is no longer pink, turning once.

4 If desired, line 4 dinner plates with romaine leaves. Divide cabbage among plates. Place 2 chicken kabobs on each plate. Divide tomato and cucumber among the plates. Shake dressing well; drizzle over chicken and vegetables. Sprinkle with green onions, peanuts, and remaining cilantro.

Nutrition Facts per serving: 186 cal., 3 g total fat (1 g sat. fat), 66 mg chol., 466 mg sodium, 11 g carbo., 4 g fiber, 30 g pro. Daily Values: 31% vit. A, 72% vit. C, 10% calcium, 9% iron

Stay outdoors and keep the stove and oven off—grill thick slices of zucchini for a great side dish to this hot-and-sweet combo.

Fiery Chicken and Potato Fingers

Prep: 20 minutes **Marinate:** 30 minutes to 24 hours **Grill:** 24 minutes **Makes:** 4 servings

4 medium skinless, boneless chicken
   breast halves (about 1 pound total)
3 tablespoons olive oil
3 tablespoons bottled hot pepper
   sauce
2 tablespoons snipped fresh parsley
   (optional)
1 tablespoon honey or brown sugar

3 cloves garlic, minced
½ teaspoon salt
½ teaspoon ground red pepper
½ teaspoon cracked black pepper
2 large baking potatoes
   (about 1 pound total)

1 Cut each chicken breast half lengthwise into 3 strips. Place chicken in a self-sealing plastic bag set in a shallow dish. For marinade, combine oil, hot pepper sauce, parsley (if desired), honey or brown sugar, garlic, salt, red pepper, and black pepper. Pour 2 tablespoons of the marinade over chicken; seal bag. Marinate in refrigerator at least 30 minutes or up to 24 hours, turning bag occasionally. Cover and chill remaining marinade for basting.

2 Drain chicken, discarding marinade. Just before grilling, cut each potato lengthwise into 8 wedges. Lightly brush wedges with some of the reserved marinade.

3 Grill potatoes on the rack of an uncovered grill directly over medium coals for 15 minutes. Turn potatoes. Add chicken to grill. Grill for 9 to 12 minutes more or until chicken and potatoes are tender and chicken is no longer pink, turning chicken and brushing once with the remaining reserved marinade halfway through grilling. Discard any remaining marinade.

Nutrition Facts per serving: 335 cal., 12 g total fat (2 g sat. fat), 59 mg chol., 340 mg sodium, 32 g carbo., 1 g fiber, 25 g pro. Daily Values: 2% vit. A, 41% vit. C, 2% calcium, 15% iron

Polynesian Honey-Pineapple Chicken

Prep: 25 minutes **Marinate:** 6 to 24 hours **Grill:** 50 minutes **Makes:** 6 to 8 servings

½ cup unsweetened pineapple juice
¼ cup honey
4 cloves garlic, minced
3 tablespoons Worcestershire sauce

1 tablespoon grated fresh ginger or
   1 teaspoon ground ginger
1 teaspoon salt
12 chicken drumsticks and/or thighs
   (about 3 pounds total)

1 For marinade, in a large saucepan stir together pineapple juice, honey, garlic, Worcestershire sauce, ginger, and salt. Bring to boiling; reduce heat. Simmer, uncovered, about 15 minutes or until the marinade is reduced to ½ cup, stirring occasionally. Let mixture cool to room temperature.

2 Place chicken in a self-sealing plastic bag set in a shallow dish. Pour marinade over chicken. Seal bag. Marinate in refrigerator at least 6 hours or up to 24 hours, turning bag occasionally. Drain chicken pieces, reserving marinade.

3 Arrange medium-hot coals around a drip pan. Test for medium heat above pan. Place chicken on the grill rack over drip pan. Cover; grill for 50 to 60 minutes or until chicken is tender and no longer pink (180°), brushing occasionally with the reserved marinade for the first 30 minutes of grilling. Discard any remaining marinade.

Nutrition Facts per serving: 424 cal., 22 g total fat (6 g sat. fat), 129 mg chol., 553 mg sodium, 16 g carbo., 37 g pro. Daily Values: 27% vit. C, 16% iron

While this recipe gets its inspiration from the exotic sweet and spicy flavors found in the beautiful, lush islands of the South Pacific, it requires few ingredients—and you probably already have several of them on hand. Now that's paradise!

Fresh Ginger Forever

Good news: Whole gingerroot stays fresh for two to three weeks in the refrigerator when wrapped loosely in a paper towel. Better news: It lasts almost indefinitely when frozen. To freeze, place unpeeled gingerroot in a freezer bag. There is no need to thaw before using, just grate or slice the fresh ginger while it is frozen.

When grilling chicken pieces, such as in this lime-sparked curry chicken, it's best to leave the skin on. The skin holds a great deal of flavor and helps retain the moistness of the meat.

Curried Barbecued Chicken

Prep: 15 minutes **Marinate:** 4 to 24 hours **Grill:** 50 minutes **Makes:** 4 to 6 servings

2½ to 3 pounds meaty chicken pieces
      (breasts, thighs, and drumsticks)
  2 teaspoons finely shredded lime peel
  ⅓ cup lime juice
  1 tablespoon curry powder
  1 tablespoon cooking oil

  2 cloves garlic, minced
  ½ teaspoon salt
  ¼ teaspoon ground cumin
  ¼ teaspoon ground coriander
  ⅛ teaspoon ground red pepper

1 Place chicken in a self-sealing plastic bag set in a shallow dish. For marinade, stir together the lime peel, lime juice, curry powder, oil, garlic, salt, cumin, coriander, and red pepper. Pour over chicken. Seal bag. Marinate in refrigerator at least 4 hours or up to 24 hours, turning bag occasionally. Drain chicken, reserving marinade.

2 Arrange medium-hot coals around a drip pan. Test for medium heat above the pan. Place chicken pieces, bone sides down, on grill rack over pan. Cover and grill for 50 to 60 minutes or until chicken is tender and no longer pink (170° for breasts, 180° for thighs and drumsticks), brushing with some of the marinade during the first 40 minutes of grilling. Discard any remaining marinade.

Nutrition Facts per serving: 366 cal., 20 g total fat (5 g sat. fat), 130 mg chol., 382 mg sodium, 4 g carbo., 1 g fiber, 42 g pro. Daily Values: 5% vit. A, 13% vit. C, 3% calcium, 16% iron

Indirect Grilling

Cooking by indirect heat means placing the coals around the edges of where the food will cook, rather than directly under the food. It is most often used for foods such as large roasts, ribs, whole chickens, and whole fish. To set up the grill for indirect cooking, light the coals as recommended by the grill manufacturer. Arrange glowing coals around the grill perimeter using long-handled tongs. When the coals are covered with gray ash and test the temperature specified in the recipe, set a drip pan in the center of the grill, surrounded by coals, directly under where the food will be placed.

Rosemary Chicken

Prep: 15 minutes **Marinate:** 6 to 24 hours **Grill:** 35 minutes **Makes:** 6 servings

2 to 2½ pounds meaty chicken pieces (breasts, thighs, and drumsticks)
½ cup dry white wine
2 tablespoons olive oil
4 cloves garlic, minced
4 teaspoons snipped fresh rosemary

1 tablespoon finely shredded lemon peel
¼ teaspoon salt
¼ teaspoon pepper

1 Place chicken in a self-sealing plastic bag set in a shallow dish. For marinade, in a blender container or food processor bowl combine wine, oil, garlic, rosemary, lemon peel, salt, and pepper. Cover and blend or process about 15 seconds or until well mixed. Pour over chicken in bag. Seal bag, turning to coat chicken with marinade. Marinate in refrigerator at least 6 hours or up to 24 hours, turning bag occasionally.

2 Drain chicken, reserving marinade. Grill chicken, bone sides up, on the rack of an uncovered grill directly over medium coals for 35 to 45 minutes or until chicken is tender and no longer pink (170° for breasts, 180° for thighs and drumsticks), turning once and brushing with marinade halfway through grilling. Discard any remaining marinade.

Nutrition Facts per serving: 192 cal., 10 g total fat (3 g sat. fat), 69 mg chol., 93 mg sodium, 0 g carbo., 0 g fiber, 22 g pro. Daily Values: 2% vit. A, 1% vit. C, 1% calcium, 6% iron

Travelers to the Mediterranean are apt to describe their dining experiences there as simple and sublime. With its rosemary, garlic, and lemon (a favorite flavor trio found in the Mediterranean), this chicken dish is likely to elicit similar praise.

Pineapple-Rum Turkey Kabobs

Prep: 15 minutes **Marinate:** 4 to 24 hours **Grill:** 12 minutes **Makes:** 4 servings

¾ pound turkey breast tenderloin
    steaks, cut ½ inch thick, or
    boneless turkey breast
⅓ cup unsweetened pineapple juice
3 tablespoons rum or unsweetened
    pineapple juice
1 tablespoon brown sugar
1 tablespoon finely chopped
    lemongrass or 2 teaspoons finely
    shredded lemon peel

1 tablespoon olive oil
1 medium red onion, cut into thin
    wedges
3 plums or 2 nectarines, pitted and
    cut into thick slices
2 cups fresh or canned pineapple
    chunks
    Hot cooked rice with green sweet
    pepper slivers (optional)

1 Cut turkey into 1-inch cubes. Place turkey in a self-sealing plastic bag set in a shallow dish. For marinade, combine the ⅓ cup pineapple juice, the 3 tablespoons rum or pineapple juice, the brown sugar, lemongrass or lemon peel, and oil. Pour over turkey. Seal bag. Marinate in refrigerator at least 4 hours or up to 24 hours, turning bag occasionally.

2 Drain turkey, reserving marinade. In a small saucepan bring reserved marinade to boiling. Boil gently, uncovered, for 1 minute. Remove from heat. On four 12-inch metal skewers*, alternately thread turkey and onion, leaving about a ¼-inch space between pieces. Alternately thread plums and pineapple onto 4 more skewers.

3 Grill turkey and fruit kabobs on the rack of an uncovered grill directly over medium coals until turkey and onion are tender, turkey is no longer pink, and fruit is heated through, turning once and brushing occasionally with the heated marinade during the last half of grilling. (Allow 12 to 14 minutes for turkey and onion and about 5 minutes for fruit.) If desired, serve over hot cooked rice.

Nutrition Facts per serving: 235 cal., 6 g total fat (1 g sat. fat), 37 mg chol., 37 mg sodium, 24 g carbo., 2 g fiber, 17 g pro. Daily Values: 1% vit. A, 34% vit. C, 2% calcium, 8% iron

*Note: To use wooden skewers, soak eight 12-inch wooden skewers in water for 30 minutes. Thread as directed above.

Rum lends a Caribbean flavor, while lemongrass tastes distinctly Asian. And then there's the pineapple-brown sugar twist so loved in the South Seas. Is it more East than West, or vice versa? You decide! (Or simply dig in and call it delicious.)

Turkey and cranberries on the grill? You bet. With a little tequila, lime peel, and smoky-hot chipotle peppers, the traditional Thanksgiving duo transcends seasonal boundaries. Try it any time of year.

Cranberry-Sauced Turkey Legs

Prep: 20 minutes **Marinate:** 2 to 24 hours **Grill:** 45 minutes **Makes:** 6 servings

6 turkey drumsticks (about 3 pounds total)
¼ cup cranberry juice
¼ cup tequila
1 tablespoon finely shredded lime peel
¼ cup lime juice
2 cloves garlic, minced
1 teaspoon salt
¼ teaspoon ground red pepper (optional)
1 16-ounce can whole cranberry sauce
2 or 3 canned chipotle peppers in adobo sauce, mashed

1 Place turkey in a self-sealing plastic bag set in a shallow dish. For marinade, combine cranberry juice, 2 tablespoons of the tequila, 1½ teaspoons of the lime peel, 2 tablespoons of the lime juice, the garlic, salt, and, if desired, red pepper. Pour over turkey. Seal bag. Marinate in refrigerator at least 2 hours or up to 24 hours, turning bag occasionally. Drain turkey, discarding marinade.

2 For sauce, in a small saucepan combine remaining tequila, remaining lime peel, remaining lime juice, the cranberry sauce, and chipotle peppers. Bring to boiling; reduce heat. Simmer, uncovered, for 5 minutes. Set aside 1¼ cups of the sauce.

3 Arrange medium-hot coals around a drip pan. Test for medium heat above the pan. Place turkey on the grill rack over drip pan. Cover; grill for 45 to 60 minutes or until tender and no longer pink (180°), turning and brushing occasionally with the remaining sauce during the last 10 minutes of grilling. To serve, reheat the reserved sauce; pass with turkey.

Nutrition Facts per serving: 372 cal., 9 g total fat (3 g sat. fat), 105 mg chol., 290 mg sodium, 32 g carbo., 1 g fiber, 36 g pro. Daily Values: 6% vit. A, 12% vit. C, 4% calcium, 21% iron

Hot Peppers in Cold Storage

If a recipe only calls for a few chipotle chile peppers, freeze the rest for future use. In a freezer container, cover remaining peppers with the liquid from the can. Seal, label, and freeze up to 2 months; thaw in the refrigerator. You can freeze leftover bottled roasted red peppers and canned green chile peppers too.

Turkey and Couscous Salad

Prep: 15 minutes Marinate: 4 to 24 hours Grill: 50 minutes Makes: 4 servings

1 turkey thigh (about 1 pound)	1 stalk celery, chopped
2 cups chicken broth	½ cup whole pitted kalamata or ripe
3 tablespoons lemon juice	olives (sliced, if desired)
2 tablespoons olive oil	2 tablespoons thinly sliced green
1 clove garlic, minced	onion
¼ teaspoon salt	2 tablespoons snipped fresh mint
¼ teaspoon ground red pepper	Shredded lettuce (optional)
1 cup quick-cooking couscous	1 medium tomato, seeded and
	chopped

1 Place turkey in a self-sealing plastic bag set in a deep bowl. For marinade, in a screw-top jar combine ½ cup of the chicken broth, the lemon juice, oil, garlic, salt, and red pepper. Cover and shake well. Pour ¼ cup of the marinade over turkey. Seal bag. Marinate in refrigerator at least 4 hours or up to 24 hours, turning bag occasionally. Cover and chill the remaining marinade for dressing.

2 Drain turkey, discarding marinade. Arrange medium-hot coals around a drip pan. Test for medium heat above the pan. Place turkey on the grill rack over drip pan. Cover and grill for 50 to 60 minutes or until tender and no longer pink (180°). Remove turkey from grill. When turkey is cool enough to handle, remove skin and bone; shred meat or cut into cubes.

3 Meanwhile, in a medium saucepan bring remaining broth to boiling; stir in couscous. Remove from heat. Cover; let stand about 5 minutes or until liquid is absorbed.

4 Transfer couscous to a large bowl. Add turkey, celery, olives, green onion, and mint; toss to combine. Drizzle with reserved marinade; toss to coat. Serve warm. (Or cover and chill in refrigerator up to 24 hours.) If desired, serve on shredded lettuce. Sprinkle with chopped tomato.

Nutrition Facts per serving: 398 cal., 12 g total fat (3 g sat. fat), 68 mg chol., 688 mg sodium, 40 g carbo., 9 g fiber, 30 g pro. Daily Values: 3% vit. A, 21% vit. C, 4% calcium, 21% iron

If it's just the two of you for dinner, why not make this lively olive- and mint-sparked salad for a casual dinner alfresco tonight? The leftovers keep well and will make a satisfying lunch to tote to work tomorrow.

Caramelized Salmon with Citrus Salsa

Prep: 20 minutes **Chill:** 8 to 24 hours **Grill:** 12 minutes **Makes:** 4 servings

1	1½-pound fresh or frozen salmon fillet (with skin), 1 inch thick
2	tablespoons sugar
2½	teaspoons finely shredded orange peel
1	teaspoon salt
¼	teaspoon freshly ground black pepper

2	oranges, peeled, sectioned, and coarsely chopped
1	cup chopped fresh pineapple or canned crushed pineapple, drained
2	tablespoons snipped fresh cilantro
1	tablespoon finely chopped shallot
1	fresh jalapeño pepper,* seeded and finely chopped

1 Thaw fish, if frozen. Rinse fish; pat dry with paper towels. Place fish, skin side down, in a shallow dish. For rub, combine sugar, 1½ teaspoons of the orange peel, the salt, and black pepper. Sprinkle rub evenly over fish (not on skin side); rub in with your fingers. Cover and chill in refrigerator at least 8 hours or up to 24 hours.

2 Meanwhile, for salsa, in a small bowl stir together the remaining orange peel, the oranges, pineapple, cilantro, shallot, and jalapeño pepper. Cover and chill in refrigerator until ready to serve or up to 24 hours. Drain fish, discarding liquid.

3 Arrange medium-hot coals around a drip pan. Test for medium heat above the pan. Place fish, skin side down, on a greased grill rack over drip pan. Cover and grill about 12 minutes or until fish flakes easily when tested with a fork.

4 To serve, cut fish into 4 serving-size pieces, cutting to but not through the skin. Carefully slip a metal spatula between fish and skin, lifting fish up and away from skin. Serve fish with salsa.

Nutrition Facts per serving: 145 cal., 4 g total fat (1 g sat. fat), 20 mg chol., 424 mg sodium, 10 g carbo., 1 g fiber, 17 g pro. Daily Values: 5% vit. A, 31% vit. C, 2% calcium, 6% iron

*Note: See tip on handling chile peppers, page 18.

Fragrant and delicious, this do-ahead recipe is especially impressive because the orange-scented sugar rub turns golden during grilling. Because jalapeños vary in their level of heat, you might want to taste the salsa before adding all the jalapeño.

Maple-Brined Turkey (page 151), Kumquat Cranberry Sauce (page 150), Mashed Turnips and Sweets (page 154), steamed green beans, and Peppery White Cheddar Biscuits (page 155)

Stress-Free Holidays

Every season brings reason to celebrate, and every recipe in this chapter gives you a head start on the festivities. These menus and timetables will ensure impressive results—and plenty of time to join in the fun too.

In This Chapter

TAKE A BREAK LUNCH

Chicken Waldorf Salad
   (below)
Cinnamon-Spiced
   Pumpkin Soup
   (page 147)
Tuscan Cornmeal
   Cookies (page 149)

Up to 3 months ahead:
● Prepare cookies; freeze.
1 day ahead:
● Prepare salad and soup; chill.
1 hour ahead:
● Thaw cookies.

30 minutes ahead:
● Heat soup.
Just before serving:
● Spoon salad onto lettuce leaves.
● Ladle soup into cups or bowls.

Chicken Waldorf Salad

Start to finish: 20 minutes **Makes:** 4 servings

¾ **pound cooked chicken breast, cubed
      or shredded (about 2 cups)**
2 **medium red and/or green apples,
      coarsely chopped (2 cups)**
⅓ **cup coarsely chopped pecans or
      peanuts**
¼ **cup thinly sliced celery**

⅓ **cup fat-free mayonnaise dressing or
      salad dressing**
⅓ **cup fat-free dairy sour cream**
1 **tablespoon lemon juice**
1 **tablespoon honey**
1 **to 1½ teaspoons dried rosemary,
      crushed**
   Radicchio leaves

1 In a medium bowl combine chicken, apples, nuts, and celery. For dressing, in a small
  bowl stir together mayonnaise dressing, sour cream, lemon juice, honey, and rosemary.
Stir dressing into chicken mixture just until coated.

2 To serve, arrange lettuce leaves on 4 salad plates. Spoon chicken-dressing mixture onto
  lettuce leaves.

Nutrition Facts per serving: 295 cal., 10 g total fat (1 g sat. fat), 72 mg chol., 240 mg sodium,
23 g carbo., 3 g fiber, 29 g pro. Daily Values: 2% vit. A, 11% vit. C, 6% calcium, 8% iron

This soup and salad
luncheon is the perfect
menu for guests who have
a busy afternoon ahead of
them. It's not heavy
enough to require an after-
feast nap, yet it's enough
to make everyone feel
graciously indulged.

To Make Ahead

**Prepare Chicken Waldorf
Salad as directed
through step 1. Cover;
refrigerate up to 24 hours.**

To Serve

Serve as directed.

Cinnamon-Spiced Pumpkin Soup

Start to finish: 15 minutes **Makes:** 6 side-dish servings

1	15-ounce can pumpkin	1	tablespoon light brown sugar
1	14½-ounce can reduced-sodium chicken broth	¼	teaspoon salt
1	cup fat-free milk	¼	teaspoon ground cinnamon
		⅛	to ¼ teaspoon ground nutmeg

1 In a large saucepan stir together pumpkin, chicken broth, and milk. Stir in brown sugar, salt, cinnamon, and nutmeg. Bring just to boiling; reduce heat. Simmer, uncovered, for 5 minutes.

2 To serve, pour pumpkin mixture into cups or soup bowls. If desired, garnish with fresh chives.

Nutrition Facts per serving: 49 cal., 0 g total fat, 1 mg chol., 299 mg sodium, 10 g carbo., 2 g fiber, 3 g pro. Daily Values: 314% vit. A, 6% vit. C, 7% calcium, 6% iron

There's a lot to like about this soup. It's filled with fall-inspired flavor, it comes together in just 15 minutes, and it's low in fat.

To Make Ahead

Prepare Cinnamon-Spiced Pumpkin Soup as directed through step 1. Cool 30 minutes. Transfer to an airtight container; seal. Refrigerate up to 24 hours.

To Serve

Transfer soup to a large saucepan. Bring to boiling. Ladle into cups or soup bowls. If desired, garnish with fresh chives.

Tuscan Cornmeal Cookies

Prep: 25 minutes **Bake:** 9 minutes per batch **Makes:** 42 cookies

⅓ cup butter, softened
⅔ cup packed brown sugar
½ cup granulated sugar
1 teaspoon baking powder
¼ teaspoon ground nutmeg
1 egg

1 teaspoon vanilla
½ cup yellow or white cornmeal
¼ cup finely ground toasted almonds
1⅓ cups whole wheat pastry flour or
    all-purpose flour

1 In a large bowl beat butter with an electric mixer on medium to high speed for 30 seconds. Add brown sugar, granulated sugar, baking powder, and nutmeg. Beat until combined. Beat in egg and vanilla until combined. Beat in cornmeal, almonds, and as much of the flour as you can with the mixer. Stir in remaining flour.

2 Shape dough into 42 balls; place balls 2 inches apart on lightly greased cookie sheets. Flatten cookies with a fork dipped in additional granulated sugar.

3 Bake in a 350° oven about 9 minutes or until lightly browned. Transfer cookies to wire racks; cool completely.

Nutrition Facts per cookie: 58 cal., 2 g total fat (1 g sat. fat), 9 mg chol., 28 mg sodium, 9 g carbo., 1 g fiber, 1 g pro. Daily Values: 1% vit. A, 2% calcium, 2% iron

Add extra crunch to these notoriously crunchy cookies by using stone-ground cornmeal. Find stone-ground cornmeal in specialty baking catalogs or at a local mill.

To Make Ahead

Prepare Tuscan Cornmeal Cookies as directed. Place cooled cookies in freezer container, or wrap in moisture- and vaporproof wrap. Seal, label, and freeze up to 3 months.

To Serve

Thaw cookies in container or wrap at room temperature.

Photo opposite page: Chicken Waldorf Salad (page 146), Cinnamon-Spiced Pumpkin Soup (page 147), and Tuscan Cornmeal Cookies (above)

THANKSGIVING FEAST

Up to 3 months ahead:
- Prepare biscuits; freeze.

Up to 1 week ahead:
- Prepare and assemble cake; freeze.

Up to 2 days ahead:
- Prepare cranberry sauce and soup; chill.

Up to 1 day ahead:
- Prepare turkey; marinate.
- Prepare vegetable mixture for mashed vegetables; chill.
- Thaw cake in the refrigerator.

3½ hours ahead:
- Roast turkey.

30 minutes ahead:
- Transfer cranberry sauce to serving dish; let stand at room temperature.
- Prepare relish for mashed vegetables; reheat vegetables in microwave. Transfer to serving dish; add relish.
- Remove turkey from oven; let stand at room temperature.

20 minutes ahead:
- Reduce oven temperature; reheat biscuits. Transfer to bread basket.
- Reheat and finish soup. Ladle into soup bowls.
- Steam green beans; transfer to serving bowl. Season with butter.

Just before serving:
- Carve turkey.
- Let cake stand at room temperature.

Kumquat Cranberry Sauce

From the kumquats in the cranberry sauce to the candied pecans on the carrot cake, this menu will make your holidays memorable.

To Make Ahead

Prepare Kumquat Cranberry Sauce as directed. Cover and refrigerate up to 2 days.

To Serve

Let sauce stand at room temperature 30 minutes.

Start to finish: 20 minutes **Makes:** 3¼ cups

12 ounces fresh kumquats, halved crosswise and seeded (2 cups)	1 cup cranberry juice
1 cup packed brown sugar	2 inches stick cinnamon
	8 ounces fresh cranberries (2 cups)

1 In a large saucepan combine kumquats, brown sugar, cranberry juice, and stick cinnamon. Bring to boiling; reduce heat. Simmer, uncovered, about 3 minutes or until kumquats have softened slightly. Stir in cranberries. Bring to boiling; reduce heat. Simmer, uncovered, 5 to 6 minutes or until syrup begins to thicken. Remove cinnamon. Serve sauce warm or at room temperature.

Nutrition Facts per ¼ cup: 96 cal., 0 g total fat, 0 mg chol., 13 mg sodium, 26 g carbo., 3 g fiber, 0 g pro. Daily Values: 3% vit. A, 32% vit. C, 3% calcium, 4% iron

Maple-Brined Turkey

Prep: 20 minutes **Marinate:** 12 to 24 hours **Roast:** 2¾ hours **Stand:** 20 minutes
Makes: 12 servings

1½ gallons water (24 cups)
1½ cups maple-flavored syrup
 1 cup coarse salt

 ¾ cup packed brown sugar
 1 10-pound turkey (not self-basting)
    Cooking oil

1 For brine, in a stockpot large enough to hold the turkey combine water, syrup, salt, and brown sugar; stir to dissolve sugar and salt.

2 Rinse turkey inside and out; remove any excess fat from cavity. Carefully add turkey to brine. Cover and marinate in refrigerator at least 12 hours or up to 24 hours.

3 Remove turkey from brine; discard brine. Rinse turkey and pat dry with paper towels. Place turkey, breast side up, on a rack in a roasting pan. Tuck the ends of the drumsticks under the band of skin across the tail. (If the band of skin is not present, tie the drumsticks securely to the tail.) Twist wing tips under the back. Brush with oil. Insert a meat thermometer into the center of one of the inside thigh muscles.

4 Cover turkey loosely with foil. Roast turkey in a 325° oven for 2¾ to 3 hours or until thermometer registers 180°. After 2¼ hours, remove foil and cut band of skin or string between the drumsticks so thighs will cook evenly. When done, drumsticks should move very easily in their sockets. Cover turkey; let stand at room temperature 20 minutes before carving.

Nutrition Facts per serving: 280 cal., 11 g total fat (3 g sat. fat), 101 mg chol., 1,250 mg sodium, 7 g carbo., 0 g fiber, 36 g pro. Daily Values: 4% calcium, 13% iron

Innovative chefs have discovered that brining—an ancient technique used for preserving foods—adds moisture and flavor to poultry. This recipe follows their lead for a juicy bird.
  Tip: The test kitchen found that a 10-quart stockpot worked best to hold the turkey and brining mixture.

Roasted Corn and Pepper Soup

Start to finish: 1 hour **Makes:** 12 appetizer or side-dish servings

1 16-ounce package frozen whole kernel corn	½ teaspoon dried thyme, crushed
1 tablespoon cooking oil	⅛ to ¼ teaspoon ground red pepper
2 cups chopped onion	⅓ cup all-purpose flour
1½ cups coarsely chopped red sweet pepper	½ cup whipping cream
4 14½-ounce cans chicken broth (7¼ cups)	⅔ cup cooked crabmeat, cut into bite-size pieces, cartilage removed (about ¼ pound)

1 Thaw frozen corn; pat dry with paper towels. Line a 15×10×1-inch baking pan with foil; use a little of the cooking oil to lightly grease the foil. Spread corn in prepared pan. Roast, uncovered, in a 450° oven for 10 minutes; stir. Continue to roast about 10 minutes more or until golden, stirring once or twice. Set aside.

2 In a 4-quart Dutch oven cook onion and sweet pepper in remaining oil over medium heat for 3 to 4 minutes or until nearly tender. Add the corn, 3 cans of the broth (about 5½ cups), the thyme, and ground red pepper. Bring to boiling; reduce heat. Simmer, uncovered, for 15 minutes.

3 In a screw-top jar combine remaining chicken broth and the flour; cover and shake well. Add to soup; cook and stir until slightly thickened and bubbly. Cook and stir for 1 minute more. Stir cream into soup; heat through. Stir in crabmeat. To serve, ladle soup into soup bowls. If desired, garnish with fresh thyme sprigs.

Nutrition Facts per serving: 133 cal., 6 g total fat (3 g sat. fat), 22 mg chol., 496 mg sodium, 14 g carbo., 1 g fiber, 7 g pro. Daily Values: 14% vit. A, 39% vit. C, 2% calcium, 5% iron

Roasting intensifies the corn's flavor and lends a savory sweetness to this soup. If you're really strapped for time, skip roasting the corn; the soup will still be luscious. (How could it not be—after all, there's crabmeat in the mix!)

To Make Ahead

Prepare Roasted Corn and Pepper Soup as directed through step 2. Cool. Transfer to an airtight container. Seal. Refrigerate up to 2 days.

To Serve

Transfer soup to a 4-quart Dutch oven. Heat to simmering. Continue as directed in step 3.

Mashed Turnips and Sweets

Start to finish: 55 minutes **Makes:** 12 side-dish servings

To Make Ahead

Prepare Mashed Turnips and Sweets as directed through step 1. Place in a microwave-safe 2- to 2½-quart dish; cool slightly. Cover and refrigerate up to 24 hours.

To Serve

Microwave vegetables, covered, on 70% power (medium-high) for 20 to 25 minutes or until heated through, stirring twice. Make relish and serve as directed.

3 pounds sweet potatoes, peeled and cut into 1-inch cubes (about 9½ cups)	2 medium tart red cooking apples, cored and coarsely chopped
2½ pounds turnips, peeled and cut into 1-inch cubes (about 8½ cups)	½ cup whole pitted dates, snipped
5 tablespoons butter	¼ cup packed brown sugar
1 teaspoon salt	1 tablespoon lemon juice

1 In a 6- to 8-quart Dutch oven combine sweet potatoes, turnips, and enough water to cover. Bring to boiling; reduce heat. Cover; simmer 12 to 15 minutes or until tender. Drain well in a very large colander. Return vegetables to Dutch oven; add 3 tablespoons of the butter and the salt. Mash with a potato masher until nearly smooth.

2 For relish, in a medium skillet melt the remaining butter. Add apples, dates, and brown sugar. Cook and stir until sugar is dissolved and apples are just tender. Stir in lemon juice. To serve, mound vegetables in serving bowl; spoon relish into center.

Nutrition Facts per serving: 239 cal., 6 g total fat (3 g sat. fat), 14 mg chol., 317 mg sodium, 46 g carbo., 7 g fiber, 3 g pro. Daily Values: 436% vit. A, 57% vit. C, 6% calcium, 6% iron

Praline Sauce

Start to finish: 10 minutes **Makes:** ⅓ cup

Simple yet superb, this sauce is equally delicious as a filling in Towering Praline Carrot Cake (page 157) or drizzled over rich vanilla ice cream.

3 tablespoons butter	2 tablespoons whipping cream
3 tablespoons brown sugar	1 teaspoon vanilla

1 In small saucepan melt butter over medium heat. Stir in brown sugar and whipping cream. Bring to full boil, stirring constantly; reduce heat. Boil gently 3 minutes, stirring occasionally. Stir in vanilla. Cool.

Nutrition Facts per tablespoon: 108 cal., 10 g total fat (6 g sat. fat), 28 mg chol., 79 mg sodium, 6 g carbo., 0 g fiber, 0 g pro. Daily Values: 7% vit. A, 1% calcium, 1% iron

Peppery White Cheddar Biscuits

Prep: 25 minutes **Bake:** 13 minutes **Makes:** 18 biscuits

4 cups all-purpose flour	2 to 3 teaspoons coarsely ground
2 tablespoons baking powder	black pepper
½ teaspoon salt	1½ cups milk
½ cup shortening	1 beaten egg
¼ cup butter	1 teaspoon water
1½ cups shredded sharp white cheddar	
cheese (6 ounces)	

1 In a large bowl combine flour, baking powder, and salt. Using a pastry blender, cut in shortening and butter until mixture resembles coarse crumbs. Stir in shredded cheese and pepper. Make a well in center of flour mixture. Add milk all at once; stir just until moistened.

2 Turn out onto a lightly floured surface. Quickly knead dough by gently folding and pressing for 10 to 12 strokes or until dough is almost smooth. Divide dough in half. Roll or pat each half into a 6-inch square; cut square into nine 2-inch squares. Place on lightly greased baking sheets. Combine egg and water; brush over biscuits. Bake in a 400° oven for 13 to 15 minutes or until tops are golden. Transfer to a wire rack. Serve warm.

Nutrition Facts per biscuit: 247 cal., 14 g total fat (6 g sat. fat), 34 mg chol., 314 mg sodium, 24 g carbo., 1 g fiber, 7 g pro. Daily Values: 8% vit. A, 19% calcium, 11% iron

While cooking for a holiday crowd, why not bake an extra batch of these peppery biscuits? They'll add a festive touch to soups and stews served during the winter nights.

To Make Ahead

Prepare Peppery White Cheddar Biscuits as directed through step 2, except cool completely. Place biscuits in a freezer container or self-sealing freezer bag. Seal, label, and freeze up to 3 months.

To Serve

Wrap frozen biscuits in foil and bake in a 300° oven 20 to 25 minutes or until warm.

Towering Praline Carrot Cake

Prep: 1½ hours **Bake:** 35 minutes **Makes:** 16 servings

  3 **cups sliced carrots**
  3 **cups all-purpose flour**
2¾ **cups sugar**
  1 **tablespoon ground cinnamon**
1½ **teaspoons baking powder**
1½ **teaspoons baking soda**
  1 **teaspoon salt**
1⅓ **cups cooking oil**
  6 **eggs**

  1 **8-ounce can crushed pineapple,
       drained**
  1 **tablespoon vanilla**
  1 **cup chopped pecans**
  ½ **cup flaked coconut**
  2 **recipes Cream Cheese Frosting
       (page 203)**
  1 **recipe Praline Sauce (page 154)**

1 Grease and lightly flour three 9×1½-inch round baking pans; set aside. In a covered medium saucepan cook carrots in a moderate amount of boiling water about 20 minutes or until very tender. Drain. Cool carrots slightly; coarsely mash a with potato masher.

2 In a very large bowl stir together flour, sugar, 2 teaspoons of the cinnamon, the baking powder, baking soda, and salt. Make a well in center of flour mixture. Add oil, eggs, pineapple, and vanilla. Beat with an electric mixer on low speed until all ingredients are combined. Fold in mashed carrots, pecans, and coconut.

3 Spread batter evenly in prepared pans. Bake in a 350° oven 35 to 40 minutes or until a toothpick inserted in centers comes out clean. Cool in pans on wire racks 10 minutes. Remove from pans; cool completely on racks. While layers are cooling, prepare Cream Cheese Frosting; beat or stir remaining cinnamon into frosting.

4 To assemble, place one cake layer, top side up, on a cake plate. Using about 1 cup of the frosting, pipe or spoon a rim about 1 inch wide and ½ inch high around outer edge of layer. Spoon about 2 tablespoons frosting into center, leaving an unfrosted ring. Spread about half of the Praline Sauce into the unfrosted ring (sauce will not fill ring). Add second cake layer, top side up; repeat frosting and filling steps using another 1 cup of the frosting and remaining Praline Sauce.

5 Add third cake layer, top side up. Frost top and side with remaining frosting. If desired, garnish with additional chopped pecans. Cover; store in refrigerator.

Nutrition Facts per serving: 918 cal., 49 g total fat (18 g sat. fat), 145 mg chol., 546 mg sodium, 116 g carbo., 2 g fiber, 7 g pro. Daily Values: 136% vit. A, 7% vit. C, 9% calcium, 14% iron

No time? That's no excuse not to make this impressive cake, for it comes with make-ahead directions for both refrigerating and freezing.

To Make Ahead

Prepare Towering Praline Carrot Cake as directed through step 5, assembling cake on the base of a cake container with a tight-fitting lid or on a baking sheet. Do not garnish with pecans. Cover and refrigerate up to 3 days. (Or freeze just until frosting is firm. Cover with container lid or moisture- and vaporproof wrap. Freeze up to 1 week.)

To Serve

To serve, let refrigerated cake stand, covered, at room temperature for 30 minutes. (Or thaw frozen cake, covered, in refrigerator overnight. Let stand at room temperature for 30 minutes.) If desired, garnish with additional chopped pecans.

WINTER HOLIDAY

Hot Artichoke Dip
(below)
Marinated Prime Rib
(page 159)
Honey-Glazed Carrots
(page 160)
Walnut-Sage Potatoes
au Gratin (page 162)
Cranberry-Pear Pie
(page 163)

Up to 4 months ahead:
● Prepare pie; freeze.
1 day ahead:
● Prepare dip; chill.
● Marinate prime rib.
● Prepare carrots; chill.
● Prepare potatoes; chill.
5 hours ahead:
● Bake pie; cool to room temperature.
2¼ to 3½ hours ahead:
● Roast prime rib.

1 hour 35 minutes ahead:
● Place potatoes in oven.
1¼ hours ahead:
● Set carrots out at room temperature.
As guests arrive:
● Microwave dip.
15 minutes before serving:
● Let prime rib stand at room temperature. Carve and garnish.
● Glaze carrots.
10 minutes before serving:
● Let potatoes stand at room temperature

Hot Artichoke Dip

With a succulent prime rib as its centerpiece, this menu will bring comfort and joy (plus a touch of elegance) to any holiday meal.

To Make Ahead

Prepare Hot Artichoke Dip as directed through step 1. Cover and refrigerate up to 24 hours.

To Serve

Microwave, covered, on 70% power (medium-high) 6 to 8 minutes or until heated through, turning dish halfway through cooking time. (Or bake as directed.)

Prep: 15 minutes **Bake:** 20 minutes **Makes:** about 3½ cups

1 medium leek, quartered lengthwise and thinly sliced, or ⅓ cup sliced green onions
2 teaspoons margarine or butter
1 14-ounce can artichoke hearts, drained and coarsely chopped
1 cup grated Parmesan cheese

1 7-ounce jar roasted red sweet peppers, drained and chopped
1 cup mayonnaise or salad dressing
⅛ teaspoon ground black pepper
2 tablespoons grated Parmesan cheese
1 tablespoon snipped fresh parsley
   Assorted vegetable dippers, flat breads, and/or crackers

1 In a skillet cook leek in hot margarine until tender. Remove from heat. Stir in artichoke hearts, the 1 cup Parmesan cheese, red peppers, mayonnaise, and black pepper. Transfer mixture to an 8-inch quiche dish or 9-inch pie plate, spreading evenly. Sprinkle with the 2 tablespoons Parmesan cheese and the parsley.

2 Bake, uncovered, in a 350° oven about 20 minutes or until heated through. Serve with assorted dippers.

Nutrition Facts per tablespoon dip: 40 cal., 4 g total fat (1 g sat. fat), 4 mg chol., 71 mg sodium, 1 g carbo., 0 g fiber, 1 g pro. Daily Values: 2% vit. A, 10% vit. C, 3% calcium

Marinated Prime Rib

Prep: 10 minutes **Marinate:** 6 to 24 hours **Roast:** 2 hours **Stand:** 15 minutes
Makes: 12 to 16 servings

¾ cup dry red wine or beef broth	1½ teaspoons snipped fresh rosemary or
½ cup chopped onion	½ teaspoon dried rosemary,
¼ cup water	crushed
¼ cup lemon juice	½ teaspoon dried marjoram, crushed
1 tablespoon Worcestershire sauce	¼ teaspoon garlic salt
	1 4- to 6-pound beef rib roast

1 For marinade, in a small bowl stir together wine or broth, onion, water, lemon juice, Worcestershire sauce, rosemary, marjoram, and garlic salt.

2 Place meat in a self-sealing plastic bag set in a shallow dish. Pour marinade over meat. Seal bag. Marinate in refrigerator at least 6 hours or up to 24 hours, turning bag occasionally.

3 Drain meat, discarding marinade. Place meat, fat side up, in a large roasting pan. Insert a meat thermometer into center without touching bones.

4 Roast in a 325° oven to desired doneness. [Allow 2 to 2¾ hours for rare (140°) or 2¼ to 3¼ hours for medium (155°).] Transfer meat to a cutting board. Cover with foil and let stand for 15 minutes before carving. (The temperature of the meat will rise 5° during standing.) If desired, garnish with additional fresh rosemary.

Nutrition Facts per serving: 162 cal., 9 g total fat (4 g sat. fat), 53 mg chol., 67 mg sodium,
0 g carbo., 0 g fiber, 18 g pro. Daily Values: 2% vit. C, 11% iron

These tender-sweet baby carrots are lightly coated with a buttery-sweet glaze for a timeless treat young and old alike will love.

To Make Ahead

Prepare Honey-Glazed Carrots as directed through step 1. Cover and refrigerate up to 24 hours.

To Serve

Bring carrots to room temperature (takes about 1 hour). Glaze carrots as directed in step 2, except heat carrots in glaze for 4 to 5 minutes. Serve as directed.

Honey-Glazed Carrots

Start to finish: 50 minutes **Makes:** 8 to 10 side-dish servings

6 cups water	2 tablespoons butter
¾ teaspoon salt	2 tablespoons honey
3 pounds young, small carrots with tops trimmed to 2 inches, peeled or scrubbed*	

1 Line a baking sheet with paper towels. In a 12- or 14-inch heavy skillet combine the water and salt. Bring to boiling. Add carrots. Return to boiling; reduce heat. Cover and simmer 10 to 12 minutes or just until carrots are tender. Drain carrots. Carefully turn out onto prepared baking sheet. Pat dry with additional paper towels.

2 To glaze carrots, in the same skillet combine butter and honey. Stir constantly over medium heat until butter is melted. Carefully add carrots. Toss gently for 2 to 3 minutes or until carrots are well coated with glaze and heated through.

3 To serve, arrange carrots in a shallow bowl or on a platter; drizzle with remaining glaze from skillet.

Nutrition Facts per serving: 116 cal., 3 g total fat (2 g sat. fat), 8 mg chol., 160 mg sodium, 22 g carbo., 5 g fiber, 2 g pro. Daily Values: 864% vit. A, 18% vit. C, 4% calcium

*Note: If you can't find small carrots with tops, use 3 pounds packaged peeled baby carrots.

Photo on opposite page: Marinated Prime Rib (page 159), Honey-Glazed Carrots (above), and Walnut-Sage Potatoes au Gratin (162)

With a sprinkling of walnuts and a snip of sage, the traditional French side dish becomes more magnificent than ever.

To Make Ahead

Peel potatoes for Walnut-Sage Potatoes au Gratin, if desired; thinly slice. (You should have 6 cups.) Cook potatoes in boiling, salted water for 5 minutes; drain. Continue as directed through step 3. Cover and refrigerate up to 24 hours.

To Serve

Bake and serve as directed.

Walnut-Sage Potatoes au Gratin

Prep: 30 minutes **Bake:** 1 hour 25 minutes **Stand:** 10 minutes **Makes:** 8 side-dish servings

6	medium potatoes (2 pounds)	¼	teaspoon pepper
½	cup chopped onion	2½	cups milk
2	cloves garlic, minced	3	tablespoons snipped fresh sage
2	tablespoons walnut oil or cooking oil	1	cup shredded Gruyère cheese
3	tablespoons all-purpose flour		(4 ounces)
¾	teaspoon salt	⅓	cup broken walnuts

1 Peel potatoes, if desired; thinly slice. (You should have 6 cups.) Place slices in a colander. Rinse with cool water; set aside to drain.

2 For sauce, in a medium saucepan cook onion and garlic in hot oil until tender. Stir in flour, salt, and pepper. Add milk all at once. Cook and stir until thickened and bubbly. Remove from heat; stir in sage.

3 Layer half of the potatoes in a greased 2-quart casserole. Cover with half of the sauce. Sprinkle with half of the cheese. Repeat layering with remaining potatoes and sauce. (Cover and chill remaining cheese in refrigerator until needed.)

4 Bake casserole, covered, in a 325° oven for 1 hour. Uncover; bake for 25 to 30 minutes more or just until potatoes are tender. Sprinkle remaining cheese and walnuts over top. Let stand 10 minutes before serving.

Nutrition Facts per serving: 285 cal., 13 g total fat (4 g sat. fat), 21 mg chol., 310 mg sodium, 33 g carbo., 2 g fiber, 10 g pro. Daily Values: 7% vit. A, 28% vit. C, 26% calcium, 4% iron

Cranberry-Pear Pie

Prep: 35 minutes **Bake:** 55 minutes **Makes:** 8 servings

1 recipe Pastry for Double-Crust Pie
  (below)
1 cup granulated sugar
3 tablespoons quick-cooking tapioca

5 cups thinly sliced, peeled, and cored
  pears
1½ cups cranberries
1 tablespoon milk
  Coarse sugar

1 Prepare Pastry for Double-Crust Pie. Line a 9-inch pie plate with half of the pastry. Set aside. In a large saucepan combine the 1 cup granulated sugar and the tapioca. Stir in pears and cranberries until coated; let stand about 15 minutes or until a syrup begins to form, stirring occasionally. Bring to boiling over high heat; reduce heat. Cover and simmer for 3 to 5 minutes or just until pears have softened and cranberries begin to pop, stirring occasionally.

2 Transfer cranberry mixture to the pastry-lined pie plate. Trim pastry to edge of pie plate. If desired, with a 1-inch holiday cookie cutter, cut shapes from center of remaining pastry circle, reserving cutouts. (Cut slits in pastry if not using cookie cutter.) Place pastry on filling. Seal and flute edge.

3 Brush pastry with milk. Sprinkle with coarse sugar. Top with holiday cutouts, if using. Brush cutouts with milk. To prevent overbrowning, cover the edge of the pie with foil.

4 Bake in a 375° oven for 25 minutes. Remove foil. Bake for 30 to 35 minutes more or until the top is golden. Cool on a wire rack. Serve warm or at room temperature.

Pastry for Double-Crust Pie: In a medium bowl stir together 2 cups all-purpose flour and ½ teaspoon salt. Using a pastry blender, cut in ⅔ cup shortening until pieces are the size of small peas. Using 6 to 7 tablespoons cold water total, sprinkle 1 tablespoon water over mixture; toss with fork. Push to side of bowl. Repeat until all is moistened. Divide dough in half. On a lightly floured surface, roll each half of the pastry into a 12-inch circle. Cover until needed. Use as directed in recipe.

Nutrition Facts per serving: 442 cal., 18 g total fat (4 g sat. fat), 0 mg chol., 135 mg sodium, 69 g carbo., 4 g fiber, 4 g pro. Daily Values: 1% vit. A, 12% vit. C, 2% calcium, 9% iron

Feeling a little bah-humbug this season? Two of winter's best-loved fruits team up for a lively holiday pie, while the sprinkling of sugar on the crust shimmers like snow. It's sure to lift your spirits.

To Make Ahead

Prepare Cranberry-Pear Pie as directed through step 2, except cool filling slightly (about 10 minutes) before adding to pastry-lined pie plate, and do not cut shapes or slits in top crust. Cover unbaked pie with inverted 10-inch paper plate. Place in a self-sealing freezer bag. Seal, label, and freeze up to 4 months.

To Serve

Remove paper plate from frozen pie and cut slits in crust. Brush with milk; sprinkle with coarse sugar. Cover edge with foil; bake in a 450° oven for 15 minutes. Reduce oven temperature to 375°; bake 15 minutes. Remove foil; bake 30 to 35 minutes or until golden. Cool; serve as directed.

NEW YEAR'S EVE

Up to 3 months ahead:
● Prepare steaks; freeze.
2 days ahead:
● Prepare chowder; chill.
1 day ahead:
● Prepare salad; chill.
● Prepare potatoes; chill.
● Prepare rolls; chill.
● Prepare tart; chill.
1¾ hours ahead:
● Let rolls stand at room temperature.

1 hour ahead:
● Bake rolls; cool.
40 minutes ahead:
● Increase oven temperature; bake steaks.
25 minutes ahead:
● Reheat and finish chowder.
20 minutes ahead:
● Microwave potatoes.
10 minutes ahead:
● Make sauce for steaks.
● Finish salad.

Beet & Apple Salad

This festive menu offers
plenty of reasons to pop
a cork—including the fact
that the wow-inspiring main
course freezes well up to
3 months!

To Make Ahead

**Prepare Beet & Apple
Salad as directed through
step 1, except refrigerate
up to 24 hours.**

To Serve

Serve as directed.

Prep: 50 minutes **Chill:** 2 hours **Makes:** 8 side-dish servings

6 medium beets (about 2 pounds) or two 16-ounce cans sliced beets	2 green onions, sliced
⅓ cup salad oil	2 tablespoons snipped fresh mint or 2 teaspoons dried mint, crushed
⅓ cup white wine vinegar	2 teaspoons honey
2 teaspoons shredded orange peel	4 cups torn romaine
¼ cup orange juice	2 medium tart green apples, chopped

1 In a large covered saucepan cook whole beets in a large amount of boiling water for 40 to 50 minutes or until tender; drain. Cool slightly; slip off skins. Slice beets. (Or rinse and drain canned beets.) Meanwhile, for dressing, in a screw-top jar combine salad oil, white wine vinegar, orange peel, orange juice, green onions, mint, and honey. Cover and shake well. In a medium bowl combine beet slices and half of the dressing. Cover and refrigerate the beet mixture and the remaining dressing for at least 2 hours.

2 To serve, in a large bowl combine romaine and apples. Toss apple mixture with remaining dressing. Using a slotted spoon, spoon beet mixture over apple mixture.

Nutrition Facts per serving: 167 cal., 9 g total fat (1 g sat. fat), 0 mg chol., 88 mg sodium,
19 g carbo., 4 g fiber, 3 g pro. Daily Values: 16% vit. A, 31% vit. C, 4% calcium, 9% iron

Beef Steaks Wellington

Prep: 40 minutes   **Bake:** 12 minutes   **Stand:** 10 minutes   **Makes:** 8 servings

1	17¼-ounce package (2 sheets) frozen puff pastry	¼	teaspoon garlic salt
			Dash pepper
8	5-ounce beef tenderloin steaks, cut 1 inch thick	1½	cups sliced fresh mushrooms
		½	cup sliced green onions
1	tablespoon cooking oil	¼	cup butter or margarine
1	3½-ounce can liver pâté (½ cup)	4	teaspoons cornstarch
¼	cup soft bread crumbs	½	cup dry white wine or beef broth
1	tablespoon snipped fresh parsley	½	cup water
½	teaspoon dried basil, crushed	1½	teaspoons instant beef bouillon granules

1 Thaw pastry according to package directions. Meanwhile, in a large skillet brown steaks, half at a time, in hot oil over medium-high heat for 1 minute on each side. Drain on paper towels. Cool. In a small bowl stir together pâté, crumbs, parsley, basil, garlic salt, and pepper. Spread 1 tablespoon of the pâté mixture on top of each steak.

2 On a lightly floured surface, roll each sheet of puff pastry into an 11-inch square; cut each into four 5½-inch squares. Place pastry squares on top of steaks; fold under meat. If necessary, trim pastry so only ½ inch remains folded under the meat. If desired, cut small shapes from pastry trimmings; moisten and place on top of bundles.

3 Place bundles, pastry sides up, on a rack in a shallow baking pan. Bake, uncovered, in a 450° oven 12 to 15 minutes or until pastry is brown and meat is medium-rare (140°). If necessary to prevent overbrowning, cover loosely with foil during the last 5 minutes of baking. Let stand 10 minutes before serving. (The temperature of the meat will rise 5° during standing.)

4 Meanwhile, for sauce, in a medium saucepan cook mushrooms and green onions in hot butter until tender. Stir in cornstarch. Add wine, water, and bouillon granules. Cook and stir until thickened and bubbly; cook and stir for 2 minutes more. Serve with meat.

Nutrition Facts per serving: 596 cal., 38 g total fat (8 g sat. fat), 135 mg chol., 607 mg sodium, 26 g carbo., 0 g fiber, 35 g pro. Daily Values: 7% vit. A, 5% vit. C, 2% calcium, 30% iron

---

Already-rich beef tenderloin that's spread with liver pâté, wrapped in a buttery crust, and served with a lovely mushroom-wine sauce is unbelievably good. What's even better is that such elegance can be made ahead and frozen.

To Make Ahead

Prepare Beef Steaks Wellington as directed through step 2. Cover and freeze on baking sheet about 1 hour or until firm. Transfer to self-sealing freezer bags or freezer containers. Seal, label, and freeze up to 3 months.

To Serve

Place frozen bundles, pastry sides up, on a rack in a shallow baking pan. Bake, uncovered, in a 450° oven 30 to 35 minutes or until pastry is brown and meat is medium-rare (140°). If necessary, cover loosely with foil during the last 10 minutes. Let stand 10 minutes before serving. Meanwhile, prepare sauce as directed. Serve with meat.

Put away your measuring spoons. The secret to this rich and wonderful side dish—made with only three ingredients—is Boursin cheese, a triple-cream cheese that's flavored with plenty of garlic and herbs.

To Make Ahead

Prepare Boursin Mashed Potatoes as directed through step 1. Spoon into a microwave-safe 2-quart casserole. Cover; refrigerate up to 24 hours.

To Serve

Uncover potatoes. Cover with vented plastic wrap. Microwave on 100% power (high) for 15 to 18 minutes or until heated through, stirring once. (Or bake, covered, in a 350° oven about 1½ hours or until heated through.)

Boursin Mashed Potatoes

Prep: 40 minutes **Bake:** 25 minutes **Makes:** 8 to 10 side-dish servings

3½ pounds potatoes, peeled and cut into 2-inch chunks (about 10 medium potatoes)

2 5.2-ounce packages Boursin cheese with garlic and herbs

½ cup milk, half-and-half, or light cream

1 In a large saucepan or Dutch oven cover potatoes with boiling water. Cover and cook for 20 to 25 minutes or until tender. Drain; return potatoes to pan. Mash with a potato masher or beat with an electric mixer on low speed until smooth. Add cheese; beat until combined. Beat in milk until combined. Season to taste with salt and pepper.

2 Spoon into a 2-quart casserole. Cover and bake in a 350° oven about 25 minutes or until heated through.

Nutrition Facts per serving: 297 cal., 16 g total fat (11 g sat. fat), 2 mg chol., 304 mg sodium, 33 g carbo., 4 g fiber, 8 g pro. Daily Values: 1% vit. A, 45% vit. C, 4% calcium, 9% iron

Photo on opposite page: Beef Steaks Wellington (page 165), Beet & Apple Salad (page 164), Rosemary Satin Dinner Rolls (page 169), and Boursin Mashed Potatoes (above)

You'll love the way pancetta brings extra flavor to this creamy soup. Hailing from Italy, pancetta is a little like bacon, except that it's not smoked; its flavor comes from being cured with salt and other seasonings. Find pancetta in Italian food shops.

To Make Ahead

Prepare Mushroom, Leek, & Seafood Chowder as directed through step 2. Cover and refrigerate up to 2 days.

To Serve

In a Dutch oven bring chilled soup mixture to simmering. Continue as directed in step 3.

Mushroom, Leek, & Seafood Chowder

Start to finish: 50 minutes   **Makes:** 8 appetizer or side-dish servings

1½ ounces thinly sliced pancetta or bacon (1½ slices), chopped	¼ teaspoon pepper
2 cups sliced fresh shiitake or other mushrooms	1 small carrot, shredded
2 leeks, thinly sliced (white parts only)	2 tablespoons all-purpose flour
2 small cloves garlic, minced	2 tablespoons margarine or butter, melted
2⅓ cups chicken broth	1½ cups half-and-half or light cream
2 medium potatoes, chopped	¾ pound peeled and deveined shrimp and/or bay scallops*

1 In a 4-quart Dutch oven cook pancetta until browned. Remove with a slotted spoon, reserving drippings in pan. Drain on paper towels; cover and chill. Add mushrooms, leeks, and garlic to the Dutch oven; cook and stir about 3 minutes or until mushrooms and leeks are tender.

2 Carefully add broth, potatoes, and pepper to Dutch oven. Bring to boiling; reduce heat. Cover and simmer about 15 minutes or until potatoes are tender. Stir in carrot.

3 Stir together flour and melted margarine. Add flour mixture and half-and-half to Dutch oven. Cook and stir over medium heat until bubbly. Add shrimp and/or scallops and pancetta. Cook and stir 2 to 3 minutes more or until shrimp are pink and scallops are opaque. Ladle into bowls. If desired, garnish with lemon slices and/or fresh thyme.

Nutrition Facts per serving: 231 cal., 13 g total fat (5 g sat. fat), 85 mg chol., 453 mg sodium. 18 g carbo., 2 g fiber, 13 g pro. Daily Values: 47% vit. A, 12% vit. C, 8% calcium, 11% iron

*Note: If you use frozen shrimp and/or scallops, thaw them before adding to the chowder.

Rosemary Satin Dinner Rolls

Prep: 45 minutes **Rise:** 1½ hours **Bake:** 12 minutes **Makes:** 12 rolls

2½ to 3 cups all-purpose flour
  1 package active dry yeast
⅔ cup cream-style cottage cheese
¼ cup water
¼ cup butter
  2 tablespoons finely chopped onion

½ teaspoon salt
½ teaspoon dried rosemary, crushed
  1 egg
  1 slightly beaten egg yolk
  1 tablespoon water

1 In a large bowl stir together ¾ cup of the flour and the yeast; set aside. In a small saucepan combine cottage cheese, the ¼ cup water, the butter, onion, salt, and rosemary. Heat and stir until warm (120° to 130°) and butter is almost melted. Add cottage cheese mixture to flour mixture. Add whole egg. Beat with an electric mixer on low speed for 30 seconds. Beat on high speed for 3 minutes. Using a wooden spoon, stir in as much of the remaining flour as you can.

2 Turn the dough out onto a lightly floured surface. Knead in enough of the remaining flour to make a moderately stiff dough that is smooth and elastic (6 to 8 minutes total). Shape into a ball. Place in a greased bowl, turn once to grease surface of dough. Cover and let rise in a warm place until double in size (about 1 hour)

3 Grease a baking sheet or twelve 2½-inch muffin cups; set aside. Punch dough down. Cover; let rest 10 minutes. Divide dough into 12 portions. Shape dough portions into your favorite dinner roll shapes and place on prepared baking sheet or shape into balls and place each ball in a prepared muffin cup.

4 Stir together egg yolk and the 1 tablespoon water; brush onto rolls. Cover; let rise in a warm place until almost double in size (about 30 minutes). Bake in a 400° oven for 12 to 15 minutes or until rolls are golden.

Nutrition Facts per roll: 147 cal., 5 g total fat (3 g sat. fat), 47 mg chol., 181 mg sodium, 19 g carbo., 1 g fiber, 5 g pro. Daily Values: 7% vit. A, 1% calcium, 9% iron

Thanks to the cottage cheese, these rolls have a lush moistness; thanks to a duo of onion and rosemary, they have a piquant flavor. And thanks to make-ahead directions, you can prepare the dough up to 24 hours in advance.

To Make Ahead

Prepare dough for Rosemary Satin Dinner Rolls as directed through step 3. Cover and refrigerate at least 2 hours or up to 24 hours.

To Serve

Stir together egg yolk and the 1 tablespoon water; brush onto rolls. Let stand at room temperature for 40 minutes. Bake as directed, allowing an additional 3 to 5 minutes if necessary.

Chocolate-Grand Marnier Tart

Prep: 35 minutes **Cool:** 30 minutes **Chill:** 2 hours **Makes:** 10 to 12 servings

¾ cup whipping cream
6 ounces semisweet chocolate,
    chopped, or one 6-ounce package
    semisweet chocolate pieces (1 cup)
2 tablespoons Grand Marnier or other
    orange liqueur (optional)

⅓ cup orange marmalade
1   recipe Almond Crust (below)

1 In a small saucepan heat whipping cream over medium heat just until simmering. Remove from heat; whisk in semisweet chocolate until smooth. If desired, whisk in Grand Marnier. Cool about 30 minutes or until filling begins to thicken but is still pourable. Spread marmalade over bottom of Almond Crust. Pour chocolate filling over marmalade. Cover and chill in refrigerator about 2 hours or until set.

2 To serve, remove side of pan. Use a sharp knife to cut tart into wedges. If desired, garnish each wedge with a kumquat half and a sprig of fresh herb.

Almond Crust: In a small bowl combine 1½ cups toasted blanched almonds and ¼ cup packed brown sugar. Place a portion at a time in a food processor bowl or blender container; cover and process or blend until nuts are finely ground. Transfer to a medium bowl. Stir in ¼ cup all-purpose flour. Add ¼ cup melted unsalted butter or regular butter, stirring until well combined. Press mixture onto bottom and 1 inch up side of a 9-inch tart pan with a removable bottom or a 9-inch springform pan. Bake in a 325° oven about 20 minutes or until golden and firm to the touch. Cool crust in pan on a wire rack.

Nutrition Facts per serving: 359 cal., 26 g total fat (10 g sat. fat), 38 mg chol., 17 mg sodium, 24 g carbo, 5 g fiber, 5 g pro. Daily Values: 9% vit. A, 1% vit. C, 7% calcium, 5% iron

This is the type of dreamy finale you'd expect to find (and pay top dollar for) on a dessert cart at an elegant restaurant. Fresh kumquats add a striking note to the presentation; their citrus flavor and baby-orange appearance highlight the overall orange motif at work in the recipe.

To Make Ahead

Prepare Chocolate-Grand Marnier Tart as directed through step 1, except refrigerate up to 24 hours.

To Serve

Serve as directed.

BACKYARD PICNIC

Up to 3 months ahead:
● Prepare biscuits; freeze.
Up to 2 weeks ahead:
● Prepare ice cream; store in freezer.
1 day ahead:
● Prepare kabobs; chill.
● Prepare salad; chill.
● Prepare chicken; marinate. (This allows maximum marinating time. If you want your chicken less spicy, modify the timetable.)

1½ hours ahead:
● Thaw biscuits.
45 minutes ahead:
● Assemble kabobs; cover and chill.
35 minutes ahead:
● Coat and cook chicken; keep warm.
Just before serving:
● Garnish and toss salad.
● Let ice cream stand at room temperature about 20 minutes; prepare topping.

Cool Antipasto Kabobs

Make sure the lazy days of summer stay that way. Enjoy a do-in-advance barbecue that kicks off with a recipe you don't even have to cook. Here, you can simply set out a batch of great nibbles and let guests make skewers of their own favorites.

Prep: 20 minutes **Marinate:** 1 to 24 hours **Makes:** 6 appetizer servings

2 cups assorted fresh vegetables (such as baby carrots with tops, radishes, 1-inch red sweet pepper pieces, or tiny pattypan squash)
4 ounces firm cheese (such as peppercorn cheese, smoked Gouda, or kasseri), cut into ½-inch chunks

¼ pound summer sausage, cut into ¾-inch slices and halved
2 tablespoons refrigerated basil pesto
1 tablespoon white wine vinegar

1 Place vegetables, cheese, and summer sausage in a large self-sealing plastic bag set in a deep bowl. For the marinade, stir together pesto and vinegar. Spoon over vegetable mixture in plastic bag. Seal bag. Marinate in refrigerator at least 1 hour or up to 24 hours, turning bag occasionally.

2 To serve, alternately thread vegetables, cheese, and summer sausage onto twelve 8-inch bamboo skewers.

Nutrition Facts per serving: 161 cal., 12 g total fat (6 g sat. fat), 26 mg chol., 483 mg sodium, 5 g carbo., 1 g fiber, 7 g pro. Daily Values: 117% vit. A, 40% vit. C, 14% calcium, 2% iron

Layered Vegetable Salad

Prep: 25 minutes **Chill:** 2 hours **Makes:** 6 to 8 side-dish servings

5 cups torn mixed salad greens	¼ cup sliced green onions
1 medium carrot	½ cup mayonnaise or salad dressing
1 cup sliced fresh mushrooms	¼ cup plain low-fat yogurt
½ cup crumbled feta cheese (2 ounces)	1 teaspoon finely shredded orange peel
½ cup coarsely chopped pitted	½ to ¾ teaspoon crushed red pepper
kalamata olives	⅛ to ¼ teaspoon ground black pepper
1 medium cucumber, halved, seeded,	1 medium orange, peeled and sliced
and sliced ¼ inch thick	¼ cup coarsely chopped walnuts

1 Place salad greens in a 2½- to 3-quart straight-sided clear bowl or soufflé dish. Using a vegetable peeler, carefully cut carrot into long, paper-thin ribbons; set aside. Layer over the salad greens in the following order: mushrooms, ¼ cup of the cheese, the olives, cucumber, carrot ribbons, and green onions.

2 For dressing, in a small bowl combine the mayonnaise, yogurt, orange peel, red pepper, and black pepper. Spread dressing over top of salad, sealing to edge of bowl. Sprinkle with the remaining cheese. Cover salad tightly with plastic wrap. Chill in refrigerator at least 2 hours.

3 To serve, top with orange slices and walnuts. If desired, garnish with orange peel strips. Just before serving toss to coat vegetables.

Nutrition Facts per serving: 236 cal., 23 g total fat (5 g sat. fat), 16 mg chol., 268 mg sodium, 8 g carbo., 2 g fiber, 4 g pro. Daily Values: 39% vit. A, 31% vit. C, 10% calcium, 8% iron

With a crumbling of feta and a sprinkling of olives, this tried-and-true potluck favorite gets a worldly update. To get the best-looking layers, use a bowl that is taller than it is wide.

To Make Ahead
Prepare Layered Vegetable Salad as directed through step 2, except refrigerate up to 24 hours.

To Serve
Serve as directed.

Whether you're
serving tender-
tongued tots or fire-
hardened chileheads, this
recipe lets you adjust the
heat level according to
who will be gathered
around the table. The
longer the chicken chills in
the hot pepper sauce, the
hotter it gets.

Firecracker Fried Chicken

Prep: 15 minutes **Marinate:** 1 to 24 hours **Cook:** 25 minutes **Makes:** 6 servings

12 chicken drumsticks (about 3 pounds total)	½ cup all-purpose flour
1 2-ounce bottle hot pepper sauce (¼ cup)	3 tablespoons yellow cornmeal
	¾ teaspoon salt
	Cooking oil (about 3 cups)

1 If desired, remove and discard skin from drumsticks. Place chicken in a large self-sealing plastic bag set in a shallow dish. Pour hot pepper sauce over chicken. Seal bag. Marinate in refrigerator at least 1 hour or up to 24 hours, turning bag occasionally.

2 Drain chicken, discarding marinade. In another plastic bag combine the flour, cornmeal, and salt. Add chicken, a few pieces at a time, shaking to coat.

3 In a 12-inch skillet heat ½ inch oil over medium heat until a bread cube dropped into oil sizzles. Carefully add chicken to skillet. Cook, uncovered, over medium heat for 25 to 30 minutes or until chicken is tender and no longer pink, turning occasionally to brown evenly. Drain on paper towels; transfer to a serving platter.

Nutrition Facts per serving: 401 cal., 24 g total fat (4 g sat. fat), 124 mg chol., 434 mg sodium, 11 g carbo., 1 g fiber, 35 g pro. Daily Values: 3% vit. A, 7% vit. C, 2% calcium, 12% iron

**Photo on opposite page: Firecracker Fried Chicken (above),
Cool Antipasto Kabobs (page 172), and
South-of-the-Border Corn Biscuits (page 176)**

Biscuits top the list of traditional country fare—and they're even more hearty and satisfying when packed with whole kernel corn and rich cheddar cheese. For a little kick, serve them with jalapeño pepper jelly.

To Make Ahead

Prepare South-of-the-Border Corn Biscuits as directed. Cool biscuits. Transfer to a self-sealing freezer bag or freezer container. Seal, label, and freeze up to 3 months.

To Serve

Thaw at room temperature. (Or wrap in foil and reheat in a 300° oven for 15 to 20 minutes or until warm.) Serve as directed.

South-of-the-Border Corn Biscuits

Prep: 25 minutes **Bake:** 12 minutes **Makes:** 10 to 12 biscuits

1½ cups all-purpose flour
½ cup yellow cornmeal
2 teaspoons baking powder
¼ teaspoon baking soda
¼ teaspoon salt
½ cup butter

½ cup shredded cheddar cheese (2 ounces)
1 12-ounce can whole kernel corn, drained
½ cup buttermilk or dairy sour cream
Jalapeño pepper jelly (optional)

1 In a medium bowl stir together flour, cornmeal, baking powder, baking soda, and salt. Using a pastry blender, cut in butter until mixture resembles coarse crumbs. Stir in cheese. Make a well in the center of the flour mixture; set aside.

2 In a small bowl stir together corn and buttermilk or sour cream. Add corn mixture all at once to the flour mixture. Stir just until moistened.

3 Turn the dough out onto a lightly floured surface. Quickly knead dough by gently folding and pressing for 10 to 12 strokes or until dough is almost smooth. Pat or lightly roll dough to ½-inch thickness. Cut with a floured 2½-inch biscuit cutter, dipping the cutter into flour between cuts.

4 Place biscuits on an ungreased baking sheet. Bake in a 450° oven 12 to 15 minutes or until golden. Serve hot. If desired, pass jalapeño pepper jelly.

Nutrition Facts per biscuit: 218 cal., 12 g total fat (7 g sat. fat), 33 mg chol., 415 mg sodium, 22 g carbo., 2 g fiber, 5 g pro. Daily Values: 9% vit. A, 2% vit. C, 11% calcium, 7% iron

Peaches 'n' Cream Ice Cream

Prep: 20 minutes **Chill:** 2 hours **Freeze:** 30 minutes **Ripen:** 4 hours **Makes:** 10 servings

2½ cups half-and-half or light cream
¾ cup granulated sugar
½ cup packed brown sugar
2 beaten eggs
1 8-ounce package cream cheese or
reduced-fat cream cheese
(Neufchâtel), softened

2 cups sliced peeled fresh peaches or
frozen unsweetened peach slices,
thawed
½ teaspoon finely shredded lemon peel
1 tablespoon lemon juice
1 teaspoon vanilla
2 rolled sugar ice-cream cones
¼ cup sliced almonds, toasted

1 In a large saucepan combine 1½ cups of the half-and-half, the granulated sugar, brown sugar, and eggs. Cook and stir over medium heat just until boiling; remove from heat. (Mixture will appear curdled.) Set aside.

2 In a large bowl beat cream cheese with an electric mixer on medium speed until smooth. Gradually beat in the hot mixture. Cover and chill in refrigerator for 2 hours.

3 Place half of the peaches in a blender container or food processor bowl. Cover and blend or process until nearly smooth. Coarsely chop remaining peaches; set aside.

4 Stir remaining half-and-half, the pureed peaches, lemon peel, lemon juice, and vanilla into chilled mixture. Freeze in a 4- or 5-quart ice cream freezer according to manufacturer's directions. Remove dasher from freezer. Stir in chopped peaches. Ripen ice cream 4 hours (see step 4, page 230).

5 Meanwhile, for topping, in a plastic bag crush ice-cream cones with a rolling pin. Combine crushed ice-cream cones and toasted almonds.

6 To serve, scoop ice cream into individual serving bowls and sprinkle with topping. If desired, garnish with additional peach slices.

Nutrition Facts per serving: 339 cal., 18 g total fat (10 g sat. fat), 90 mg chol., 109 mg sodium, 41 g carbo., 2 g fiber, 6 g pro. Daily Values: 20% vit. A, 10% vit. C, 11% calcium, 5% iron

Cream cheese complements the sweetness of the fruit in this peachy-keen ice cream. Can't choose between a sophisticated sundae and a simple-hearted ice cream cone? The topping lets you have it both ways.

To Make Ahead

Prepare Peaches 'n' Cream Ice Cream as directed through step 4. Transfer ice cream to a freezer container. Seal, label, and freeze up to 2 weeks.

To Serve

Let ice cream stand at room temperature about 20 minutes to soften slightly. Prepare topping. Serve over ice cream as directed.

SPRINGTIME BRUNCH

Apricot-Apple Sipper
(below)
**Double-Coffee Coffee
Cake (page 179)**
**Mushroom and
Asparagus Strata
(page 180)**
**Sweet Melon Cups
(page 182)**

Up to 3 days ahead:
● Prepare coffee cake; cover and chill.
1 day ahead:
● Prepare sipper; chill.
● Prepare strata; chill.
● Prepare melon cups; chill.
55 minutes ahead:
● Bake strata.
45 minutes ahead:
● Let coffee cake stand at room temperature.

● Assemble and garnish melon cups; cover and chill.
10 minutes ahead:
● Let baked strata stand at room temperature for 10 minutes.
Just before serving:
● Sift powdered sugar over coffee cake.
● Pour and garnish sipper.
● Garnish strata.

From Easter to Mother's Day, the season blooms with plenty of reasons to gather around the table. This do-ahead menu makes it all as easy as a breezy spring day.

To Make Ahead

**Prepare Apricot-Apple
Sipper as directed
through step 2, except
refrigerate up to 24 hours.**

To Serve

**Serve and garnish
as directed.**

Apricot-Apple Sipper

Prep: 20 minutes **Chill:** 4 hours **Makes:** about 10 (6-ounce) servings

4 cups apple cider or apple juice
4 cups apricot nectar
2 tablespoons lemon juice
2 tablespoons honey

1 teaspoon whole cloves
1 teaspoon whole allspice
4 inches stick cinnamon, broken
   Fresh strawberries (optional)

1 In a large saucepan combine apple cider, apricot nectar, lemon juice, and honey. For spice bag, place cloves, allspice, and stick cinnamon on a double-thick, 6-inch square of 100% cotton cheesecloth. Bring corners together and tie with clean kitchen string. Add the spice bag to cider mixture.

2 Bring the mixture to boiling; reduce heat. Cover and simmer for 10 minutes. Discard spice bag. Cool the mixture; chill in refrigerator at least 4 hours.

3 Serve chilled mixture in glasses. If desired, garnish each glass with a fresh whole strawberry.

Nutrition Facts per serving: 116 cal., 0 g total fat, 0 mg chol., 6 mg sodium, 30 g carbo., 1 g fiber, 0 g pro. Daily Values: 26% vit. A, 5% vit. C, 1% calcium, 4% iron

Double-Coffee Coffee Cake

Prep: 20 minutes **Bake:** 50 minutes **Makes:** 12 servings

4 teaspoons instant coffee crystals	1¾ cups sugar
2 teaspoons hot water	1 8-ounce carton dairy sour cream
3 cups all-purpose flour	3 eggs
1½ teaspoons baking powder	¼ cup buttermilk or sour milk (see tip, page 214)
1½ teaspoons baking soda	
½ teaspoon salt	¼ cup applesauce
¾ cup butter	1 teaspoon vanilla
	1 recipe Coffee Streusel (below)

1 Dissolve coffee crystals in the hot water; set aside. In a medium bowl combine flour, baking powder, baking soda, and salt; set aside.

2 In a large bowl beat butter with an electric mixer on medium to high speed for 30 seconds. Add sugar. Beat until light and fluffy. Add sour cream, eggs, buttermilk, applesauce, vanilla, and coffee-water mixture; beat well. Add flour mixture, a little at a time, beating well after each addition.

3 Pour half of the batter into a greased and floured 10-inch fluted tube pan. Sprinkle with 1 cup of the Coffee Streusel. Top with remaining batter; sprinkle with remaining streusel. Bake in a 350° oven about 50 minutes or until a toothpick inserted near center comes out clean. Cool in pan on wire rack for 10 minutes; remove from pan. Cool completely on wire rack. If desired, sift powdered sugar over coffee cake just before serving.

Coffee Streusel: In a small bowl stir together 1 cup chopped walnuts, ¼ cup granulated sugar, ¼ cup packed brown sugar, 2 teaspoons ground cinnamon, and 2 teaspoons instant coffee crystals; set aside.

Nutrition Facts per serving: 483 cal., 23 g total fat (6 g sat. fat), 62 mg chol., 461 mg sodium, 64 g carbo., 1 g fiber, 1 g pro. Daily Values: 21% vit. A, 8% calcium, 14% iron

Brunch isn't complete without a sweet bread or coffee cake somewhere on the table. Try this version at your next gathering. Your guests will love the way coffee percolates throughout the tender cake.

To Make Ahead

Prepare Double-Coffee Coffee Cake as directed through step 3, except do not sift powdered sugar over cake. Cover coffee cake and refrigerate up to 3 days.

To Serve

Let coffee cake stand at room temperature about 45 minutes before serving. Sift powdered sugar over coffee cake as directed.

This recipe brims with fresh asparagus. Remember it as a great make-ahead lunch or brunch dish for Easter, Mother's Day, a bridal luncheon—or simply to celebrate sunny days.

To Make Ahead

Prepare Mushroom and Asparagus Strata as directed through step 3, except refrigerate up to 24 hours.

To Serve

Uncover. Bake and serve as directed.

Mushroom and Asparagus Strata

Prep: 25 minutes **Chill:** 2 hours **Bake:** 45 minutes **Stand:** 10 minutes **Makes:** 6 to 8 servings

1 pound asparagus spears	2 tablespoons snipped fresh dill or
1 tablespoon olive oil	1 teaspoon dried dillweed
4 cups sliced fresh mushrooms (such as button and/or shiitake)	6 slices French or Italian bread, cut into 4×1×½-inch sticks
2 cloves garlic, minced	6 eggs
¼ teaspoon salt	2¼ cups half-and-half, light cream, or milk
¼ teaspoon freshly ground white or black pepper	¼ cup finely shredded Romano, Parmesan, or other hard grating cheese (1 ounce)
2 cups shredded Swiss and/or Edam cheese (8 ounces)	

1 Clean asparagus; snap off woody bases. If spears are thick, cut in half lengthwise. Cut spears into 3-inch-long pieces. In a large saucepan bring a small amount of water to boiling. Add asparagus. Cook, uncovered, for 1 minute. Drain; rinse with cold water. Drain on paper towels.

2 In a large skillet heat oil. Add mushrooms, garlic, salt, and pepper. Cook, uncovered, over medium-high heat for 4 to 5 minutes or until nearly all of the liquid has evaporated, stirring often; set aside. In a bowl toss together the Swiss cheese and dill. Arrange half of the bread in the bottom of a lightly greased 2-quart rectangular baking dish. Top with the mushroom mixture, the cheese mixture, and the asparagus. Top with remaining bread.

3 In a medium bowl beat together eggs and half-and-half. Pour mixture over layers in dish. Press lightly with back of a spoon to thoroughly moisten bread. Sprinkle Romano cheese over top. Cover and chill in refrigerator at least 2 hours.

4 Bake, uncovered, in a 325° oven about 45 minutes or until a knife inserted near the center comes out clean. Let stand 10 minutes before cutting.

Nutrition Facts per serving: 484 cal., 31 g total fat (16 g sat. fat), 284 mg chol., 521 mg sodium, 27 g carbo., 2 g fiber, 27 g pro. Daily Values: 35% vit. A, 26% vit. C, 48% calcium, 23% iron

Photo on opposite page:
Double Coffee Coffee Cake (page 179)
Sweet Melon Cups (page 192)
and Mushroom and Asparagus Strata (above)

Who doesn't love a pretty cup of sweet fresh fruit? A splash of white wine and a whisper of ginger make this melon medley all the more worthy of affection. You'll also love the way you can make it up to 24 hours in advance.

To Make Ahead

Prepare Sweet Melon Cups as directed through step 1, except refrigerate up to 24 hours. Prepare cantaloupe and honeydew balls; place cantaloupe and honeydew balls in separate self-sealing plastic bags or airtight storage containers. Seal and refrigerate up to 24 hours.

To Serve

Combine and serve as directed.

Sweet Melon Cups

Prep: 25 minutes **Chill:** 2 hours **Makes:** 6 servings

1 cup dry white wine or white grape juice
¼ cup sugar
½ teaspoon grated fresh ginger

4 cups cantaloupe balls
2 cups honeydew balls
Crystallized ginger strips (optional)

1 In a small saucepan combine wine or grape juice, sugar, and ginger. Bring to boiling; reduce heat. Cover and simmer for 5 minutes. Remove from heat. Strain ginger from mixture. Discard ginger. Cover and chill in refrigerator at least 2 hours.

2 To serve, in a medium bowl combine cantaloupe, honeydew, and wine or juice mixture. Toss gently to coat. Divide mixture evenly among 6 cups or dinner plates. If desired, garnish with strips of crystallized ginger.

Nutrition Facts per serving: 116 cal., 0 g total fat, 0 mg chol., 17 mg sodium, 23 g carbo., 1 g fiber, 1 g pro. Daily Values: 34% vit. A, 98% vit. C, 1% calcium, 2% iron

BREAKFASTS & BRUNCHES

No make-ahead book would be complete without a selection of special brunch and breakfast dishes; that's where the do-ahead idea really rises and shines. Prepare any of these recipes the night before, and you can sleep well knowing you've got a terrific crowd-pleaser set to dazzle your friends and family in the morning.

In addition to the Springtime Brunch menu, you'll find breakfast and brunch recipes on pages 183 through 191.

Ham & Cheese Strata

Prep: 30 minutes **Chill:** 2 hours **Bake:** 45 minutes **Makes:** 6 servings

8 ½-inch-thick slices (each about 4×3 inches) cinnamon-raisin bread or rustic white bread

2 tablespoons butter, softened (optional)

6 ounces thinly sliced cooked ham

1 small pear or tart apple, peeled, cored, and chopped

¼ cup finely chopped onion

1 cup shredded sharp cheddar or Gruyère cheese (4 ounces)

4 eggs

2 cups milk

1½ teaspoons Dijon-style mustard

½ teaspoon Worcestershire sauce

¼ teaspoon pepper

Cinnamon-raisin bread and a touch of apple add a little sophistication to this traditional brunch dish. But never fear—at its heart, this recipe still retains its rustic, homey appeal.

To Make Ahead

Prepare Ham & Cheese Strata as directed through step 2, except refrigerate up to 24 hours.

To Serve

Bake as directed.

1 If desired, lightly spread one side of each bread slice with butter. Divide ham evenly among 4 of the bread slices, placing ham on buttered side of each slice. Top ham with remaining bread, buttered sides down. Quarter each sandwich diagonally to form a total of 16 triangles. Arrange triangles, cut sides up, in a buttered 2-quart square baking dish. Sprinkle pear or apple and onion over triangles. Sprinkle with cheese.

2 In a medium bowl combine eggs, milk, mustard, Worcestershire sauce, and pepper; pour over the bread. Cover dish and chill in refrigerator at least 2 hours.

3 Bake, covered with foil, in a 350° oven for 20 minutes. Remove foil. Bake about 25 minutes more or until puffed and golden and a knife inserted into center comes out clean.

Nutrition Facts per serving: 508 cal., 15 g total fat (7 g sat. fat), 183 mg chol., 598 mg sodium, 70 g carbo., 7 g fiber, 26 g pro. Daily Values: 15% vit. A, 6% vit. C, 30% calcium, 24% iron

With eggs to poach and hollandaise sauce to keep from separating, traditional eggs benedict can be tricky—and not exactly do-ahead fare. This easy dish offers the same much-loved flavors as the classic (and an extra bonus of smoked salmon) but none of the hassle. And it's definitely in the do-ahead category.

To Make Ahead

Prepare Salmon and Eggs Benedict as directed through step 2. Cover and chill the sauce and egg mixture separately in the refrigerator up to 24 hours. Prepare crumb topping. Cover; refrigerate up to 24 hours.

To Serve

Assemble egg stacks as directed in step 3. Sprinkle crumb topping over egg stacks. Bake, covered, in a 350° oven about 25 minutes or until heated through. If desired, garnish with snipped fresh chives.

Salmon and Eggs Benedict

Prep: 30 minutes **Bake:** 15 minutes **Makes:** 6 servings

1 1⅛-ounce or 0.9-ounce envelope hollandaise sauce mix (to make about 1¼ cups sauce)
2 tablespoons capers, drained
½ teaspoon finely shredded lemon peel
6 eggs
¼ cup milk

⅛ teaspoon pepper
2 tablespoons margarine or butter
3 English muffins, split and toasted
6 ounces thinly sliced smoked salmon (lox-style) or Canadian-style bacon
¾ cup soft bread crumbs (1 slice)

1 For sauce, prepare hollandaise sauce mix according to package directions. Stir in capers and lemon peel. Cover and set aside.

2 In a medium bowl beat together eggs, milk, and pepper. In a large skillet melt 1 tablespoon of the margarine over medium heat. Pour in egg mixture. Cook, without stirring, until mixture begins to set on bottom and around edge. Using a spatula or a large spoon, lift and fold the partially cooked eggs so the uncooked portion flows underneath. Continue cooking for 3 to 4 minutes or until eggs are cooked through but are still glossy and moist.

3 Spread about ½ cup of the sauce over bottom of a 2-quart rectangular baking dish. Arrange muffins, cut sides up, on top of sauce in dish. Divide smoked salmon or Canadian-style bacon into 6 equal portions. Place one portion, folding as necessary, on each muffin half. Spoon eggs onto muffin stacks, dividing evenly. Spoon remaining sauce over eggs.

4 For crumb topping, melt remaining margarine. Add bread crumbs, tossing lightly to coat. Sprinkle over muffin stacks.

5 Bake, uncovered, in a 350° oven about 15 minutes or until heated through. If desired, garnish with snipped fresh chives.

Nutrition Facts per serving: 243 cal., 11 g total fat (3 g sat. fat), 220 mg chol., 1,065 mg sodium, 20 g carbo., 1 g fiber, 14 g pro. Daily Values: 11% vit. A, 1% vit. C, 10% calcium, 10% iron

This hearty, down-home casserole is a satisfying come-and-get-it-style crowd-pleaser. Because it starts with refrigerated hash browns, getting it to the table is extra easy.

To Make Ahead

Prepare Mexicali Potato Brunch Bake as directed through step 3. Cover and refrigerate up to 24 hours.

To Serve

Bake, covered, in a 375° oven for 25 minutes. Uncover and bake for 5 minutes more.

Mexicali Potato Brunch Bake

Prep: 20 minutes **Bake:** 25 minutes **Makes:** 6 servings

3 cups refrigerated shredded hash brown potatoes
5 eggs
1 cup shredded Monterey Jack cheese with jalapeño peppers (4 ounces)
½ cup ricotta cheese or cream cheese, softened

¾ cup milk, half-and-half, or light cream
⅛ teaspoon salt
⅛ teaspoon ground black pepper
2 tablespoons margarine or butter
1 tablespoon all-purpose flour
1 4½-ounce can diced green chile peppers, drained

1 Stir together the potatoes, 1 of the eggs, and ½ cup of the shredded cheese. Spread mixture in bottom of a greased 2-quart square baking dish. Carefully spread with ricotta or cream cheese.

2 In a medium bowl beat together the remaining eggs, ¼ cup of the milk, the salt, and black pepper. In a medium skillet melt 1 tablespoon of the margarine over medium heat; add egg mixture. Cook, without stirring, until mixture begins to set on the bottom and around edge. Using a spatula or a large spoon, lift and fold the partially cooked eggs so the uncooked portion flows underneath. Continue cooking for 3 to 4 minutes or until eggs are cooked through but are still glossy and moist. Spoon eggs evenly over mixture in dish.

3 In same skillet melt remaining margarine; stir in flour. Add remaining milk and the chile peppers; cook and stir until thickened and bubbly. Add remaining shredded cheese, stirring until melted. Spoon evenly over the eggs.

4 Bake casserole, uncovered, in a 375° oven for 25 minutes. If desired, garnish with fresh parsley sprigs.

Nutrition Facts per serving: 289 cal., 16 g total fat (7 g sat. fat), 203 mg chol., 406 mg sodium, 22 g carbo., 2 g fiber, 16 g pro. Daily Values: 22% vit. A, 143% vit. C, 23% calcium, 8% iron

Caramel Apple Breakfast Pudding

Prep: 35 minutes **Chill:** 3 hours **Bake:** 40 minutes **Stand:** 15 minutes **Makes:** 8 servings

2 large tart apples (such as Jonathan or Granny Smith)	¼ cup pecan pieces
¼ cup water	3 beaten eggs
¾ teaspoon ground cinnamon	1¼ cups milk
½ cup packed brown sugar	1 teaspoon vanilla
2 tablespoons light-colored corn syrup	¼ teaspoon ground nutmeg
2 tablespoons margarine or butter	8 to 10½-inch-thick slices Italian or French bread

1 Peel, core, and slice apples. (You should have 2 cups sliced apples.) In a small saucepan combine apple slices and the water. Bring to boiling; reduce heat to medium-low. Cover and cook for 5 to 7 minutes or until apples are tender, stirring occasionally. Drain in a colander. Transfer cooked apples to a small bowl. Gently stir cinnamon into cooked apples. Set aside.

2 In the same small saucepan combine brown sugar, corn syrup, and margarine. Cook and stir over medium heat just until mixture comes to a boil. Remove from heat. Pour mixture into a 2-quart square baking dish. Sprinkle with pecans.

3 In a medium bowl combine the eggs, milk, vanilla, and nutmeg. Arrange half of the bread slices in the baking dish on top of the brown sugar mixture, trimming bread to fit. Spoon cooked apples evenly over bread layer. Arrange remaining bread slices on top. Carefully pour the egg mixture over bread. Press lightly with back of a spoon to thoroughly moisten bread. Cover with plastic wrap; chill in refrigerator at least 3 hours.

4 Bake, uncovered, in a 325° oven for 40 to 45 minutes or until a knife inserted in center comes out clean. Remove from oven; run a knife around edge to loosen. Let stand 15 minutes. Carefully invert pudding onto a platter. (Spoon any remaining caramel mixture in dish over pudding.) Cut into triangles. Serve warm, or cool to room temperature before serving.

Nutrition Facts per serving: 208 cal., 7 g total fat (2 g sat. fat), 83 mg chol., 168 mg sodium, 31 g carbo., 0 g fiber, 5 g pro. Daily Values: 9% vit. A, 7% calcium, 8% iron

Pudding for breakfast? By all means! Think of this as a cross between French toast and caramel rolls, without the hassle of rolling the dough or the mess of dipping the bread. You'll love the way it comes together the night before baking, not to mention the way the luscious caramel-pecan layer starts on the bottom and ends on the top.

To Make Ahead
Prepare Caramel Apple Breakfast Pudding as directed through step 3, except refrigerate up to 24 hours.

To Serve
Bake and serve as directed.

Pain Perdu is what the French call French toast. But this is no ordinary version. Here, a cream-cheese filling oozes from between the bread slices, bringing a luscious dimension to the Franco-American breakfast favorite.

To Make Ahead

Prepare and cook bread slices for Pain Perdu as directed, except do not spread with cream cheese. Place the cooked slices of toast on a baking sheet and freeze just until firm. Place in freezer container. Seal, label, and freeze up to 3 months.

To Serve

To reheat, place frozen slices in a single layer on an ungreased baking sheet. Bake, uncovered, in a 400° oven for 10 to 12 minutes or until heated through. Meanwhile, prepare Cream Cheese Filling. Fill and serve as directed.

Pain Perdu (French Toast)

Prep: 20 minutes **Cook:** 4 minutes per batch **Makes:** 9 servings

- 1 5-ounce can (⅔ cup) evaporated milk
- ⅓ cup milk
- ¼ cup butter or margarine
- 3 slightly beaten eggs
- ¾ cup sugar
- 1 teaspoon vanilla
- 1 8-ounce French bread baguette, cut into 18 slices about ¾ inch thick
- 2 tablespoons cooking oil
- 1 recipe Cream Cheese Filling (below) Maple-flavored or fruit-flavored syrup

1 In a small saucepan heat evaporated milk, milk, and butter just until butter melts. In a medium bowl combine eggs, sugar, vanilla, and warm milk mixture; pour into a shallow baking dish. Place bread slices in egg mixture, turning to coat both sides. Let stand about 5 minutes to thoroughly soak bread.

2 In a large skillet heat oil over medium heat. Add several bread slices and cook for 2 to 3 minutes on each side or until golden. Keep warm in a 300° oven. Repeat with remaining bread, adding more oil if necessary. Working with half of the slices of toast, spread about 1 heaping tablespoon of the Cream Cheese Filling on each slice; top with remaining toast slices. Serve with desired syrup.

Cream Cheese Filling: In a food processor bowl or a large bowl combine one 8-ounce package cream cheese, softened; ¼ of an 8-ounce container frozen whipped dessert topping, thawed; 2 tablespoons sugar; and 2 tablespoons dairy sour cream. Cover and process or beat with an electric mixer on low to medium speed until smooth.

Nutrition Facts per serving: 379 cal., 23 g total fat (13 g sat. fat), 120 mg chol., 330 mg sodium, 36 g carbo., 1 g fiber, 8 g pro. Daily Values: 20% vit. A., 1% vit. C., 10% calcium, 7% iron

There's no need to be stuck in the kitchen when you have guests for brunch. The make-ahead directions for these raisin-and-nut-studded delights allow you to be exactly where you want to be—gathered with your guests around the table sharing good times.

To Make Ahead

Prepare Company Cinnamon Rolls as directed through step 4, except do not let rolls rise. Cover with oiled waxed paper, then with plastic wrap. Refrigerate at least 8 hours or up to 24 hours.

To Serve

Let stand for 20 minutes at room temperature. Uncover and puncture any surface bubbles with a greased toothpick. Bake and serve as directed.

Company Cinnamon Rolls

Prep: 25 minutes **Rise:** 1½ hours **Bake:** 25 minutes **Makes:** 12 rolls

3½ to 4 cups all-purpose flour	2 tablespoons butter, softened
1 package active dry yeast	¾ cup packed brown sugar
1 cup milk	2 teaspoons ground cinnamon
⅓ cup granulated sugar	½ cup raisins
⅓ cup butter	½ cup chopped nuts
½ teaspoon salt	4 teaspoons half-and-half or light
1 egg	cream

1 In a large bowl, combine 1½ cups of the flour and the yeast; set aside. In a small saucepan heat milk, granulated sugar, the ⅓ cup butter, and the salt until warm (120° to 130°) and butter is almost melted. Add to flour mixture along with egg. Beat with an electric mixer on low speed 30 seconds, scraping bowl. Beat on high speed 3 minutes. Stir in as much of the remaining flour as you can with a wooden spoon.

2 Turn dough out onto a lightly floured surface. Knead in enough of the remaining flour to make a moderately soft dough that is smooth and elastic (3 to 5 minutes total). Shape dough into a ball. Place dough in a lightly greased bowl; turn once to grease surface of dough. Cover and let rise in a warm place until double in size (1 to 1½ hours).

3 Punch dough down. Turn out onto a lightly floured surface. Cover; let rest 10 minutes. Roll dough into an 18×10-inch rectangle. Spread with the 2 tablespoons softened butter. Combine brown sugar and cinnamon; sprinkle over dough. Sprinkle with raisins and nuts. Starting from a long side, tightly roll into a spiral. Pinch seam to seal.

4 Cut dough crosswise into 12 even slices. Arrange slices, cut sides down, in a greased 13×9×2-inch baking pan. Cover and let rise until nearly double (30 to 40 minutes).

5 Brush rolls with half-and-half. Bake in a 350° oven for 25 to 30 minutes or until golden. Invert rolls onto a wire rack or serving platter. Cool slightly.

Nutrition Facts per roll: 319 cal., 12 g total fat (6 g sat. fat), 42 mg chol., 192 mg sodium, 49 g carbo., 2 g fiber, 6 g pro. Daily Values: 10% vit. A, 1% vit. C, 4% calcium, 15% iron

Orange Breakfast Granola

Prep: 20 minutes **Bake:** 30 minutes **Makes:** about 5 cups (ten ½-cup servings)

3 cups regular rolled oats	⅓ cup orange juice
½ cup toasted wheat germ	½ teaspoon ground cinnamon
½ cup coarsely chopped hazelnuts (filberts) or sliced almonds	1 cup coconut
⅓ cup honey	Berries or sliced fruit (optional)
½ teaspoon finely shredded orange peel	Plain or vanilla yogurt (optional)

1 In a large bowl stir together the oats, wheat germ, and hazelnuts. In a small saucepan stir together the honey, orange peel, orange juice, and cinnamon. Heat just until boiling; remove from heat. Pour honey mixture over oat mixture, tossing gently until coated.

2 Coat a 15×10×1-inch baking pan with nonstick cooking spray. Spread oat mixture evenly in pan. Bake in a 325° oven for 15 minutes. Stir coconut into oat mixture. Bake for 15 to 20 minutes more or until lightly browned, stirring once. Remove from oven and immediately turn out onto a large piece of foil; cool.

3 To serve, spoon granola into cereal bowls. If desired, top each serving with fresh berries or sliced fresh fruit and plain or vanilla low-fat yogurt.

Nutrition Facts per serving: 224 cal., 8 g total fat (3 g sat. fat), 0 mg chol., 3 mg sodium, 33 g carbo., 1 g fiber, 7 g pro. Daily Values: 7% vit. C, 2% calcium, 13% iron

Expecting overnight guests around the holidays? Consider keeping a batch of this granola on hand for breakfast anytime. Whether they're leepyheads or early risers, guests will appreciate the flexibility of grabbing scoopfuls whenever they're ready to eat.

To Make Ahead

Prepare Orange Breakfast Granola as directed through step 2. Transfer to an airtight container; seal and store at room temperature up to 2 weeks. (Or transfer to self-sealing freezer bags. Seal, label, and freeze up to 3 months.)

To Serve

Thaw frozen granola at room temperature. Serve as directed.

Recipes for gift giving are on pages 192 through 199.

GIFTS IN GOOD TASTE

Give the gifts that money can't buy: exquisite edibles that come straight from the heart. You can make most of these recipes up to 3 months in advance. At holiday time you'll have memorable gifts on hand for friends and family.

Lemon-Nut Biscotti

K now someone who's nuts about pistachios? Bake a batch of these delicious dunkers studded with that delectable nut. Present them as a gift in a colorful mug with a bag of gourmet coffee beans.

To Make Ahead

Prepare Lemon-Nut Biscotti as directed through step 3, except do not drizzle with icing. Transfer to self-sealing freezer bags or arrange in layers separated by waxed paper in a freezer container. Seal, label, and freeze up to 3 months.

To Serve

Thaw biscotti at room temperature 15 minutes. Drizzle with icing.

Prep: 35 minutes **Bake:** 36 minutes **Stand:** 30 minutes **Makes:** about 36 cookies

⅓ cup butter, softened	1 teaspoon vanilla
⅔ cup granulated sugar	2 cups all-purpose flour
2 teaspoons baking powder	1½ cups unsalted pistachio nuts
2 eggs	1 cup sifted powdered sugar
4 teaspoons finely shredded lemon peel	Lemon juice or milk

1 Line 2 cookie sheets with parchment paper or lightly grease the cookie sheets; set aside. In a large bowl beat butter with an electric mixer on medium to high speed for 30 seconds. Add granulated sugar, baking powder, and ½ teaspoon salt; beat until combined, scraping side of bowl occasionally. Beat in eggs, lemon peel, and vanilla until combined. Beat in as much of the flour as you can with the mixer. Using a wooden spoon, stir in any remaining flour and the pistachio nuts.

2 On a lightly floured surface, divide dough into 3 portions. Shape each portion into an 8-inch-long loaf. Place loaves at least 3 inches apart on prepared cookie sheets. Flatten loaves to about 2½ inches wide. Bake in a 375° oven for 20 to 25 minutes or until golden and tops are cracked. (Loaves will spread slightly.) Let stand on cookie sheets on wire racks for 30 minutes. Reduce oven temperature to 325°.

3 Transfer loaves to a cutting board. Cut each loaf diagonally into ½-inch-thick slices. Place slices, cut sides down, on the same parchment-lined or greased cookie sheets. Bake in the 325° oven for 8 minutes. Turn slices over and bake 8 to 10 minutes more or until dry and crisp. Transfer to wire racks; cool. For icing, stir together powdered sugar and enough lemon juice or milk (1 to 2 tablespoons) to make icing of drizzling consistency. Drizzle over biscotti. Let stand until frosting is set.

Nutrition Facts per biscotti: 96 cal., 4 g total fat (1 g sat. fat), 17 mg chol., 76 mg sodium, 13 g carbo., 1 g fiber, 2 g pro. Daily Values: 2% vit. A, 1% vit. C, 2% calcium, 3% iron

This rich and buttery cream cheese spread, rolled in coconut for a seasonal effect, tastes heavenly on shortbread. For a stunning presentation, offer each snowball in a cut-glass sherbet dish wrapped in cellophane and bedecked with beaded wire. Complete the gift with a package of your favorite home-baked or purchased shortbread.

To Make Ahead

Prepare Cherry-Hazelnut Snowballs as directed. Cover and store in refrigerator up to 3 days. (Or place each ball in a self-sealing freezer bag or freezer container. Seal, label, and freeze up to 3 months.)

To Serve

Thaw frozen balls at room temperature in freezer bags or containers for 15 minutes.

Cherry-Hazelnut Snowballs

Prep: 20 minutes **Chill:** 20 minutes **Makes:** 2 balls (32 one-tablespoon servings)

1 8-ounce package cream cheese, softened
½ cup butter, softened
¼ cup sifted powdered sugar
1 tablespoon milk
⅓ cup snipped dried cherries and/or finely chopped dried figs
⅓ cup toasted hazelnuts (filberts) or almonds, chopped
¾ cup coconut

1 In a medium bowl combine cream cheese, butter, powdered sugar, and milk. Beat with an electric mixer on medium speed about 1 minute or until combined. Stir in cherries and/or figs and hazelnuts.

2 Chill in refrigerator for 20 to 30 minutes or until easy to handle. Using your hands, shape mixture into 2 balls. Roll balls in coconut. Serve immediately or store in refrigerator until serving time.

Nutrition Facts per 1-tablespoon serving: 74 cal., 7 g total fat (4 g sat. fat), 16 mg chol., 53 mg sodium, 3 g carbo., 0 g fiber, 1 g pro. Daily Values: 4% vit. A, 1% calcium, 1% iron

Ultimate Chocolate Brownies

Prep: 10 minutes **Makes:** 1 gift jar (enough for 16 brownies)

 1 cup all-purpose flour
 ½ teaspoon baking powder
 ¼ teaspoon salt
 1½ cups Vanilla Sugar (below)
 ¼ cup unsweetened cocoa powder

 6 ounces candy-coated semisweet
    chocolate pieces; miniature
    chocolate-covered mint creams,
    quartered; any chocolate-covered
    candy bar, coarsely chopped; or
    a combination to total 1 cup
 ½ cup coconut, toasted nuts, or
    miniature marshmallows

1 Layer ingredients in order listed in a 1-quart glass jar, tapping jar gently on the counter to settle each layer before adding the next one. If necessary, fill any small gaps at top of jar by adding additional candy, nuts, or miniature marshmallows. Secure lid. Include recipe directions for preparing brownies with gift.

2 Recipe Directions: In a large bowl combine ½ cup butter, melted and cooled, and 2 slightly beaten eggs. Add jar contents, stirring gently until combined. Spread in a greased and floured 8×8×2-inch baking pan. Bake in a 350° oven for 35 minutes. Cool in pan and cut into bars. Makes 16 brownies.

Vanilla Sugar: Fill a quart jar with 4 cups sugar. Cut a vanilla bean in half lengthwise and insert both halves into sugar. Secure lid and store in a cool dry place for several weeks before using. Will keep indefinitely. Makes 4 cups.

Nutrition Facts per brownie: 229 cal., 10 g total fat (6 g sat. fat), 44 mg chol., 126 mg sodium, 33 g carbo., 1 g fiber, 3 g pro. Daily Values: 6% vit. A, 4% calcium, 4% iron

This brownie mix lets recipients prepare the treats at their convenience, and anyone who is already inundated with holiday sweets will appreciate that! Hint: Package the mix in any new or antique 1-quart glass jar with a tight-fitting lid. Make sure the jar is clean and dry before adding the ingredients.

To Make Ahead

Prepare Ultimate Chocolate Brownies as directed through step 1. Store up to 6 weeks at room temperature or up to 6 months in the freezer. (Or prepare brownies as directed through step 2. Cool completely. Arrange in layers separated by waxed paper in a freezer container. Seal, label, and freeze up to 3 months.)

To Serve

Use dry mixture to prepare brownies as directed in step 2. (Or thaw frozen brownies in freezer container at room temperature for 15 minutes.)

These tender rum-soaked cakes brimming with tropical fruit bits and rich macadamia nuts make sure-to-please gifts. If you keep some of these on hand in the freezer, you'll have a one-of-a-kind treat ready and waiting for last-minute gift giving.

To Make Ahead

Prepare Tropical Fruit Cakes as directed through step 5, except refrigerate up to 5 days. (Or prepare Tropical Fruit Cakes as directed through step 5, except do not sprinkle with powdered sugar. Place in self-sealing freezer bags. Seal, label, and freeze up to 3 months.)

To Serve

Thaw frozen cakes in freezer bags in the refrigerator overnight. Serve as directed.

Tropical Fruit Cakes

Prep: 30 minutes **Bake:** 20 minutes **Cool:** 1 hour **Chill:** 2 days
Makes: 6 or 8 cakes (24 servings)

1½ cups all-purpose flour	2 tablespoons light-colored corn syrup
½ teaspoon baking powder	1 teaspoon grated fresh ginger
¼ teaspoon baking soda	1 teaspoon vanilla
½ cup butter	1¾ cups mixed dried tropical fruit bits
¾ cup packed brown sugar	½ cup chopped macadamia nuts or Brazil nuts
2 eggs	
¼ cup rum or pineapple juice	⅓ cup rum or pineapple juice
¼ cup pineapple juice	¼ cup rum or pineapple juice

1 Grease and lightly flour eight 1-cup fluted tube pans or six 4½×2½×1½-inch individual loaf pans. Set pans aside.

2 In a medium bowl combine flour, baking powder, and baking soda; set aside. In a large bowl beat butter with an electric mixer on medium to high speed for 30 seconds. Add brown sugar; beat until combined. Add eggs, one at a time, beating on medium speed until combined. (The batter may appear curdled.) Combine ¼ cup rum or pineapple juice, ¼ cup pineapple juice, the corn syrup, ginger, and vanilla. Add flour mixture and rum mixture alternately to butter mixture, beating on low speed after each addition just until combined. Fold in fruit bits and nuts. Spread batter in prepared pans.

3 Bake in a 325° oven for 20 to 25 minutes for fluted tube pans or 30 to 35 minutes for loaf pans or until a toothpick inserted into centers comes out clean. Cool cakes in pans on wire racks for 10 minutes. Remove from pans; cool at least 1 hour on racks.

4 Poke holes in cakes using a wooden toothpick or bamboo skewer. Soak six or eight 8-inch-square pieces of double thickness 100% cotton cheesecloth with the ⅓ cup rum or pineapple juice. Wrap each cake in rum- or juice-soaked cheesecloth. Wrap each cake tightly in foil or seal in a plastic bag. Chill in refrigerator for 24 hours.

5 Remove foil or remove cakes from bags; drizzle with ¼ cup rum or pineapple juice. Rewrap with foil or return to plastic bags and refrigerate at least 24 hours. Remove cheesecloth before serving. If desired, sprinkle with sifted powdered sugar.

Nutrition Facts per serving: 165 cal., 7 g total fat (3 g sat. fat), 29 mg chol., 87 mg sodium, 21 g carbo., 0 g fiber, 2 g pro. Daily Values: 4% vit. A, 1% vit. C, 2% calcium, 4% iron

Here's a surefire way to spread holiday cheer. Make a few batches of these sweet-spicy scones to share with friends at tea time. When they ask you for the recipe, just smile—and offer a bag of this homemade mix.

To Make Ahead

Prepare Gingerbread Scones as directed through step 1. Store in an airtight container up to 6 weeks at room temperature or in a freezer container up to 6 months in the freezer. (Or prepare scones as directed through step 3. Cool completely. Place in self-sealing freezer bags or arrange in layers separated by waxed paper in a freezer container. Seal, label, and freeze up to 3 months.)

To Serve

Using 1¾ cups of dry mixture for each recipe, prepare scones as directed in step 3. (Or thaw frozen scones in freezer bags or containers at room temperature.)

Gingerbread Scones

Prep: 15 minutes **Makes:** 3 gift bags (enough for 18 scones)

3¾ cups all-purpose flour
 ½ cup packed brown sugar
 2 tablespoons baking powder
 2 teaspoons ground ginger
 1 teaspoon ground cinnamon

 ½ teaspoon salt
 ¼ teaspoon baking soda
 ¼ teaspoon ground cloves
 ¼ teaspoon ground nutmeg
 ¾ cup shortening

1 In a large bowl combine flour, brown sugar, baking powder, ginger, cinnamon, salt, soda, cloves, and nutmeg. Using a pastry blender, cut in shortening until mixture resembles coarse crumbs.

2 For each gift, measure about 1¾ cups of the mixture into a self-sealing plastic bag or airtight container. Seal bags or containers. Include recipe directions for scones with each gift.

3 Recipe Directions: Pour gingerbread mix from gift bag or container into a medium bowl. Make a well in center of dry mixture. Combine 1 beaten egg, 2 tablespoons milk, and 1 tablespoon molasses; add to dry mixture. Stir just until moistened. Turn dough out onto lightly floured surface. Quickly knead dough by folding and pressing it gently for 10 to 12 strokes or until dough is almost smooth. Pat or lightly roll dough into a 6-inch circle. Cut into 6 wedges. Place wedges 1 inch apart on an ungreased baking sheet. Brush with milk; sprinkle with coarse or granulated sugar. Bake in a 400° oven for 10 to 12 minutes or until bottoms are brown. Serve warm. Makes 6 scones.

Nutrition Facts per scone: 211 cal., 10 g total fat (3 g sat. fat), 36 mg chol., 186 mg sodium, 27 g carbo., 1 g fiber, 4 g pro. Daily Values: 11% calcium, 11% iron

Nut Rocha

Start to finish: 40 minutes **Makes:** about 40 servings

2 **cups butter**
2 **cups sugar**
⅓ **cup water**
2 **tablespoons light-colored corn syrup**

1 **11½-ounce package (1¾ cups) milk chocolate pieces**
1 **cup finely chopped, toasted nuts (such as almonds, pecans, walnuts, and/or cashews)**

1 Line a 15×10×1-inch baking pan with foil, extending the foil over edges of pan. Set baking pan aside.

2 In a 3-quart saucepan melt butter. Stir in sugar, water, and corn syrup. Cook over medium-high heat to boiling, stirring until sugar is dissolved. Avoid splashing side of saucepan. Carefully clip a candy thermometer to pan. Cook over medium heat, stirring frequently, until thermometer registers 290°, soft-crack stage (about 15 minutes). Mixture should boil at a moderate, steady rate with bubbles over entire surface. Remove from heat; remove thermometer.

3 Carefully pour mixture into prepared pan; spread evenly. Cool about 5 minutes or until top is set. Sprinkle with chocolate pieces; let stand 2 minutes. Spread softened chocolate over candy. Sprinkle with nuts; press into chocolate. Let stand at room temperature several hours or until set. Use foil to lift candy out of pan; break into pieces.

Nutrition Facts per serving: 181 cal., 13 g total fat (7 g sat. fat), 25 mg chol., 128 mg sodium, 16 g carbo., 0 g fiber, 1 g pro. Daily Values: 9% vit. A, 2% calcium, 1% iron

A spectacular gift to pack and mail, this toffee stacks easily in airtight containers. And when the recipient bites into the crunchy brittle coated with silken chocolate, you may well be out of sight—but you certainly won't be out of mind.

To Make Ahead

Prepare Nut Rocha as directed through step 3. Stack in layers separated by waxed paper in an airtight container. Seal and store at cool room temperature up to 1 month.

Baklava (page 222)

Sweets
In Store

When you need a cheesecake to dazzle dinner guests, cookies to satisfy sudden cravings, or a cake for an upcoming celebration, choose from this stash of goodies to delight any sweet tooth—at a moment's notice.

In This Chapter

Here's convenience cooking at its best. Blueberries and citrus peel transform a simple lemon cake mix into a moist and delectable treat. Of course, a luscious cream cheese frosting doesn't hurt anything either!

To Make Ahead

Prepare Blueberry-Citrus Cake as directed through step 2, assembling cake on the base of a cake container with a tight-fitting lid or on a baking sheet. Freeze 2 to 3 hours or just until frosting is firm. Cover with cake container lid or with moisture- and vaporproof wrap. Label and freeze up to 1 week.

To Serve

Thaw cake, covered, overnight in the refrigerator. If desired, garnish with orange peel curls.

Blueberry-Citrus Cake

Prep: 25 minutes **Bake:** 25 minutes **Makes:** 12 servings

1 package 2-layer-size lemon cake mix
1 tablespoon finely shredded orange peel (set aside)
½ cup orange juice
½ cup water
⅓ cup cooking oil

3 eggs
1½ cups fresh or frozen blueberries
1 tablespoon finely shredded lemon peel
1 recipe Citrus Frosting (below)

1 Grease and lightly flour two 8×1½-inch or 9×1½-inch round baking pans; set aside. In a large bowl combine cake mix, orange juice, water, oil, and eggs. Beat with an electric mixer on low speed for 30 seconds. Beat 2 minutes on medium speed. Gently fold in blueberries, lemon peel, and orange peel. Divide batter between prepared pans.

2 Bake in a 350° oven for 25 to 35 minutes or until a toothpick inserted near the centers comes out clean. (Centers may dip slightly.) Cool in pans on wire racks for 10 minutes. Remove from pans. Cool completely on wire racks. Place one cake layer, blueberry side down, on a cake plate. Fill and frost cake with Citrus Frosting.

3 If desired, garnish frosted cake with orange peel curls. Cover and store frosted cake in refrigerator up to 2 days.

Citrus Frosting: Finely shred 2 tablespoons orange peel and 1 tablespoon lemon peel; set aside. In a large bowl beat one 3-ounce package cream cheese, softened, and ¼ cup butter, softened, with an electric mixer on low to medium speed until fluffy. Add 3 cups sifted powdered sugar and 2 tablespoons orange juice. Beat until combined. In a medium chilled bowl beat ¾ cup whipping cream with same beaters of an electric mixer on medium speed until soft peaks form; add to cream cheese mixture. Beat on low speed until combined. Stir in shredded orange peel and lemon peel. Makes 3 cups.

Nutrition Facts per serving: 470 cal., 22 g total fat (10 g sat. fat), 92 mg chol., 355 mg sodium, 65 g carbo., 1 g fiber, 4 g pro. Daily Values: 12% vit. A, 20% vit. C, 11% calcium, 6% iron

Gingered Carrot Cake

Prep: 40 minutes **Bake:** 30 minutes **Makes:** 12 to 15 servings

2 cups all-purpose flour
2 cups sugar
2 teaspoons baking powder
½ teaspoon baking soda
3 cups finely shredded carrot
4 beaten eggs
¾ cup cooking oil

¾ cup mixed dried fruit bits
2 teaspoons grated fresh ginger or
    ¾ teaspoon ground ginger
1 recipe Cream Cheese Frosting
    (below)
1 cup finely chopped pecans, toasted
    (optional)

1 Grease and flour two 9×1½-inch round baking pans.* Set aside. In a large bowl stir together the flour, sugar, baking powder, and baking soda. In a medium bowl combine the carrot, eggs, oil, fruit bits, and ginger. Stir the egg mixture into the flour mixture. Pour batter into the prepared pans.

2 Bake in a 350° oven 30 to 35 minutes or until a toothpick inserted near centers comes out clean. Cool in pans on wire racks for 10 minutes. Remove cakes from pans. Cool completely on wire racks.

3 Fill and frost cake with Cream Cheese Frosting. If desired, press pecans onto the side of the cake. Cover loosely and store frosted cake in refrigerator up to 2 days.

Cream Cheese Frosting: In large bowl beat two 3-ounce packages cream cheese, softened; ½ cup butter, softened; and 1 tablespoon apricot brandy or orange juice with and an electric mixer on medium speed until combined. Gradually beat in enough of 4½ to 4¾ cups sifted powdered sugar to make spreading consistency. Stir in ½ teaspoon finely shredded orange peel. Makes about 2¾ cups.

Nutrition Facts per serving: 652 cal., 29 g total fat (11 g sat. fat), 108 mg chol., 281 mg sodium, 95 g carbo., 1 g fiber, 6 g pro. Daily Values: 167% vit. A, 6% vit. C, 9% calcium, 10% iron

*Note: To avoid spillovers during baking, the round baking pans must be at least 1½ inches deep. If your round pans aren't deep enough, pour all of the batter into one greased 13×9×2-inch baking pan. Bake in a 350° oven about 40 minutes or until toothpick inserted near the center comes out clean. Place pan on wire rack; cool completely. Frost with Cream Cheese Frosting. (There may be some leftover frosting.) If desired, sprinkle with nuts. Store as above.

Make this impressive cake the next time you need a special dessert. Mixed dried fruit bits and fresh ginger bring an out-of-the-ordinary touch to the ever-popular carrot cake. With the choice of storing in the refrigerator or the freezer, it's easy to fit the preparation into your schedule.

To Make Ahead

Prepare Gingered Carrot Cake as directed through step 3, assembling cake on the base of a cake container with a tight-fitting lid or on a baking sheet. Freeze about 1 hour or just until frosting is firm. Cover with cake container lid or moisture- and vaporproof wrap. Label and freeze up to 1 week.

To Serve

Thaw cake, covered, overnight in the refrigerator.

Chocolate can be both regal and whimsical, and this recipe proves it! Hint: If you don't have three 8-inch square baking pans, you can use three 9×1½-inch round baking pans instead.

To Make Ahead

Prepare Triple Chocolate Cake as directed through step 3, assembling cake on the base of a cake container with a tight-fitting lid or on a baking sheet. Freeze about 1 hour or just until frosting is firm. Cover with cake container lid or moisture- and vaporproof wrap. Label and freeze up to 1 week.

To Serve

Thaw cake, covered, overnight in the refrigerator. Let stand at room temperature for 30 minutes before serving. Coarsely chop or halve some of the malted milk balls. Decorate the cake with whole malted milk balls and pieces.

Triple Chocolate Cake

Prep: 40 minutes **Bake:** 17 minutes **Chill:** 3 hours **Makes:** 20 servings

½ cup unsweetened cocoa powder	4 ounces unsweetened chocolate, melted and cooled
2 cups all-purpose flour	2 teaspoons vanilla
1 teaspoon baking powder	1½ cups milk
½ teaspoon baking soda	1 recipe Chocolate Malt Frosting (below)
⅔ cup butter, softened	2 cups malted milk balls
1¾ cups sugar	
3 eggs	

1 Grease three 8×8×2-inch baking pans; lightly dust each pan with 1 teaspoon of the cocoa powder (1 tablespoon total). In a medium bowl stir together remaining cocoa powder, the flour, baking powder, and baking soda. Set aside.

2 In a large bowl beat butter with an electric mixer on medium to high speed for 30 seconds. Add sugar; beat until combined. Add eggs, one at a time, beating on medium speed for 30 seconds after each. Beat in chocolate and vanilla. Add flour mixture and milk alternately to beaten mixture, beating on low speed until combined. Pour batter into prepared pans; spread evenly.

3 Bake in a 350° oven for 17 to 20 minutes or until a toothpick inserted near the centers comes out clean. Cool in pans on wire rack for 10 minutes. Remove from pans. Cool completely on wire racks. Fill and frost cake with Chocolate Malt Frosting.

4 Coarsely chop or halve some of the malted milk balls. Decorate the cake with remaining whole malted milk balls and pieces. Cover and store in refrigerator up to 3 days.

Chocolate Malt Frosting: In a medium saucepan heat 2 cups whipping cream over medium-high heat just until boiling. Stir in ⅓ cup malted milk powder. Add two 11.5-ounce packages milk chocolate pieces (do not stir). Cover; set aside 5 minutes. Stir until smooth. Transfer to a large bowl. (Mixture will be thin.) Cover and refrigerate 3 hours or until well chilled, stirring occasionally. Set the large bowl in a larger bowl of ice water. Beat with an electric mixer on medium speed about 3 minutes or until fluffy and of spreading consistency. (The frosting will turn light brown as it is beaten.)

Nutrition Facts per serving: 591 cal., 34 g total fat (19 g sat. fat), 90 mg chol., 227 mg sodium, 66 g carbo., 2 g fiber, 9 g pro. Daily Values: 14% vit. A, 1% vit. C, 16% calcium, 7% iron

Ultimate Nut and Chocolate Chip Tart

Prep: 35 minutes **Bake:** 40 minutes **Makes:** 8 to 10 servings

½ of a 15-ounce package (1 crust) folded refrigerated unbaked piecrust

3 eggs

1 cup light-colored corn syrup

½ cup packed brown sugar

⅓ cup butter, melted and cooled

1 teaspoon vanilla

1 cup coarsely chopped salted mixed nuts

½ cup miniature semisweet chocolate pieces

⅓ cup miniature semisweet chocolate pieces

1 tablespoon shortening

Vanilla ice cream (optional)

1 Let refrigerated piecrust stand at room temperature according to package directions. Ease piecrust into an 11-inch tart pan with removable bottom. Trim piecrust even with the rim of the pan. Do not prick piecrust.

2 For filling, in a large bowl beat eggs slightly with a rotary beater or fork. Stir in the corn syrup. Add the brown sugar, butter, and vanilla, stirring until sugar is dissolved. Stir in the nuts and the ½ cup chocolate pieces.

3 Place pastry-lined tart pan on a baking sheet on oven rack. Carefully pour filling into pan. Bake in a 350° oven about 40 minutes or until a knife inserted near the center comes out clean. Cool on a wire rack.

4 To serve, cut tart into wedges and transfer to dessert plates. In a small, heavy saucepan cook and stir the ⅓ cup chocolate pieces and the shortening over very low heat until chocolate begins to melt. Immediately remove from heat; stir until smooth. Cool slightly. Transfer chocolate mixture to a small, heavy plastic bag. Snip a very small hole in one corner of the bag. Drizzle some of the melted chocolate in zigzag lines across each tart wedge. If desired, serve tart with vanilla ice cream.

Nutrition Facts per serving: 574 cal., 31 g total fat (13 g sat. fat), 106 mg chol., 312 mg sodium, 65 g carbo., 4 g fiber, 6 g pro. Daily Values: 9% vit. A, 1% vit. C, 3% calcium, 5% iron

A little like another all-time favorite, pecan pie, this rich tart mixes several kinds of nuts and chocolate pieces in a caramel custard filling. Served with a scoop of ice cream, it's heavenly. Its ability to withstand freezing for up to 3 months makes it a spectacular dessert indeed.

To Make Ahead

Prepare Ultimate Nut and Chocolate Chip Tart as directed through step 3. Wrap in moisture- and vaporproof wrap or place in a self-sealing freezer bag. Seal, label, and freeze up to 3 months.

To Serve

Remove from wrap or bag. Thaw at room temperature. Serve as directed.

Summer-fresh peaches nestle inside a flaky crust with a sugary nut topping to add a little extra sweetness.

To Make Ahead

Prepare Peach Pie with Candied Pecans as directed through step 2, except do not cut slits in top crust. Cover unbaked pie with inverted 10-inch paper plate. Place in a self-sealing freezer bag. Seal, label, and freeze up to 4 months.

To Serve

Remove frozen pie from bag, remove paper plate, and cut slits in top crust. Cover edge of pie with foil; place on a baking sheet. Bake in a 450° oven for 15 minutes. Reduce oven temperature to 375°; bake 15 minutes. Remove foil; bake about 30 minutes more or until top is golden and filling bubbles through slits in top crust. Prepare pecan topping; spread over pie. Bake 5 minutes. Cool on wire rack.

Peach Pie with Candied Pecans

Prep: 35 minutes **Bake:** 55 minutes **Makes:** 8 servings

½ to ⅔ cup granulated sugar*
2 tablespoons quick-cooking tapioca
¼ teaspoon ground cinnamon
¼ teaspoon ground nutmeg
6 cups thinly sliced, peeled peaches or frozen unsweetened peach slices

1 recipe Pastry for Double-Crust Pie (page 163)
⅓ cup packed brown sugar
2 tablespoons butter
1 tablespoon water
1 teaspoon cornstarch
¾ cup broken pecans

1 For filling, in a large bowl stir together granulated sugar, tapioca, cinnamon, and nutmeg. Add peaches; gently toss until coated. Let mixture stand 20 minutes, stirring once or twice.

2 Meanwhile, prepare and roll out Pastry for Double-Crust Pie. Line a 9-inch pie plate with half of the pastry. Transfer peach mixture to the pastry-lined pie plate. Trim pastry to edge of pie plate. Cut slits in the top crust. Place top crust on filling. Seal and flute edge.

3 To prevent overbrowning, cover edge of pie with foil. Place pie plate on a baking sheet to catch any drips. Bake in a 375° oven for 25 minutes (50 minutes if using frozen fruit). Remove foil. Bake 25 to 30 minutes more or until golden.

4 Meanwhile, for pecan topping, in a small saucepan stir together brown sugar, butter, water, and cornstarch. Cook and stir over medium heat until bubbly. Stir in pecans. Spread warm pecan mixture over hot pie. Bake for 5 minutes more. Cool completely on a wire rack. Cover and refrigerate any leftovers.

Nutrition Facts per serving: 556 cal., 28 g total fat (7 g sat. fat), 8 mg chol., 169 mg sodium, 76 g carbo., 7 g fiber, 6 g pro. Daily Values: 23% vit. A, 20% vit. C, 3% calcium, 12% iron

*Note: If you prefer a sweeter pie or if your peaches are not completely ripe, use the ⅔ cup sugar.

When the farmers' market brims with berries, stash a few in this pie and freeze it up to 4 months. When autumn rolls around, you'll be glad you did!

To Make Ahead

Prepare Mixed Berry Pie as directed through step 2, except do not cut slits in top crust. Cover unbaked pie with inverted 10-inch paper plate. Place pie in a self-sealing freezer bag. Seal, label, and freeze up to 4 months.

To Serve

Remove frozen pie from bag, remove paper plate, and cut slits in top crust. Cover edge of pie with foil; place on a baking sheet. Bake in a 450° oven for 15 minutes. Reduce oven temperature to 375°; bake 30 minutes. Remove foil; bake 40 to 50 minutes or until top is golden and filling bubbles through slits in top crust. Cool on wire rack.

Mixed Berry Pie

Prep: 35 minutes **Bake:** 45 minutes **Makes:** 8 servings

1 cup sugar	2 cups sliced fresh strawberries
¼ cup quick-cooking tapioca	2 cups fresh blackberries or raspberries
1 teaspoon finely shredded orange peel	1 cup fresh blueberries
½ teaspoon ground cinnamon	1 recipe Pastry for Double-Crust Pie (page 163)
¼ teaspoon ground nutmeg	
⅛ teaspoon ground ginger	

1 For filling, in a large bowl combine sugar, tapioca, orange peel, cinnamon, nutmeg, and ginger. Add strawberries, blackberries, and blueberries. Gently toss until coated. Let stand 20 minutes, stirring once or twice.

2 Meanwhile, prepare and roll out Pastry for Double-Crust Pie. Line a 9-inch pie plate with half of the pastry. Transfer berry mixture to the pastry-lined pie plate. Trim pastry to the edge of pie plate. Cut slits in the top crust. Place top crust on filling. Seal; flute edge.

3 To prevent overbrowning, cover edge of pie with foil. Place pie plate on a baking sheet to catch any drips. Bake in a 375° oven 25 minutes. Remove foil. Bake 20 to 25 minutes more or until top is golden and filling is bubbly. Cool completely on rack.

Nutrition Facts per serving: 409 cal., 18 g total fat (4 g sat. fat), 0 mg chol., 136 mg sodium, 61 g carbo., 4 g fiber, 4 g pro. Daily Values: 2% vit. A, 51% vit. C, 3% calcium, 10% iron

The Starch Switch for Frozen Pies

Fruit pies freeze well as long as you choose the right starch to thicken the filling. Quick-cooking tapioca is the best choice because, unlike cornstarch and flour, it keeps its thickening power when frozen. To thicken pies with tapioca in place of flour or cornstarch, follow these guidelines:

● For every 2 tablespoons of flour, use 1 tablespoon quick-cooking tapioca.

● For every 4 teaspoons of cornstarch, use 1 tablespoon quick-cooking tapioca.

Candy Bar Pie

Prep: 30 minutes **Cool:** 1 hour **Freeze:** 5 hours **Makes:** 8 to 10 servings

6 1- to 1¾-ounce bars milk chocolate with almonds, chopped	1 cup whipping cream
15 marshmallows or 1½ cups tiny marshmallows	½ teaspoon vanilla Whipped cream
½ cup milk	Coarsely chopped milk chocolate bars with almonds
1 recipe Walnut Crust (below)	

1 For filling, in a medium saucepan combine the 6 chopped chocolate bars, the marshmallows, and milk. Heat and stir over medium-low heat until chocolate is melted. Remove from heat. Let the chocolate mixture stand until cooled to room temperature (about 1 hour). Meanwhile, prepare Walnut Crust. Chill a large bowl and the beaters for an electric mixer.

2 In the chilled bowl beat the 1 cup cream and the vanilla with an electric mixer on medium speed just until soft peaks form (tips curl). Fold whipped cream mixture into cooled chocolate mixture. Spoon chocolate mixture into Walnut Crust. Freeze pie at least 5 hours or until firm.

3 To serve, let pie stand at room temperature about 10 minutes to soften slightly. Cut pie into wedges.* Top each serving with additional whipped cream and chopped chocolate bars.

Walnut Crust: In a medium bowl combine 1½ cups coarsely ground walnuts (6 ounces); 3 tablespoons butter or margarine, melted; and 2 tablespoons sugar. Press onto the bottom and side of a 9-inch pie plate to form a firm, even crust. Bake in a 325° oven about 10 minutes or until edge is golden. Cool on a wire rack.

Nutrition Facts per serving: 563 cal., 43 g total fat (19 g sat. fat), 69 mg chol., 105 mg sodium, 36 g carbo., 2 g fiber, 11 g pro. Daily Values: 16% vit. A, 2% vit. C, 13% calcium, 7% iron

*****Note:** For easier serving, set the pie on a warm, damp towel for several minutes before cutting the first wedge.

Definitely an indulgence, this treat is the choice when having dessert lovers over for dinner. It's tempting to cut corners by using a pastry crust, but it's the walnut crust that makes this pie exquisite.

To Make Ahead

Prepare Candy Bar Pie as directed through step 2. When firmly frozen, wrap pie in moisture- and vaporproof wrap or store in a freezer container. Seal, label, and freeze up to 1 week.

To Serve

Serve as directed.

To Make Ahead

Prepare Margarita Pie as directed through step 4. When firmly frozen, wrap pie in moisture- and vaporproof wrap or store in a freezer container. Seal, label, and freeze up to 1 week.

To Serve

Serve as directed.

Margarita Pie

Prep: 40 minutes **Bake:** 13 minutes **Freeze:** 4½ hours **Stand:** 20 minutes **Makes:** 8 servings

1 15-ounce package (2 crusts) folded refrigerated unbaked piecrust	⅓ cup frozen margarita mix concentrate, thawed
1 teaspoon all-purpose flour	2 tablespoons tequila (optional)
3 cups vanilla ice cream	1½ cups lime sherbet
	Lime slices (optional)

1 Let refrigerated piecrust stand at room temperature according to package directions. Trim 1 of the piecrusts to a 9-inch circle. Sprinkle 1 side of the circle with the flour. Center the circle, flour side down, in the bottom of a 9-inch pie plate. Using a 2-inch fluted round cutter, cut remaining piecrust into 20 rounds. Brush edge of crust in pie plate with water. Arrange and overlap the 2-inch rounds around edge of piecrust to form an edge; press rounds to the edge of piecrust circle to seal. Using a fork, prick the bottom and side of the piecrust.

2 Line pastry with a double thickness of foil. Bake in a 450° oven for 8 minutes. Remove foil; bake 5 to 6 minutes more or until golden. Cool completely on a wire rack. In a chilled medium bowl stir ice cream just enough to soften. Stir in margarita mix concentrate. Return to freezer; freeze about 30 minutes or until nearly firm.

3 Meanwhile, if desired, stir tequila into lime sherbet. Return to freezer; freeze about 30 minutes or until nearly firm.

4 To assemble pie, randomly drop spoonfuls of lime sherbet into ice cream mixture, folding with a spatula just to marble slightly. Do not overmix. If mixture seems soft, return to freezer and freeze until nearly firm. Gently transfer ice cream mixture to the baked piecrust. Cover; freeze at least 4 hours or until firm.

5 To serve, let pie stand at room temperature about 20 minutes to soften slightly. Cut into wedges. If desired, garnish with lime slices.

Nutrition Facts per serving: 416 cal., 20 g total fat (10 g sat. fat), 33 mg chol., 253 mg sodium, 57 g carbo., 0 g fiber, 3 g pro. Daily Values: 5% vit. A, 6% vit. C, 8% calcium, 1% iron

The sweetness of the apples mellows the rhubarb, while the rhubarb's tartness perks up the apple flavor. This recipe makes eight individual tarts, so you can bake as many as needed and keep the rest frozen.

To Make Ahead

Prepare Rhubarb Hand Tarts as directed through step 5, except bake for 20 minutes; cool. Arrange on a baking sheet in a single layer. Cover and freeze until firm. Transfer to freezer container or self-sealing freezer bag. Seal, label, and freeze up to 4 months.

To Serve

Line a large baking sheet with foil; grease foil. Remove frozen tarts from freezer container or bag. Arrange on prepared baking sheet. Cover with foil. Bake in a 375° oven for 10 minutes. Uncover; bake 10 to 15 minutes more or until filling is bubbly and pastry is golden. Serve as directed.

Rhubarb Hand Tarts

Prep: 50 minutes **Bake:** 30 minutes **Cool:** 30 minutes **Makes:** 8 tarts

1 cup granulated sugar
2 tablespoons quick-cooking tapioca
1 teaspoon grated fresh ginger
  Dash ground nutmeg
3 cups ½-inch slices fresh rhubarb or
  frozen sliced rhubarb

1 cup sliced, peeled tart apples
1 recipe Pastry for Double-Crust Pie
  (page 163)
Milk
Coarse sugar

1 In a large saucepan stir together granulated sugar, tapioca, ginger, and nutmeg. Stir in rhubarb and apples until coated; let stand about 15 minutes or until a syrup begins to form, stirring occasionally. Cover and cook over medium heat about 15 minutes or just until fruit is softened, stirring occasionally. Remove from heat. Cool filling completely.

2 Prepare Pastry for Double-Crust Pie; divide in half. On a lightly floured surface roll out each portion to a 12-inch square. Cut each portion into four 6-inch squares.

3 Line a large baking sheet with foil; grease foil and set aside. Spoon about ¼ cup of the cooked rhubarb mixture onto half of one pastry square, leaving a 1-inch border around edges of pastry. Brush edges of square with water. Fold pastry over filling, forming a rectangle or triangle. Press edges gently to seal. Brush edges lightly with water again. Fold edges up and over about ¼ inch. Press edges with tines of a fork to seal again.

4 Place tart on prepared baking sheet. Repeat with remaining squares of pastry and remaining rhubarb mixture. Prick top of each 2 or 3 times with the tines of a fork to let steam escape. Gently pat down top to get rid of excess air around filling. Brush tops with milk; sprinkle with coarse sugar.

5 Bake in a 375° oven for 30 to 35 minutes or until golden. Remove tarts from baking sheet and cool on a wire rack about 30 minutes. Serve warm.

Nutrition Facts per tart: 382 cal., 18 g total fat (4 g sat. fat), 0 mg chol., 137 mg sodium, 54 g carbo., 2 g fiber, 3 g pro. Daily Values: 1% vit. A, 7% vit. C, 5% calcium, 8% iron

Berry Icebox Dessert

Prep: 1½ hours **Chill:** 8 hours **Makes:** 9 servings

1½ cups coarsely crushed crisp
    chocolate chip cookies
	2 cups chilled white grape juice or
	    lemonade

3 tablespoons butter, melted	1 8-ounce package cream cheese, softened
1⅓ cups boiling water	½ cup whipping cream

1 6-ounce package or two 3-ounce
    packages sparkling wild-berry-
    flavored gelatin
	Fresh strawberries (optional)
	    Mint sprigs (optional)

1 In a medium bowl stir together crushed cookies and butter. Line an 8×8×2-inch baking pan with heavy foil. Press crumbs into bottom of foil-lined pan; set aside.

2 In a large bowl combine boiling water and gelatin; stir until gelatin dissolves. Stir in the chilled grape juice or lemonade. Chill in refrigerator until partially set (the consistency of unbeaten egg whites).

3 Meanwhile, in a large bowl beat cream cheese until fluffy. With electric mixer on low speed, gradually beat in partially set gelatin. Wash beaters; chill. Chill a small bowl.

4 In the chilled small bowl beat whipping cream with chilled beaters of an electric mixer on medium speed until soft peaks form (tips curl); fold into gelatin mixture. Chill again until mixture mounds when spooned.

5 Turn gelatin mixture into crumb-lined pan. Cover and chill in refrigerator about 8 hours or until firm.

6 Using foil, lift dessert from pan. To serve, cut dessert into squares. If desired, garnish with fresh strawberries and mint sprigs.

Nutrition Facts per serving: 329 cal., 20 g total fat (12 g sat. fat), 58 mg chol., 205 mg sodium, 35 g carbo., 1 g fiber, 5 g pro. Daily Values: 20% vit. A, 5% vit. C, 3% calcium, 4% iron

Kids especially love this dessert. It starts with a chocolate chip cookie crumb crust and keeps getting better from there, with whipped cream and cream cheese folded into sparkling wild-berry gelatin.

To Make Ahead

Prepare Berry Icebox Dessert as directed through step 5, except chill in refrigerator up to 24 hours.

To Serve

Serve as directed.

Lemon Poppyseed Shortcakes

Prep: 25 minutes **Bake:** 12 minutes **Makes:** 12 servings

Think of how nice it will be to have a batch of these tender, lemony shortcakes on hand in the freezer. With the shortcakes out of the way, choose whatever fruit strikes your fancy at the market and come home to quickly put together the quintessential summer dessert.

To Make Ahead

Prepare Lemon Poppyseed Shortcakes as directed through step 1. Place shortcakes on a baking sheet; freeze until firm. Place in self-sealing freezer bags or wrap in heavy foil. Seal, label, and freeze up to 3 months.

To Serve

Remove shortcakes from freezer bags or wrap. To thaw, let stand at room temperature for 1 hour. Assemble and serve as directed.

1	15.6-ounce package lemon poppyseed quick bread mix
3	tablespoons butter
1	slightly beaten egg
⅓	cup buttermilk or sour milk (see tip below)
8	cups assorted fresh fruits (such as sliced nectarines; peeled, sliced peaches; sliced strawberries; sliced bananas; and/or blueberries)
¼	cup strawberry jelly
½	cup whipping cream, whipped

1 Pour bread mix into a large bowl. Using a pastry blender, cut in butter until mixture resembles coarse crumbs. Combine egg and buttermilk; add to dry mixture. Stir just until moistened. Drop the batter into 12 mounds, 2 inches apart, on greased large baking sheet. Bake in a 400° oven for 12 to 15 minutes or until golden. Transfer shortcakes to a wire rack and cool completely.

2 Meanwhile, in a large bowl combine the fruits. In a small saucepan heat the jelly over low heat just until melted, stirring frequently. Pour jelly over fruits, tossing gently to mix.

3 To serve, place each shortcake in an individual bowl. Divide fruit mixture evenly among bowls and top with whipped cream.

Nutrition Facts per serving: 294 cal., 12 g total fat (5 g sat. fat), 5 mg chol., 198 mg sodium, 44 g carbo., 2 g fiber, 4 g pro. Daily Values: 11% vit. A, 28% vit. C, 4% calcium, 8% iron

Making Sour Milk

When you don't have buttermilk on hand to use in a recipe, substitute sour milk instead. For 1 cup sour milk, place 1 tablespoon lemon juice or vinegar in a glass measuring cup. Add enough milk to make 1 cup liquid; stir. Let the mixture stand for 5 minutes before using it.

Chocolate-Peanut Butter Pudding Cake

Prep: 15 minutes **Cook:** 2 hours **Stand:** 30 minutes **Makes:** 8 servings

1 cup all-purpose flour	¾ cup peanut butter-flavored pieces
½ cup sugar	¾ cup sugar
2 tablespoons unsweetened cocoa powder	¼ cup unsweetened cocoa powder
1½ teaspoons baking powder	2 cups boiling water
½ cup milk	½ cup chunky peanut butter
2 tablespoons cooking oil	2 tablespoons chopped unsalted dry-roasted peanuts
1 teaspoon vanilla	Vanilla ice cream (optional)

1 In a medium bowl stir together flour, the ½ cup sugar, the 2 tablespoons cocoa powder, and the baking powder. Add milk, oil, and vanilla; stir until batter is smooth. Stir in the peanut butter-flavored pieces. Spread batter evenly in the bottom of a greased 3½- or 4-quart electric crockery cooker.

2 In another medium bowl combine the ¾ cup sugar and the ¼ cup cocoa powder. Stir together boiling water and peanut butter; stir into the cocoa mixture. Pour evenly over the batter in the crockery cooker.

3 Cover; cook on high-heat setting for 2 to 2½ hours or until a toothpick inserted 1 inch into the center of the cake comes out clean. Let stand, uncovered, 30 to 40 minutes to cool slightly.

4 To serve, spoon pudding cake into dessert dishes. Sprinkle with peanuts. If desired, serve with ice cream.

Nutrition Facts per serving: 417 cal., 18 g total fat (4 g sat. fat), 1 mg chol., 196 mg sodium, 56 g carbo., 2 g fiber, 10 g pro. Daily Values: 1% vit. C, 12% calcium, 12% iron

T his pudding cake is a dessert lover's dream. A warm chocolate-peanut butter pudding develops under the cake layer as it bakes in a crockery cooker. Served with ice cream, it is the best!

The time-honored English trifle traditionally layers cake, jam, and custard. Paying tribute to today's fresh-is-best approach, we've substituted fresh fruit for the jam, making the dessert a wonderful way to show off fresh berries.

To Make Ahead

Prepare cake layers for Strawberry Crown Trifle as directed through step 1. Place layers on a baking sheet. Freeze until firm. Place each layer in a self-sealing freezer bag or wrap in moisture- and vaporproof wrap. Seal, label, and freeze up to 3 months.

To Serve

Remove layers from freezer bags or wrap. Thaw at room temperature. Assemble and serve as directed.

Strawberry Crown Trifle

Prep: 45 minutes **Bake:** 20 minutes **Chill:** 8 to 24 hours **Makes:** 12 servings

1 cup sifted cake flour	1 teaspoon vanilla
1 teaspoon baking powder	3 pints fresh strawberries
¼ teaspoon salt	3 tablespoons sugar
½ cup milk	⅓ cup orange liqueur or orange juice
2 tablespoons butter	1 recipe Fluffy Filling (below)
2 eggs	Whipped cream
1 cup sugar	Fresh mint (optional)

1 In a medium bowl combine the cake flour, baking powder, and salt. In a small saucepan heat milk and butter until butter melts; keep hot. In a large bowl beat eggs with an electric mixer on high speed for 3 to 4 minutes or until thick and lemon-colored. Gradually add the 1 cup sugar, beating constantly on medium speed for 4 to 5 minutes. Add flour mixture to egg mixture; stir just until combined. Stir in hot milk mixture and vanilla. Turn batter into two greased and floured 8×1½-inch round baking pans. Bake in a 350° oven about 20 minutes or until a toothpick inserted near centers comes out clean. Cool on wire racks for 10 minutes; remove from pans. Cool completely.

2 Set aside a few strawberries for garnish; crush enough remaining berries to make 2 cups. Stir the 3 tablespoons sugar into crushed berries. To assemble, split cake layers in half horizontally to make 4 layers. Fit 1 layer into bottom of a 2-quart soufflé dish (8 inches in diameter); spread 1 cup of the crushed berries over. Top with second cake layer; sprinkle with half of the liqueur. Spread with Fluffy Filling. Place third cake layer on top; spread with remaining crushed berries. Sprinkle cut side of fourth cake layer with remaining liqueur; place cake, cut side down, over berries in dish. Cover; refrigerate at least 8 hours or up to 24 hours. To serve, top with whipped cream and reserved berries. If desired, garnish with fresh mint.

Fluffy Filling: In a medium saucepan combine ⅓ cup sugar, 1 tablespoon cornstarch, and ⅛ teaspoon salt. Stir in 1 cup milk. Cook and stir over medium heat until bubbly. Slowly stir ½ cup of the hot mixture into 2 beaten egg yolks. Return mixture to saucepan. Cook and stir 2 minutes more. Remove from heat. Stir in 1 tablespoon butter and 1 teaspoon vanilla. Cover surface with plastic wrap; refrigerate until completely chilled. Just before assembling trifle, in a small bowl beat ½ cup whipping cream until soft peaks form (tips curl); fold into chilled mixture.

Nutrition Facts per serving: 304 cal., 13 g total fat (7 g sat. fat), 109 mg chol., 173 mg sodium, 41 g carbo., 2 g fiber, 4 g pro. Daily Values: 12 vit. A, 69% vit. C, 9% calcium, 7% iron

Your crockery cooker is the perfect partner for creating this make-ahead dessert. Simply put all the ingredients in the cooker before you leave home. The bread pudding steams unattended for 4 hours, so you return home to an out-of-this-world taste treat.

Cranberry Bread Pudding

Prep: 25 minutes   **Cook:** 2 to 4 hours   **Makes:** 6 servings

1½ cups half-and-half or light cream
½ of a 6-ounce package (3 ounces) white baking bars or squares, coarsely chopped
⅓ cup snipped dried cranberries or dried cherries
2 beaten eggs

½ cup sugar
½ teaspoon ground ginger
3 cups dry ½-inch bread cubes (about 4½ slices)
¼ cup coarsely chopped pecans or hazelnuts (filberts)
   Whipped cream (optional)

1 In a small saucepan heat half-and-half over medium heat until very warm but not boiling. Remove from heat; add chopped white baking bars and cranberries. Stir until baking bars are melted.

2 In a medium bowl combine eggs, sugar, and ginger. Whisk in the cream mixture. Gently stir in bread cubes and nuts. Pour mixture into a 1-quart soufflé dish (dish will be full). Cover the dish tightly with foil.

3 Pour 1 cup warm water into a 3½-, 4-, or 5-quart electric crockery cooker. Tear off an 18×12-inch piece of heavy foil. Cut in half lengthwise. Fold each foil piece into thirds lengthwise. Crisscross the foil strips and place the soufflé dish in the center of the foil cross. Bringing up foil strips, lift the ends of the strips to transfer the dish and foil to the cooker. (Leave foil strips under dish.)

4 Cover; cook on low-heat setting for 4 hours or on high-heat setting for 2 hours. Using the foil strips, carefully lift dish out of cooker. Serve warm. If desired, top each serving with whipped cream and sprinkle with grated white baking bar and additional ground ginger.

Nutrition Facts per serving: 360 cal., 17 g total fat (8 g sat. fat), 98 mg chol., 177 mg sodium, 45 g carbo., 1 g fiber, 7 g pro. Daily Values: 11% vit. A, 1% vit. C, 9% calcium, 7% iron

Chocolate-Raspberry Cheesecake

Prep: 30 minutes **Bake:** 50 minutes **Cool:** 1¾ hours **Chill:** 4 to 24 hours
Makes: 16 servings

1½ cups finely crushed graham crackers
¼ cup sifted powdered sugar
⅓ cup butter, melted
3 8-ounce packages cream cheese
2 cups fresh or loose-pack frozen
      raspberries, thawed
½ teaspoon granulated sugar

1 14-ounce can sweetened condensed
      milk
4 eggs
1 teaspoon vanilla
1 cup semisweet chocolate pieces
      (6 ounces), melted and cooled

1 For crust, combine crushed graham crackers and powdered sugar; stir in butter. Press onto bottom and 2 inches up side of a 9-inch springform pan. Set aside. For filling, soften cream cheese. In a small bowl combine 1 cup of the raspberries and the granulated sugar; set aside. In a large bowl beat cream cheese and sweetened condensed milk with an electric mixer on low speed until combined. Add eggs and vanilla; beat just until combined. Divide batter in half. Stir melted chocolate into half. Pour chocolate batter into the crust-lined pan. Stir raspberry-sugar mixture into remaining batter. Spoon raspberry batter over chocolate batter. Place springform pan on shallow baking pan.

2 Bake in a 350° oven for 50 to 60 minutes or until center appears nearly set when pan is gently shaken. Cool in pan on a wire rack 15 minutes. Loosen crust from side of pan. Cool 30 minutes. Remove side of pan; cool about 1 hour or until cooled completely.

3 Cover; chill in refrigerator at least 4 hours or up to 24 hours before serving. Serve with remaining raspberries.

Nutrition Facts per serving: 382 cal., 26 g total fat (14 g sat. fat), 119 mg chol., 257 mg sodium, 32 g carbo., 1 g fiber, 8 g pro. Daily Values: 27% vit. A, 7% vit. C, 10% calcium, 9% iron

This cheesecake is so rich and decadent, it yields 16 servings. Not serving that many? Place each leftover piece in a freezer bag and store in the freezer up to 2 weeks. To serve, thaw each piece at room temperature for 20 to 30 minutes.

To Make Ahead

Prepare Chocolate-Raspberry Cheesecake as directed through step 2. (You'll use only 1 cup of the raspberries.) Place cooled, whole cheesecake in a freezer container or self-sealing freezer bag. Seal, label, and freeze up to 1 month.

To Serve

Thaw cheesecake, covered, in refrigerator overnight. Serve with 1 cup raspberries.

Bring Home the Berries

Collect a bounty of berries from the farmers' market and stash them in the freezer for a sweet touch of summer later in the year. To freeze berries, arrange washed, stemmed berries on a baking sheet. Freeze solid; transfer to freezer containers, leaving ½-inch headspace. Freeze berries up to 1 year.

This is it—the creamy and traditional version beloved by cheesecake purists. Though it's great on its own, consider serving it with a selection of fruit sauces (sometimes called "coulis") available in gourmet grocery stores or fancy food catalogs.

To Make Ahead

Prepare Classic New York-Style Cheesecake as directed through step 5. Place cooled cheesecake in a freezer container or self-sealing freezer bag. Seal, label, and freeze up to 1 month.

To Serve

Thaw cheesecake, covered, in refrigerator overnight.

Classic New York-Style Cheesecake

Prep: 45 minutes **Bake:** 55 minutes **Cool:** 2 hours **Chill:** 4 to 24 hours **Stand:** 15 minutes
Makes: 16 servings

½ cup butter, softened	1¼ cups granulated sugar
¼ cup packed brown sugar	¼ cup all-purpose flour
4 eggs	4 teaspoons vanilla
1¼ cups all-purpose flour	2 8-ounce cartons dairy sour cream
4 8-ounce packages cream cheese, softened	¼ cup granulated sugar

1 For crust, in a large bowl beat butter with an electric mixer on medium speed for 30 seconds. Add brown sugar. Beat until fluffy. Beat in 1 of the eggs. Slowly beat in the 1¼ cups flour until mixed. Divide dough in half. Cover and refrigerate one portion. Spread remaining portion in bottom of an ungreased 10-inch springform pan with side removed. Place on a baking sheet. Bake in a 350° oven 10 minutes. Cool completely.

2 When bottom crust has cooled, attach side of pan. Press chilled dough onto side to a height of about 1¾ inches. Set aside.

3 Increase oven temperature to 450°. In a large bowl beat cream cheese and the 1¼ cups granulated sugar until fluffy. Beat in the ¼ cup flour on low speed until smooth. Add the remaining eggs and 1 tablespoon of the vanilla all at once, beating on low speed just until combined. Stir in ½ cup of the sour cream. Pour batter into the crust-lined pan. Place on a shallow baking pan in oven. Bake for 10 minutes.

4 Reduce oven temperature to 300°. Bake about 30 minutes more or until center appears nearly set when pan is gently shaken. Remove from oven. Combine remaining sour cream, the ¼ cup granulated sugar, and the remaining vanilla. Spread evenly over top of baked cheesecake. Return to oven and bake for 15 minutes more.

5 Remove from oven. Cool in pan on wire rack for 15 minutes. Loosen crust from side of pan. Cool for 30 minutes more. Remove side of pan; cool about 1¼ hours or until cooled completely.

6 Cover and chill in refrigerator at least 4 hours or up to 24 hours. Let stand at room temperature 15 minutes before slicing.

Nutrition Facts per serving: 455 cal., 33 g total fat (20 g sat. fat), 144 mg chol., 260 mg sodium, 33 g carbo., 0 g fiber, 8 g pro. Daily Values: 38% vit. A, 7% calcium, 9% iron

Made with paper-thin phyllo dough, walnut filling, and a glistening honey-lemon syrup, this traditional Greek sweet never fails to impress. To cut in traditional diamond shapes, make several cuts along the length of the baking pan, then make diagonal cuts crosswise. The corners and edges will yield odd-shaped pieces.

To Make Ahead

Prepare Baklava as directed. Place in an airtight container. Store at room temperature up to 3 days. (Or place in a freezer container. Seal, label, and freeze up to 1 month.)

To Serve

Thaw frozen Baklava at room temperature for 30 minutes.

Baklava

Prep: 45 minutes **Bake:** 35 minutes **Makes:** 60 pieces

4 cups finely chopped walnuts	1 cup water
2 cups sugar	¼ cup honey
1 teaspoon ground cinnamon	½ teaspoon finely shredded lemon peel
1¼ cups butter, melted	2 tablespoons lemon juice
1 16-ounce package frozen phyllo dough, thawed	2 inches stick cinnamon

1 For filling, in a large bowl stir together chopped walnuts, ½ cup of the sugar, and the ground cinnamon. Set aside.

2 Brush the bottom of a 15×10×1-inch baking pan with some of the melted butter. Unfold phyllo dough. Keep phyllo covered with plastic wrap, removing sheets as you need them. Layer one-fourth (about 5) of the phyllo sheets in the pan, generously brushing each sheet with melted butter as you layer, and allowing phyllo to extend up the sides of the pan. Sprinkle about 1⅓ cups of the filling on top of the phyllo. Repeat layering the phyllo sheets and filling 2 more times.

3 Layer remaining phyllo sheets on the third layer of filling, brushing each sheet with butter before adding the next phyllo sheet. Drizzle any remaining butter over the top. Trim edges of phyllo to fit the pan. Using a sharp knife, cut through all the layers to make 60 diamond-, triangle-, or square-shaped pieces.

4 Bake in a 325° oven for 35 to 45 minutes or until golden. Cool slightly in pan on a wire rack.

5 Meanwhile, for syrup, in a medium saucepan stir together the remaining sugar, the water, honey, lemon peel, lemon juice, and stick cinnamon. Bring to boiling; reduce heat. Simmer, uncovered, for 20 minutes. Remove cinnamon. Pour honey mixture over slightly cooled baklava in the pan. Cool completely.

Nutrition Facts per piece: 138 cal., 9 g total fat (13 g sat. fat), 10 mg chol., 76 mg sodium, 13 g carbo., 0 g fiber, 2 g pro. Daily Values: 1% vit. C, 1% calcium, 3% iron

Chocolate and Peanut Butter Bars

Prep: 20 minutes **Bake:** 27 minutes **Makes:** 48 bars

2 cups quick-cooking rolled oats	1 12-ounce package (2 cups) semisweet
1¾ cups packed brown sugar	chocolate pieces
1 cup all-purpose flour	1 beaten egg
½ cup whole wheat flour	1 14-ounce can sweetened condensed
1 teaspoon baking powder	milk or low-fat sweetened
½ teaspoon baking soda	condensed milk
1 cup butter	⅓ cup creamy peanut butter
½ cup chopped peanuts	

1 For crumb mixture, in a large bowl combine oats, brown sugar, all-purpose flour, whole wheat flour, baking powder, and baking soda. Using a pastry blender, cut in the butter until mixture resembles fine crumbs. Stir in peanuts. For topping, combine 1¾ cups of the crumb mixture and the chocolate pieces; set aside.

2 For crust, stir the egg into the remaining crumb mixture. Press into bottom of an ungreased 15×10×1-inch baking pan. Bake in a 350° oven 15 minutes. Meanwhile, for filling, stir together sweetened condensed milk and peanut butter until smooth.

3 Pour filling over partially baked crust. Sprinkle topping evenly over filling. Bake 12 to 15 minutes more or until light brown around the edges. Cool completely in pan on a wire rack. Cut into bars.

Nutrition Facts per bar: 177cal., 9 g total fat (4 g sat. fat), 18 mg chol., 92 mg sodium, 21 g carbo., 2 g fiber, 3 g pro. Daily Values: 4% vit. A, 4% calcium, 3% iron

A chewy oat crust, a creamy peanut butter filling, and a chocolate chip-crumb topping—is this bar-cookie heaven?

To Make Ahead

Prepare Chocolate and Peanut Butter Bars as directed through step 3. Place cut bars in a freezer container or a self-sealing freezer bag. Seal, label, and freeze up to 1 month.

To Serve

Thaw, covered, at room temperature.

Phyllo Dough Know-How

Phyllo dough gives baklava its characteristic flaky layers. Fortunately, these layers are easier to achieve than they look. Follow these tips:
- **Allow frozen phyllo dough to thaw while it is still wrapped and sealed.**
- **Once unwrapped, sheets of phyllo dough dry out quickly and crumble. Keep the opened sheets of dough covered with plastic wrap until needed.**
- **Brush each sheet with melted butter or oil as directed in the recipe.**
- **Rewrap remaining sheets of dough and return them to the freezer.**

Toasted Hazelnut Bars

Prep: 15 minutes **Bake:** 50 minutes **Makes:** 48 bars

½ cup butter, softened
2 3-ounce packages cream cheese,
    softened
½ cup packed brown sugar
2 cups all-purpose flour
2 cups granulated sugar
1½ cups buttermilk or sour milk
    (see tip, page 214)
4 eggs

½ cup butter, melted
⅓ cup all-purpose flour
2 teaspoons vanilla
½ teaspoon salt
2 cups toasted chopped hazelnuts
    (filberts)
   Sifted powdered sugar

1 For crust, in a large bowl beat the ½ cup softened butter and the cream cheese with an electric mixer on medium to high speed until smooth. Beat in brown sugar until combined. Beat in the 2 cups flour until combined. (The mixture will be crumbly.) With lightly floured hands, pat mixture onto the bottom and up sides of an ungreased 15×10×1-inch baking pan. Bake in a 350° oven about 15 minutes or until light golden.

2 Meanwhile, for filling, in a medium bowl beat together granulated sugar, buttermilk, eggs, the ½ cup melted butter, the ⅓ cup flour, the vanilla, and salt with an electric mixer on low speed until combined. Stir in nuts. Pour filling over baked layer.

3 Bake about 35 minutes more or until golden. Cool completely in pan on a wire rack. Cut into bars. Sprinkle with powdered sugar. Store bars in the refrigerator.

Nutrition Facts per bar: 155 cal., 9 g total fat (4 g sat. fat), 33 mg chol., 90 mg sodium, 16 g carbo., 1 g fiber, 3 g pro. Daily Values: 5% vit. A, 1% vit. C, 2% calcium, 4% iron

Toasty Nuts

Toasting heightens the flavor of nuts. Spread the nuts in a single layer in a shallow baking pan. Bake in a 350° oven for 5 to 10 minutes or until light golden, stirring once or twice to brown evenly. To toast nuts in the microwave, place nuts in a 2-cup microwave-safe measure. Micro-cook on 100% power (high) until golden, stirring after 2 minutes, then stirring every 30 seconds.

S erve this sophisticated bar with its rich cream cheese crust and buttery hazelnut filling with the best cup of coffee you can find.
Toasting the hazelnuts will help you remove the skins. To remove the skins, place the warm nuts on a clean kitchen towel and rub vigorously until the skins come off.

To Make Ahead

Prepare Toasted Hazelnut Bars as directed through step 3, except do not sprinkle cut bars with powdered sugar. Place cut bars in an airtight container. Refrigerate up to 3 days. (Or place cut bars in a freezer container or self-sealing freezer bag. Seal, label, and freeze up to 1 month.)

To Serve

Thaw frozen bars, covered, at room temperature. To serve, sprinkle refrigerated or thawed bars with powdered sugar.

Keep a batch of these chewy and spicy supersized cookies in the freezer, and you'll have something on hand to tuck into the lunchboxes of very special people.

To Make Ahead

Prepare Giant Cherry-Oatmeal Cookies as directed through step 3. Transfer to self-sealing freezer bags or arrange in layers separated by waxed paper in a freezer container. Seal, label, and freeze up to 3 months.

To Serve

Thaw cookies in bags or container for 15 minutes at room temperature.

Giant Cherry-Oatmeal Cookies

Prep: 20 minutes **Bake:** 8 minutes per batch **Makes:** 14 cookies

½ cup shortening	¼ teaspoon salt
½ cup butter	2 eggs
¾ cup packed brown sugar	1 teaspoon vanilla
½ cup granulated sugar	1⅓ cups all-purpose flour
2 teaspoons apple pie spice or pumpkin pie spice	2½ cups regular rolled oats
	1½ cups snipped dried tart cherries or raisins
½ teaspoon baking powder	
¼ teaspoon baking soda	1 teaspoon finely shredded orange peel

1 In a large bowl beat shortening and butter with an electric mixer on medium to high speed for 30 seconds. Add brown sugar, granulated sugar, pie spice, baking powder, baking soda, and salt; beat until combined, scraping side of bowl occasionally. Beat in eggs and vanilla. Beat in flour. Stir in oats, dried cherries, and orange peel.

2 Fill a ⅓-cup dry measure with dough; drop onto a greased cookie sheet. Press into a 4-inch circle. Repeat with the remaining dough, placing cookies 3 inches apart.

3 Bake in a 375° oven for 8 to 10 minutes or until edges are golden. Let stand on cookie sheet 1 minute. Transfer cookies to wire racks; cool completely.

Nutrition Facts per cookie: 360 cal., 16 g total fat (6 g sat. fat), 49 mg chol., 163 mg sodium, 49 g carbo., 3 g fiber, 5 g pro. Daily Values: 6% vit. A, 1% vit. C, 4% calcium, 9% iron

Crackled Sugar Cookies

Prep: 25 minutes **Bake:** 18 minutes per batch **Makes:** 48 cookies

½ **cup butter, softened**	⅛ **teaspoon salt**
½ **cup shortening**	3 **egg yolks**
2 **cups sugar**	1 **tablespoon milk**
1 **teaspoon cream of tartar**	½ **teaspoon vanilla**
½ **teaspoon baking soda**	2 **cups all-purpose flour**

1 In a large bowl beat butter and shortening with an electric mixer on medium to high speed for 30 seconds. Add sugar, cream of tartar, baking soda, and salt: beat until combined, scraping side of bowl occasionally. Beat in egg yolks, milk, and vanilla until combined. Beat in as much of the flour as you can with the mixer. Using a wooden spoon, stir in any remaining flour. If necessary, knead dough until smooth.

2 Shape dough into 1-inch balls. Place balls 2 inches apart on an ungreased cookie sheet. Bake in a 300° oven about 18 minutes or until tops are slightly crackled and cookies are lightly browned. Let stand on cookie sheet for 1 minute. Transfer cookies to wire racks; cool completely.

Nutrition Facts per cookie: 90 cal., 4 g total fat (2 g sat. fat), 19 mg chol., 41 mg sodium, 12 g carbo., 0 g fiber, 1 g pro. Daily Values: 2% vit. A, 2% iron

E ven though these buttery cookies bake longer and at a lower oven temperature than most other cookies, they need to be watched carefully. To keep them tender, bake them just until light brown.

To Make Ahead

Prepare Crackled Sugar Cookies as directed through step 1. Shape dough into 1-inch balls. Arrange balls in a single layer on an ungreased cookie sheet. Cover and freeze 1 to 2 hours or until firm. Transfer balls to a self-sealing freezer bag or a freezer container. Seal, label, and freeze up to 3 months.

To Serve

Place frozen dough balls 2 inches apart on an ungreased cookie sheet. Bake in a 300° oven about 20 minutes or until tops are slightly crackled and cookies are lightly browned. Let stand on cookie sheet 1 minute. Transfer cookies to wire racks; cool completely.

Cookie-Less No More!

Great news for cookie lovers. Because baked cookies keep well—up to 3 days at room temperature and 3 months frozen, there's no need to ever go without cookies again. Follow these guidelines:

● **To store cookies short term, cool completely. In an airtight container, arrange unfrosted or frosted cookies in a single layer or in layers separated by sheets of waxed paper. Do not mix soft and crisp cookies in the same container—this can cause the crisp cookies to soften. If cookies are frosted with a cream cheese or yogurt icing, refrigerate them.**

● **To store cookies long-term, cool completely. Pack in a self-sealing freezer bag or freezer container. Before serving, thaw them in the bag or container about 15 minutes. If the cookies are to be frosted, glazed, or sprinkled with sugar, wait until they have thawed to decorate them.**

Try using a different flavor for each sandwich or even two different ice creams in one sandwich. That way, you can keep everyone's favorite on hand in the freezer.

To Make Ahead

Prepare Choose-Your-Own Ice Creamwiches as directed. Place wrapped sandwiches in a self-sealing freezer bag. Seal, label, and freeze up to 1 month.

To Serve

Let stand at room temperature 5 minutes.

Choose-Your-Own Ice Creamwiches

Prep: 30 minutes **Bake:** 7 minutes per batch **Freeze:** 2 hours **Makes:** 18 sandwiches

½   cup butter
⅓   cup granulated sugar
¼   cup packed dark brown sugar
1½ teaspoons unsweetened cocoa
      powder
¼   teaspoon baking powder
 1   egg
½   teaspoon vanilla
1½ ounces unsweetened chocolate,
      melted and cooled slightly

1   cup plus 2 tablespoons all-purpose
      flour
     Miniature chocolate-covered,
       cream-filled mint patties and/or
       assorted candies
1   pint vanilla or other flavor ice cream

1 In a large bowl beat butter with an electric mixer on medium to high speed for 30 seconds. Beat in granulated sugar, brown sugar, cocoa powder, and baking powder just until combined. Beat in egg and vanilla. Stir in melted chocolate.

2 Beat in as much of the flour as you can with the mixer. Using a wooden spoon, stir in remaining flour. Drop dough by slightly rounded teaspoons, 2 inches apart, onto an ungreased cookie sheet. Spread each dough portion to about 2 inches in diameter.

3 Bake in a 350° oven for 7 to 8 minutes or until edges are firm. Immediately (while still warm) top half of the cookies with the chocolate-covered mints or candies. Transfer cookies to a wire rack; cool completely.

4 To assemble, let ice cream stand at room temperature for 10 minutes to soften slightly. Place about 2 tablespoons ice cream on the flat side of each cookie without the candy topping. Carefully place the candy-topped cookies on top of the ice cream, candy sides up. Press each cookie gently in the center to slightly flatten sandwich. Wrap each sandwich in plastic wrap; freeze at least 2 hours. To serve, let stand at room temperature for 5 minutes.

Nutrition Facts per cookie sandwich: 149 cal., 8 g total fat (5 g sat. fat), 32 mg chol., 74 mg sodium, 18 g carbo., 0 g fiber, 2 g pro. Daily Values: 6% vit. A, 3% calcium, 4% iron

G elato, an irresistible
custard-like treat,
ranks at the top of rich and
creamy frozen desserts.
Whether served straight from
the ice cream freezer or
frozen up to 1 week ahead,
it takes ice cream lovers into
a whole new realm.

To Make Ahead

**Prepare Custard Cream
Gelato as directed
through step 3. Transfer
gelato to a freezer
container. Seal, label,
and freeze up to 1 week.**

To Serve

**Let stand at room
temperature about
20 minutes.**

Custard Cream Gelato

Prep: 25 minutes **Chill:** 6 to 24 hours **Freeze:** 40 minutes **Ripen:** 4 hours
Makes: about 2½ quarts (20 servings)

6 cups milk	1 tablespoon grated lemon or
1⅓ cups sugar	orange peel
12 beaten egg yolks	

1 In a large saucepan combine 3 cups of the milk, the sugar, and egg yolks. Cook and stir over medium heat until mixture just coats a metal spoon. Remove from the heat. Stir in remaining milk and lemon peel.

2 Cover the surface with plastic wrap. Chill in refrigerator at least 6 hours or up to 24 hours. (Or place the saucepan in a sink of ice water to chill quickly.)

3 Freeze in a 4- or 5-quart ice cream freezer according to the manufacturer's directions.

4 To ripen, remove lid and dasher; cover top of freezer can with waxed paper or foil. Plug the hole in lid with a small piece of cloth; replace lid. Pack outer freezer bucket with enough ice and rock salt to cover top of freezer can, using 4 cups ice to 1 cup salt. Let stand to ripen about 4 hours.

Nutrition Facts per serving: 122 cal., 4 g total fat (2 g sat. fat), 133 mg chol., 41 mg sodium, 16 g carbo., 0 g fiber, 4 g pro. Daily Values: 7% vit. A, 2% vit. C, 10% calcium, 2% iron

Strawberry Gelato: Prepare Custard Cream Gelato as directed, except omit lemon or orange peel. Place 3 cups cut-up strawberries in a blender container or food processor bowl. Cover and blend or process until nearly smooth. Stir strawberries and, if desired, several drops of red food coloring into cooked mixture. Chill, freeze, and ripen as directed.

Peach Gelato: Prepare Custard Cream Gelato as directed, except omit lemon or orange peel. Place 2 cups chopped, peeled, ripe peaches in a blender container or food processor bowl. Cover and blend or process until nearly smooth. Stir peaches and 1 cup peach nectar into the cooked mixture. Chill, freeze, and ripen as directed.

Index

Photographed recipes indicated in **bold**.

Home-Cooked Products

Below are guidelines for refrigerating and freezing home-baked and home-cooked products. Keep in mind that these are general guidelines only; specific instructions for individual recipes may vary. Follow the recipe's guidelines for safest and best results. For appropriate wrappings and containers for freezing and refrigerating, refer to pages 6–9. Thaw all frozen foods in the refrigerator unless otherwise specified.

Product	How to:	Refrigerate	Freeze
Breads, Yeast (baked)	See tip, page 77.	Not recommended.	Up to 3 months. Thaw at room temperature.
Breads, Quick (baked)	Place in self-sealing plastic bags; seal and store at room temperature up to 3 days. To freeze, wrap loaves tightly in heavy foil or place in self-sealing freezer bags.	Not recommended.	Up to 3 months. Wrap frozen loaves in heavy foil. Reheat in a 300° oven about 15 minutes.
Bread dough	Follow recipe through mixing and kneading stages. Form dough into a ball. Wrap in moisture- and vaporproof wrap or place in self-sealing freezer bags.	Chill dough up to 24 hours before shaping. Bring to room temperature before shaping.	Up to 3 months. Thaw dough for up to 2 hours at room temperature or overnight in the refrigerator. Shape and bake according to to recipe.
Cakes-unfrosted (layers, angel food, sponge, and chiffon cakes.)	To freeze, place cooled cake on a baking sheet; freeze until firm. Wrap and seal cake in moisture- and vaporproof wrap or place in freezer bags. Freeze angel food, sponge, and chiffon cakes unfrosted.	Not recommended unless recipe states to do so.	Up to 3 months. Thaw at room temperature.
Cakes-frosted (Buttercream and cream cheese frostings. *Note:* Do not freeze whipped cream frostings.)	To freeze, assemble and frost cake on base of a cake container with a tight-fitting lid or on a baking sheet. Freeze just until frosting is firm. Cover with appropriate wrap or container lid.	Up to 3 days.	Up to 2 weeks. Thaw, covered, at room temperature.
Casseroles-unbaked	Prepare according to recipe. Cool, if necessary. Cover with appropriate wrap. (See A Perfect Fit, page 9)	Up to 24 hours or as recipe directs.	Up to 3 months. Thaw and bake according to recipe.
Casseroles-baked	Prepare according to recipe, Cool. Cover with appropriate wrap. (See A Perfect Fit, page 9)	As recipe directs.	Up to 3 months. Thaw and bake according to recipe.

Product	How to:	Refrigerate	Freeze
Cheesecakes	To freeze, carefully transfer cooled cheesecake to a freezer-safe plate. Place whole cheesecake in a freezer bag. Or, place individual pieces in an airtight container.	Up to 3 days.	Up to 1 month (individual pieces up to 2 weeks). Thaw whole cheesecake in refrigerator overnight or pieces at room temperature 30 min.
Cookies-baked	See tip, page 227.	Up to 3 days.	Up to 3 months. To thaw, see tip, page 227.
Cookie dough	Transfer cookie dough to a freezer container or shape slice-and-bake cookies into rolls and wrap in moisture- and vaporproof wrap.	Up to 1 week.	Up to 3 months. Thaw frozen dough in refrigerator. If it is too stiff, let stand at room temperature.
Meat-cooked	Divide into smaller portions, if appropriate. Cool; wrap or place in appropriate container.	Up to 4 days.	Up to 3 months.
Poultry-cooked	Divide into smaller portions, if appropriate. Cool. Wrap or place in appropriate container.	Up to 4 days.	Up to 4 months.
Pies-baked, fruit	Cool completely. Cover with plastic wrap to refrigerate. Or, transfer to a self-sealing freezer bag to freeze.	Up to 3 days. (24 hours only if kept at room temperature.)	Up to 4 months. Thaw at room temperature. Reheat, covered, in a 325° oven.
Pies-unbaked, fruit	Assemble pie in a metal or freezer-to-oven pie plate. Place in a self-sealing freezer bag. If possible, use tapioca for thickener (see tip, page 208).	Not recommended.	Up to 4 months. Bake according to recipe or bake, covered, in a 450° oven for 15 min.; reduce temp. to 375° and bake 15 min. more. Uncover; bake 55 to 60 min. or until bubbly.
Pies-cream/custard	Cool; cover lightly with plastic wrap.	Up to 2 days.	Not recommended.
Pies-meringue	Cool 1 hour; cover loosely if chilling for longer than 6 hours.	Up to 2 days.	Not recommended.
Soups and Stews	Cool; divide into smaller portions. Transfer to appropriate containers.	Up to 4 days.	Up to 3 months.

Purchased Items

Sometimes the most time-consuming part of cooking is shopping for the ingredients. By keeping the pantry, refrigerator, and freezer well stocked, you can cut down on those last-minute trips to the store. Here are some guidelines regarding how to store commonly used ingredients.

Note: Thaw all frozen foods in the refrigerator unless otherwise specified.

Product	How to:	Refrigerate	Freeze
Dairy Products			
Butter	Refrigerate in original packaging; to freeze, overwrap with moisture- and vaporproof wrap.	1 month.	6 months.
Cheese	Do not remove rind, if present. Wrap cheese tightly in plastic wrap or foil.	Soft cheese: 5 days. Hard cheese: several weeks.	Soft cheese: 4 months. Hard cheese: 6 months.
Margarine	Refrigerate or freeze in original packaging.	4 to 5 months.	12 months.
Milk/Buttermilk	Refrigerate or freeze in original packaging.	7 days.	Milk: 3 months. Do not freeze buttermilk.
Sour cream	Refrigerate in original packaging.	7 days.	Do not freeze.
Yogurt	Refrigerate in original packaging.	7 days.	1 month.
Eggs			
Eggs, raw	Store whole eggs in carton placed in coldest part of refrigerator. Do not wash; do not store in the refrigerator door. Store whites and yolks in airtight freezer or refrigerator containers.	4 to 5 weeks (in shells). 2 to 4 days (whites/yolks).	Do not freeze whole eggs or yolks. whites: 12 months
Eggs, hard-cooked, in shells	Refrigerate uncovered.	7 days.	Do not freeze.
Meats, Poultry, and Fish			
Bacon	Refrigerate in original wrapping; overwrap in freezer wrap to freeze.	7 days.	1 to 2 months.
Sausage, raw	Refrigerate in original wrapping; overwrap in freezer wrap to freeze.	7 days.	1 to 2 months.
Sausage, smoked links/patties	Refrigerate in original wrapping; overwrap in freezer wrap to freeze.	1 to 2 days.	1 to 2 months.
Ham, cooked	Wrap in appropriate refrigerator wrap or in moisture- and vaporproof wrap to freeze.	7 days (whole). 3 to 5 days (half). 3 to 4 days (slices).	1 to 2 months.

Product	How to:	Refrigerate	Freeze
Ham, canned (keep refrigerated)	Chill, unopened, in original can or wrap in appropriate wrap.	6 to 9 months (in can). 3 to 5 days (after opening).	Do not freeze in can. 1 to 2 months.
Hot dogs/Lunch meats	Refrigerate in original wrapping; overwrap in freezer wrap to freeze.	2 weeks (unopened). 1 week (opened).	1 to 2 months.
Meat, uncooked roasts	Refrigerate in original wrapping; overwrap in freezer wrap to freeze.	3 to 5 days.	9 months.
Meat, uncooked steaks/chops/ground	Same as above.	3 to 5 days (steaks/chops). 1 to 2 days (ground).	4 to 6 months. 3 to 4 months.
Pre-stuffed pork, lamb, and chicken breasts	Refrigerate in original wrapping.	1 day.	Not recommended.
Poultry (chicken or turkey), uncooked whole	Refrigerate in original wrapping; overwrap in freezer wrap to freeze.	1 to 2 days.	12 months.
Poultry (chicken or turkey), uncooked pieces/ground	Refrigerate in original wrapping; overwrap in freezer wrap to freeze.	1 to 2 days.	9 months (pieces). 3 to 4 months (ground).
Fish	Store in moisture- and vaporproof wrap in coldest part of refrigerator.	1 to 2 days.	2 to 3 months.
Produce			
Garlic	Store in a cool, dark, dry place. Store whole garlic cloves up to 8 weeks; individual cloves 3 to 10 days. Discard shriveled, discolored, or dried-out cloves.	Do not refrigerate.	Do not freeze.
Onions and Shallots	Store in a cool, dry, well-ventilated place for up to 2 months (shallots for up to 1 month).	Do not refrigerate.	See tip, page 33, for freezing onions.
Potatoes and Root vegetables	Store for 2 to 3 weeks in a well-ventilated, cool, dark place.	Do not refrigerate.	Do not freeze.
Pantry Staples			
Olive oil or Cooking oil	Store at room temperature up to 6 months.		
Pasta and Rice, dry	Store at room temperature up to 6 months (brown rice) or 12 months (pasta and long grain rice).		
Instant chicken or beef granules	Store at room temperature up to 6 months.		
Dried herbs and spices	Store at room temperature up to 1 year. (See Spice Storage Smarts, page 34.)		

METRIC COOKING HINTS

By making a few conversions, cooks in Australia, Canada, and the United Kingdom can use the recipes in this book with confidence. The charts on this page provide a guide for converting measurements from the U.S. customary system, which is used throughout this book, to the imperial and metric systems. There also is a conversion table for oven temperatures to accommodate the differences in oven calibrations.

Product Differences: Most of the ingredients called for in the recipes in this book are available in English-speaking countries. However, some are known by different names. Here are some common U.S. American ingredients and their possible counterparts:
- Sugar is granulated or castor sugar.
- Powdered sugar is icing sugar.
- All-purpose flour is plain household flour or white flour. When self-rising flour is used in place of all-purpose flour in a recipe that calls for leavening, omit the leavening agent (baking soda or baking powder) and salt.
- Light-colored corn syrup is golden syrup.
- Cornstarch is cornflour.
- Baking soda is bicarbonate of soda.
- Vanilla is vanilla essence.
- Green, red, or yellow sweet peppers are capsicums.
- Golden raisins are sultanas.

Volume and Weight: U.S. Americans traditionally use cup measures for liquid and solid ingredients. The chart, top right, shows the approximate imperial and metric equivalents. If you are accustomed to weighing solid ingredients, the following approximate equivalents will help.
- 1 cup butter, castor sugar, or rice = 8 ounces = about 230 grams
- 1 cup flour = 4 ounces = about 115 grams
- 1 cup icing sugar = 5 ounces = about 140 grams

Spoon measures are used for smaller amounts of ingredients. Although the size of the tablespoon varies slightly in different countries, for practical purposes and for recipes in this book, a straight substitution is all that's necessary.

Measurements made using cups or spoons always should be level unless stated otherwise.

EQUIVALENTS: U.S. = AUSTRALIA/U.K.

⅕ teaspoon = 1 ml
¼ teaspoon = 1.25 ml
½ teaspoon = 2.5 ml
1 teaspoon = 5 ml
1 tablespoon = 15 ml
1 fluid ounce = 30 ml
¼ cup = 60 ml
⅓ cup = 80 ml
½ cup = 120 ml
⅔ cup = 160 ml
¾ cup = 180 ml
1 cup = 240 ml
2 cups = 475 ml
1 quart = 1 liter
½ inch = 1.25 cm
1 inch = 2.5 cm

BAKING PAN SIZES

U.S.	Metric
8×1½-inch round baking pan	20×4-cm cake tin
9×1½-inch round baking pan	23×4-cm cake tin
11×7×1½-inch baking pan	28×18×4-cm baking tin
13×9×2-inch baking pan	32×23×5-cm baking tin
2-quart rectangular baking dish	28×18×4-cm baking tin
15×10×1-inch baking pan	38×25.5×2.5-cm baking tin (Swiss roll tin)
9-inch pie plate	22×4- or 23×4-cm pie plate
7- or 8-inch springform pan	18- or 20-cm springform or loose-bottom cake tin
9×5×3-inch loaf pan	23×13×8-cm or 2-pound narrow loaf tin or pâté tin
1½-quart casserole	1.5-liter casserole
2-quart casserole	2-liter casserole

OVEN TEMPERATURE EQUIVALENTS

Fahrenheit Setting	Celsius Setting*	Gas Setting
300°F	150°C	Gas mark 2 (very low)
325°F	170°C	Gas mark 3 (low)
350°F	180°C	Gas mark 4 (moderate)
375°F	190°C	Gas mark 5 (moderately hot)
400°F	200°C	Gas mark 6 (hot)
425°F	220°C	Gas mark 7 (hot)
450°F	230°C	Gas mark 8 (very hot)
475°F	240°C	Gas mark 9 (very hot)
Broil		Grill

*Electric and gas ovens may be calibrated using Celsius. However, for an electric oven, increase the Celsius setting 10 to 20 degrees when cooking above 160°C. For convection or forced-air ovens (gas or electric), lower the temperature setting 10°C when cooking at all heat levels.